Science Observed

SCIENCE OBSERVED

Essays Out of My Mind

JEREMY BERNSTEIN

Basic Books, Inc., Publishers

NEW YORK

Library of Congress Cataloging in Publication Data

Bernstein, Jeremy, 1929-
 Science Observed.

 Bibliography: p. 353
 Includes index.
  1. Science—Philosophy—Addresses, essays, lectures.
 2. Minsky, Marvin Lee, 1927-   —Addresses, essays,
 lectures. 3. Artificial intelligence—Addresses,
 essays, lectures. I. Title.
 Q175.3.B476   501   81-68404
 ISBN 0-465-07340-9   AACR2

CONTENTS

Contents

PART III
Out of My Mind: Entertainments, Serious and Otherwise

ACKNOWLEDGMENTS

WE THANK the following publishers for having given their permission to reproduce material from the following books and articles.

The *American Scholar* for permission to quote from "A.I." in vol. 49, no. 3, Summer 1980; "The Bead Game in the Glass House" in vol. 50, no. 3, Summer 1981; "A Cosmic Flow" in vol. 48, no. 1, Winter 1978/79; "Nuclear Research: Shooting the Pussycat" in vol. 49, no. 1, Winter 1979/80; "Scientific Cranks" in vol. 47, no. 1, Winter 1977/78; and "Topless in Hamburg" in vol. 50, no. 1, Winter 1980/81.

The Dial Magazine for permission to quote from "Can TV Really Teach Science?" June 1981.

Geo Magazine for permission to quote from "Time" in vol. 1, August 1979.

Harvard University Press for permission to quote from *Robert Oppenheimer: Letters and Recollections,* ed. Alice Kimball Smith and Charles Weiner, 1980.

The *Mountain Gazette* for permission to quote from "Bubble & Squeak."

The *New Yorker* for permission to quote from "Mind and Machine."

Random House, Inc. for permission to quote from "How About a Little Game? Stanley Kubrick" and "I Am This Whole World: Erwin Schrödinger" in *A Comprehensible World: On Modern Science and Its Origins* by Jeremy Bernstein, 1961.

PART I

Mind and Machine: Profile of Marvin Minsky

Introduction

ABOUT twenty years ago, Jacques Barzun wrote a brilliant and often irritating book called *Science: The Glorious Entertainment*, in which he characterized science as a game: "Out of man's mind in free play comes the creation Science. It renews itself, like the generations, thanks to an activity which is the best game of *homo ludens:* science is in the strictest and best sense a glorious entertainment." Many of my colleagues were deeply offended by what they felt was a demeaning of their enterprise. Indeed, I took Barzun to task in a spirited review that I wrote of his book for the *New Yorker.* But in these intervening years, I have come to feel that Barzun had a point. There is something playful about science at its best. Einstein, the greatest scientist of modern times and perhaps in all of history, had an almost childlike way of manipulating nature, of almost playing with scientific concepts. One of my most delightful impressions of Einstein comes from an interview that Einstein gave in his house to the historian of science, I. Bernard Cohen. The interview took place not long after Einstein's seventy-sixth birthday and very shortly before his death.

> ...At last I was taking my leave. Suddenly [Einstein] turned and called "Wait. Wait. I must show you my birthday present." [It had been given to him by his neighbor, the Princeton physicist Eric Rogers.] Back in the study I saw Einstein take from the

3

corner of the room what looked like a curtain rod five feet tall, at the top of which was a plastic sphere about four inches in diameter. Coming up from the rod into the sphere was a small plastic tube about two inches long, terminating in the center of the sphere. Out of this tube there came a string with a little ball at the end. "You see," said Einstein, "this is designed as a model to illustrate the equivalence principle. The little ball is attached to a string, which goes into the little tube in the center and is attached to a spring. The spring pulls on the ball, but it cannot pull the ball up into the little tube because the spring is not strong enough to overcome the gravitational force which pulls down on the ball."

A big grin spread across his face and his eyes twinkled with delight as he said, "And now the equivalence principle." Grasping the gadget in the middle of the long brass curtain rod, he thrust it upwards until the sphere touched the ceiling. "Now I will let it drop," he said, "and according to the equivalence principle there will be no gravitational force. So the spring will now be strong enough to bring the little ball into the plastic tube." With that he suddenly let the gadget fall freely and vertically, guiding it with his hand, until the bottom reached the floor. The plastic sphere at the top was now at eye level. Sure enough, the ball rested in the tube.

With the demonstration of the birthday present our meeting was at an end.

The principle of equivalence was something that Einstein had formulated almost a half-century before this interview. He had hit upon it by focusing his attention on something that had been well known since Newton and Galileo but whose deep significance had never been properly appreciated. In the gravitational field of the earth—not taking into account the effects of air resistance—all objects fall with the same acceleration. Einstein illustrated this by comparing weight registered on a scale in a stationary elevator to the "weightlessness" the scale will register if the elevator cable snaps, putting into free fall the elevator, the scale, and the person being weighed. The scale will register zero. From this apparently innocuous principle Einstein was able to deduce that light will be bent in a gravitational field and that a gravitational field will also change the color of light. A reader who is curious about how these remarkable phenomena follow from the principle of equivalence might consult *Einstein: A Centenary Volume,* edited by A. P. French, or my short biography, *Einstein.* The point that I want to make here is one of style. We have here at its absolute best an example of the creative playfulness of science. We can see the anatomy of a great creative scientific discovery; a leap of the imagination. It can be understood by an intelligent and interested lay person if it is properly and honestly explained, and it is beautiful in much the same way that a Bach fugue is beautiful.

Most of the essays in this collection are attempts to explain some of the things that have struck me in recent years as best exemplifying the many aspects of scientific creativity. A few years ago Joseph Epstein, editor of the *American Scholar,* gave me the opportunity to write a biannual column for the *Scholar* that I decided to call "Out of My Mind." Joe encouraged me to write more or less on whatever was on my mind, and he permitted me to use a variety of forms—including "semi-fiction"—as vehicles for expressing lines of thought that do not quite fit into the usual molds. Joe and I share fondness for humor, and I hope that some of the columns included here will make the reader laugh. Like much humor, though, they have a serious intent.

In the past few years, there seems to have developed a growing tendency on the part of some people to see popular science writing as a kind of sensational escape literature. A spate of apparently very successful popular science magazines has appeared. If one actually takes the trouble to read them, one often finds them reflecting pop culture at its worst. (One, for example, forecasts future Nobel Prize winners, and if the guesses prove right, a little photograph of the laureate is printed with a caption that goes something like, "We spotted him two years ago when he was only an assistant professor.") The articles are superficial, frequently misleading, sometimes totally wrong, and ultimately disappointing. They often are written by or about scientific quacks. The scientific enterprise cannot sustain this kind of technicolor exposure. Real breakthroughs are rare and usually very difficult to understand. (Even their creators often don't fully understand them at first.) All of this misleading pop-culture hype will inevitably lead to disillusion and boredom. Quantum mechanics is *not* Zen Buddhism. Photons do *not* display manifestations of consciousness. Relativity theory has nothing to do with ethical relativism. Creationism is not a rival scientific theory of the origin of species. Evolution is *not* a speculation, and so on. If people read popular science with misguided expectations, in the long run this will manifest itself in a loss of popular support for, and interest in, real scientific research.

For this reason, among others, I believe that a scientist such as myself who writes for the general public has both an opportunity and a responsibility to call attention to nonsense when he comes across it. On the other hand, to write about nonsense and save the writing from degenerating into tedious polemic requires thought. Here is where the humor comes in. It is, I think, a great deal more effective and certainly a lot more fun to try humorously to make pseudo-scientific notions appear as ludicrous as, in fact, they are. In doing so, one runs the risk of being taken lightly even when one's intention is not necessarily to be funny. That is a risk I am willing to assume. On the other hand, I have discovered that the effects of writing about odd ideas in a humorous or semi-humorous style are not always what one expects. After having received a large number of crank letters I decided, in the hopes of stemming the tide, to write a generic article on the subject. (It is included in this collection.) Much to my surprise, it did the opposite. The piece was reprinted without my knowing it in a Los Angeles newspaper, and soon thereafter I began receiving communications from an entirely new set of cranks. These people often began their letters, or whatever, with the statement that they agreed with my piece, but that *they* were different. If I would only take the trouble to read *their* seventy-page manuscript I would learn that Einstein really had been wrong. There seems to be no way of winning this particular game.

From the foregoing it is clear that I owe Joe Epstein a debt of gratitude for encouraging me to write the *American Scholar* columns, and I am pleased to acknowledge it here. I also owe Marvin Minsky many thanks for his patience in explaining both his own work and the work of his friends and colleagues in the artificial intelligence community. My interviews with him resulted in the first pieces in this book, which first appeared in the *New Yorker*. I owe both William Shawn and Pat Crow, my *New Yorker* editors, a heartfelt debt of thanks, in Mr. Shawn's case for his encouragement and understanding of my attempts to describe very difficult material for a general readership, and in Pat Crow's case for his editorial skills in helping to shape the pieces.

1

A Once and

Future Hacker

"Warren," said he, "what is thee going to be?" And I said, "I don't know." "And what is thee going to do?" And again I said, "I have no idea, but there is one question I would like to answer: What is a number, that a man may know it, and a man that he may know a number?" He smiled and said, "Friend, thee will be busy as long as thee lives."
                                        —WARREN McCULLOCH

I believe that we are on the threshold of an era that will be based on, and quite possibly dominated by, the activity of intelligent problem-solving machines.
                                        —MARVIN MINSKY

IN JULY of 1979 a new backgammon champion of the world was crowned in Monte Carlo. It was a computer program called BKG 9.8, created by Hans Berliner of Carnegie-Mellon University in Pittsburgh. The program was run on a large computer at Carnegie-Mellon that was connected by satellite to a mobile robot named Gammonoid. (Gammonoid had a visual display backgammon board to exhibit its moves.) Its opponent was Luigi Villa of Italy, who, a short while before, had beaten all of his human challengers, gaining the right to meet Gammonoid. It was a five-thousand-dollar, winner-take-all match, and Gammonoid won—seven games to one. The computer had been expected to lose. Berliner, describing the experience in a recent *Scientific American* article, writes:

> Not much was expected of the programmed robot....Although the organizers [of the tournament] made Gammonoid the symbol of the tournament by putting a picture of it on their literature and little robot figures on the trophies, the players knew that [previously] existing microprocessors could not give them a good game. Why should the robot be any different?
>
> This view was reinforced at the opening ceremonies in the Summer Sports Palace in Monaco. At one point the overhead lights dimmed, the orchestra began playing the theme of the film *Star Wars* and a spotlight focused on an opening in the stage curtain through which Gammonoid was supposed to propel itself onto the stage. To my dismay the robot got entangled in the curtain and its appearance was delayed for five minutes.

This was one of the few mistakes the robot made. Backgammon is now the first board or card game with a machine champion. Checkers, chess, go, and the rest soon will follow. But what does this mean for us, for our sense of uniqueness and worth—especially as machines evolve whose output we are less and less able to distinguish from our own? Some sense of what is in store is described in a remarkable paragraph in Berliner's article:

> I could hardly believe this finish, yet the program certainly earned its victory. There was nothing seriously wrong with its play, although it was lucky to have won the third game and the last. The spectators rushed into the closed room where the match had been played. Photographers took pictures, reporters sought interviews [presumably with Berliner and not with the machine], and the assembled experts congratulated me. Only one thing marred the scene. Villa, who only a day earlier had reached the summit of his backgammon career in winning the world title, was disconsolate. I told him that I was sorry it had happened and that we both knew he was really the better player.

My own involvement with computers has been sporadic. Although a theoretical physicist, I belong to the generation that received its scientific education just prior to the time —the late 1950s—when the use of computers in scientific work really became common. I own and can operate one of the new programmable pocket calculators. I once took a brief course in FORTRAN (for formula translator) programming, and afterward the ten-year-old son of a colleague gave me an afternoon's worth of instruction in the BASIC (for beginner's all-purpose symbolic instruction code) programming language he uses to operate the typewriter-size computer in his father's study. I have whenever possible avoided physics problems that have to be run off on large machines.

Over the years, I have read a great deal of the popular and semipopular literature on the new computer revolution—the age of the microprocessor in which circuits with thousands of elements can be packed into a silicon chip so small that the chip can be inserted into the eye of a needle. The speed of machine operations is now measured in billionths of a second, and the limitations on the machines that are due to the fact that electromagnetic signals propagate with *only* the speed of light are beginning to manifest themselves. There are so many books and articles on this subject and on its implications for our view of ourselves that it is hard to distinguish one voice from the next. Yet, in all of this reading I have been constantly struck by Marvin Minsky's ideas. His words resonate in my head. Here, for example, are two extracts from a paper entitled "Matter, Mind and Models." The first is on "free will":

If one thoroughly understands a machine or a program one finds no urge to attribute *volition* to it. If one does not understand it so well, one must supply an incomplete model for expla-

11

nation. Our everyday intuitive models of higher human activity are quite incomplete and many notions in our informal explanations do not tolerate close examination. Free will or volition is one such notion—people are incapable of explaining how it differs from stochastic caprice, but feel strongly that it does. I conjecture that this idea has its genesis in a strong primitive defense mechanism. Briefly, in childhood we learn to recognize various forms of aggression and compulsion, and to dislike them, whether we submit or resist. Older, when told that our behavior is controlled by such-and-such a set of laws, we insert this fact in our model (inappropriately) along with other recognizers of compulsion. We resist *compulsion* no matter from *whom*. Although resistance is logically futile the resentment persists and is rationalized by defective explanations, since the alternative is emotionally unacceptable.

Later in the paper, Minsky writes:

When intelligent machines are constructed, we should not be surprised to find them as confused and as stubborn as men on their convictions about mind-matter, consciousness, free will and the like. For all such questions are pointed at explaining the complicated interactions between parts of the self-model. A man's or a machine's strength of conviction about such things tells us nothing about the world, or about the man, except for what it tells us about his model of himself.

I have known Marvin Minsky for thirty years. When I first met him in the late 1940s at Harvard, it was not entirely clear what his specialty was, or whether he had chosen one at all. He was taking courses in musical composition with Irving Fine. While still an undergraduate he had his own laboratories—one in the psychology department and one in the biology department—and he was in the process of writing a brilliantly original senior mathematics thesis on a problem in topology. His basic interest seemed to be in the workings of the human mind and in making machine models of the mind. Indeed, about that time he and a friend made one of the first electronic machines that could

12

actually teach itself to do something interesting. It monitored electronic "rats" that learned to run mazes. It was being financed by the navy. On one notable occasion, I remember descending to the basement of Memorial Hall, while Minsky worked on it. It had an illuminated display panel that enabled one to follow the progress of the "rats." Near the machine was a hamster in a cage. When the machine blinked, the hamster would run around its cage happily. Minsky, with his characteristic elfin grin, remarked that on the previous day the navy contract officer had been down to see the machine. Noting the man's interest in the hamster, Minsky had told him laconically: "The next one we build will look like a bird."

In recent years I had lost touch with Marvin, but when I realized that something very new in the way of technology was engulfing us, I decided to ask him about it. I knew that he had been in the field of what is now called "artificial intelligence"—A.I., for short—before it even had a name. The phrase "artificial intelligence"—meaning machines that can do things that people are inclined to call "intelligent"—is usually attributed to Minsky's former M.I.T. colleague, John McCarthy. Now at Stanford, he invented the phrase in the mid-1950s. In 1958 he and Minsky created the Artificial Intelligence Group at M.I.T. and to this day it is considered to be one of the most creative and distinguished scientific enterprises of its kind in the world. (There are other powerful groups at Stanford and Carnegie-Mellon.) In 1974 Minsky succeeded Claude Shannon, his mentor and one of the great pioneers in automata and cybernetics, as the M.I.T. Donner Professor of Science in the Department of Electrical Engineering and Computer Science, a chair that he presently holds. Along the way he was elected to both the National Academy of Sciences and the American Academy of Arts and Sciences.

Minsky is a fascinating conversationalist given to non-stop cigarette smoking that does not seem to interfere with the flow of language. He has a delightful, somewhat impish sense of humor, and a luminescent smile. His mind is one of the clearest I have ever known, capable of unraveling the most complicated ideas in simple language. We talked for many hours over several weeks. Some of our conversations took place in his office at M.I.T. and some in his nearby, sprawling house in Boston.

Minsky has three children, and his wife is Gloria Rudisch, a prominent Boston pediatrician, treating children, as she puts it, "from the cradle to college." One might deduce from the books and medical supplies at hand that a doctor lives in the Minsky house. But who else lives there would be a real puzzle to figure out. Even after several visits I felt I had only scratched the surface. On a table I noted a fireman's hat with a red light and on another a sizable, lifelike plastic shark. On a wall there was a giant wrench that I at first thought might be a sculpture of a wrench. In fact, it is a real wrench bought at an M.I.T. shop. Several musical instruments were visible. Near the wrench there was what appeared to be a brass alpine horn, and elsewhere were also two organs, two pianos, and a Moog synthesizer. Minsky spends many hours composing and improvising and plans to record some of his baroque fugues. There were innumerable recording instruments and a huge juke box. When I asked about the latter, Gloria Minsky explained that it had been a present from Marvin. It just appeared one day out of the blue complete with a set of "hits," such as "Indiff'rent" by the Platters. At first it had to be coin operated, but with the electronic skills in the household it was child's play to rewire it so that it could be used for free. The Platters and some of the other groups' records that came with the juke box have been replaced by folk music and some classical selections, although the original labels are still there. One is not quite sure what one will hear when one presses a button. Underneath the dining room table was an ancient electric hand calculator with gears and wheels, some of which were stuck. Minsky informed me that on a recent occasion he and the Nobel Prize-winning physicist Richard Feynman spent several hours trying unsuccessfully to get the thing to work. He explained it, "We were like two garage mechanics with a stuck distributor cap."

In Minsky's crowded study lay a computer with a printer whose *i*'s and *e*'s were broken. The broken letters made reading the messages coming from it a challenge. All of the prominent researchers in A.I. seem to be permanently wired to each other by computer terminal. Their network allows them to send messages all over the country. Several times when I visited Minsky, he would read his "mail"—messages on the system. Near the telephone I spotted what I naïvely thought might be some kind of hi-fi set and when Minsky saw me staring at it, he asked if I would like to listen to it. By setting a few switches, he caused the thing to make an uncanny series of increasingly complex musical sounds. If there *were* Martians it would be my idea of a Martian music box. Minsky explained its provenance. Some years ago he had got a box full of computer modules and had used them at home to construct various logic circuits. He was working in the kitchen and was having trouble "de-bugging" the circuits, since he did not have an oscilloscope—a device that projects the behavior of the circuits onto a screen. It occurred to him that if he were to run a computing circuit very fast and play it through a loudspeaker, he might actually listen to it and by the sounds tell if there were something wrong. "I connected a couple of speakers to it," Minsky explained, "and

I found that by listening to it I could actually tell if any of the flip-flops [electronic components that can take one of two stable positions] were dead. It was making all those sounds, and then I started to like the sounds. So I made various counting circuits to make little chords and tunes. This thing was going and a friend of mine named Ed Fredkin (another M.I.T professor) came in and said 'That sounds pretty good. How did you get it to make those sounds?' I showed him and then we spent the afternoon making more sounds. Fredkin had a successful electronics company, and for awhile he manufactured a few of [the 'music boxes'] as toys.''

Computer scientists call an elegant bit of programming a "hack." As Minsky once remarked, "If you do enough hacking you often get something profound." I am not sure whether his music box would be called a hack, and I am less sure if that would be the right term for some of the other innumerable inventions he has created and left behind. One summer, while still a student, Minsky went to work for the Bell Telephone Laboratories in New Jersey, where Claude Shannon then was. Shannon is fond of mechanical gadgets—for example, he had in his house near Boston a pitching machine against which he could take batting practice—so Minsky made a gadget for him, a black box with a single switch. When one turned the switch on, the lid of the box opened and a mechanical hand came out and turned the switch off. Bell was sufficiently enchanted with this device to make seventy of them to give to executives to show that the company had a sense of humor. Apparently the company's sense of humor was limited, for when Minsky asked to keep the patent rights Bell turned him down. When, a few years ago, the black boxes became popular items in novelty shops, one had to wonder where they had come from.

Minsky's office in the Artificial Intelligence Laboratory at M.I.T. is as crowded as his house, if less eclectic. There is a plastic statue of a robot that Minsky assured me does nothing. There is a surprisingly lifelike cloth plant. There is also the inevitable computer terminal. (The lab has its own very large computers that, over the years, have been rigged with about every conceivable hack.) It can open the electric doors in the lab and summon the elevators in the building; it has had mechanical arms attached to it, special television cameras to simulate vision, and a radio transmitter to operate remote controlled robots. There is also a trophy on it for a chess tournament it once won. The laboratory is now spread over three floors in a new building just across the street from the main M.I.T. campus. About a hundred people work there, including seven professors, most of them former Minsky students, twenty-five graduate students, and a corps of people whom Minsky often refers to affectionately as "hackers." The hackers are people who entered M.I.T., became infatuated with computing machines, and in some cases never bothered to get degrees of any kind. They have developed into one of the most productive groups in the laboratory.

One of the most amazing objects the hackers managed to design—in 1968—was a robot that could catch a ball. It consisted of a four-foot arm powered by a five-horsepower motor that could swing the arm through a full semicircle in about half a second. They were given the arm, which they attached to the computer, by the A.M.F. Company, which had marketed it for some purpose under the trade name "Versatran." The hackers designed a mechanical hand that they thought might be suitable for ball catching. A television camera guided the hand. It was fast enough to grab the ball, but it couldn't close its fingers around it quickly enough. The hackers tried various baskets without success until one hacker, Richard Greenblatt, thought of using a straw cornucopia of the type usually used to hold fruit. It worked splendidly: When the ball was thrown, the arm swung around and caught it in the cornucopia. The only problem, Minsky noted, was that "it began to go after people. It was quite dangerous because it was so powerful, so finally we had to fence the computer off."

Minsky once explained something of the lab's evolution when we took a little tour of the place. In 1960, the Artificial Intelligence Group consisted of just Minsky and McCarthy and a couple of students. One day he and McCarthy were standing in the hall of Building 20 at M.I.T.—one of the wooden buildings built during the Second World War that is still being used—when Jerome Weisner, then director of the electronics laboratory at M.I.T. came by and started a conversation. He learned that McCarthy was in the process of developing "time sharing" —the system by which computers can be shared by several independent users, each of whom gets a fraction of a second of the computer's undivided attention to run a program—as well as new and extremely sophisticated computer languages. Minsky described what has since become his major preoccupation, getting computers to do nonnumerical things such as reasoning by analogy. Weisner found their plans so interesting that he asked them if they needed any money to carry out the work. They replied that they could use a little for equipment and to pay students. Weisner had some sort of block grant from all of the armed services combined, and almost immediately he allocated money to their projects and gave them a key to the supply room. For many years they never had to write a research proposal. Things have changed and now the laboratory is funded—about 2.5 million dollars a year— and prospective grant recipients submit proposals that are reviewed by the various sponsoring agencies. Minsky was director of the laboratory from 1964 through 1973; when he tired of grant proposals, he turned the directorate over to one of his former students, Patrick Winston, who has run the laboratory ever since.

On my tour of the laboratory one of the first things I noticed was a giant drawing—perhaps six by fifteen feet—of what appeared at first to be the street plan of a large city. Minsky explained that it was an engineering drawing of a "chip"—a silicon wafer. The lines were circuits photoprinted on the wafer. In fact this chip is an essential part of the first micro-computer designed especially for A.I. All of the elements of the computer that process data are on this one chip. We took an elevator to the third floor of the lab to look at the chip, which is about a half-inch square. To see the circuit lines, we had to put the chip under a very powerful microscope, and even then they were just about visible. On these chips "transistors" are located wherever two lines cross. Each transistor is only slightly larger than a blood cell. The next generation of computers will use transistors about one-sixth this size.

While we were on this floor Minsky also showed me a model of a computer he had built more or less by himself. In 1970 he became convinced that a specially designed computer would be an extremely valuable educational aid in schools if it were both low enough in cost for schools to buy and powerful enough so that it could use simple programming language. This may seem paradoxical, but the simpler the programming language is to be on the surface the more powerful the machine has to be, since it must be able to do more things inside. Furthermore Minsky wanted to make an inexpensive computer that was able to produce animated visual displays. As Minsky said,

19

We had observed that children—and everyone else for that matter—became most deeply engaged in computer programming when they literally could see what they were doing by creating pictures on a screen. So I set about to make a computer that children could use to create real-time animation effects and that would have a programming language simple enough for them to use easily. The computer I built could produce two million dots per second on a screen, which is enough to make very interesting animated cartoons and other graphic presentations. A fifth grader, for example, might program a garden of plants and flowers that would appear on the screen and actually grow following the laws of growth the child would write into his program.

Most computers store and manipulate information in units known as "bytes." A typical byte might look like 10011001, a set of eight one's or zero's. The one's and zero's are what are called "bits" of information. (Pocket calculators often process information in four-bit units called "nybbles.") The basic "letters" of the computer's alphabet consist of 2^8, or 256, distinct bytes. Minsky decided that for his purposes he needed a 64,000, 16-bit word memory. The typical home computer that one now buys for about $1,000 has about a 16,000-byte memory. (In practice, such a memory is designated in the catalogues and the like as "16K bytes," where K means 1024.) For a few hundred dollars one can add some additional memory units to these computers. Minsky's machine is a rather powerful computer. The big scientific computers now have internal memories with millions of bytes and in addition there are external memories—magnetic discs and the like—that can store an almost limitless number of words. It is the internal memory that controls the operations of the computer during a given process.

Minsky decided that he would call his computer the 2500, what he thought its price would be to schools. For a year he immersed himself in computer design, until he could read circuit diagrams like novels. "By the time I finished," he noted, "I knew what happened in about two hundred different kinds of computer chips." To check circuit diagrams he used programs that analyzed them automatically for short circuits and other flaws and that had been developed by the artificial intelligence group at Stanford (which McCarthy formed in 1964). He designed the machine from his office, using the Stanford programs on his own computer console. The computer needed three hundred chips, which he ordered from the Texas Instrument Company catalogue along with twenty-four pages of drawings of the computer's circuits. These drawings Minsky digitally recorded on magnetic tape that was sent to a company in Boston which connected about three thousand wires on a board. All Minsky had to do was to plug in his three hundred chips and the thing worked.

The M.I.T. project now included Seymour Papert, a South African mathematician who had come to M.I.T. from Piaget's group in Geneva and who had a professional interest in the education of children. Papert created the LOGO language, a special mathematical language for the machine that they thought the children might like. Minsky showed me how, using LOGO, I could get the machine to draw all sorts of wonderful polygons on its display screen. Some of them can be made to rotate like propellers. (At one point Minsky, who hadn't used the program for some time, got stopped by a display that read "Poly wants more data.") Minsky and Papert tried to market the machines themselves. They formed a small company that subsequently went broke. "Neither Seymour nor I are very good at getting people to part with their money," Minsky noted. While many schools seemed to like the machine, it took often about three years for school administrators to get the appropriations through the various school committees, and the company couldn't survive the delays. Finally, they gave it to a Canadian named Guy Montpetit who renamed it Tortué Générale, and the last thing that Minsky had heard about it was that a few computers had been sold in Algeria and Quebec—but to businessmen rather than children. It turned out that they could learn programming with LOGO about as easily as children. "Seymour and I went back to being scientists," he remarked. The laboratory has since signed a contract with the Texas Instrument Company to install LOGO in the next generation of home computers.

Marvin Minsky was born in New York City on August 9, 1927. Like many gifted mathematically inclined scientists, he finds no traces of a mathematical predisposition in his family background. His father Henry Minsky was a distinguished eye surgeon who became head of the Department of Ophthalmology at The Mount Sinai Hospital in New York. (*His* father, who was born on Mott Street in Chinatown, had been a carpenter.) Minsky recalls. his father carrying on a series of futile battles with health faddists who in the 1930s encouraged people to strengthen their eyes by looking into the sun. For years he treated a stream of half-blind patients who had tried it. Minsky's mother, who has been active in Zionist affairs and now writes a weekly column, showed no special mathematical leanings, and neither does his younger sister, Ruth, a medical genetics counselor, or his older sister, Charlotte, an artist who recently sold a painting to the magazine *Creative Computing* for one of its covers.

Minsky's memories of mathematics go back to early childhood. He recalls taking what must have been an I.Q. test when he was about five. One of the questions was the following: Suppose you have lost a ball in a field where the grass is sufficiently tall so that you cannot see the ball—what is the most economical strategy for finding it? The official solution, which in later years Minsky looked up in the standard Terman Intelligence Test, was to go to the center of the field and then to execute a series of spirals out from the center until the ball is located. Minsky attempted to explain to the tester that this was not the best solution, since it would involve inspecting some areas twice. One should start from the outside and spiral in. The fact that he was not able to convince his interlocutor of what happened to Minsky to be an obvious logical point is a memory that has never left him. "Every child," he noted recently, "remembers the disillusioning experience when he first discovers that an adult isn't perfect." Nonetheless, he must have made a favorable impression, because on the basis of the test scores and his experience with the tester he was sent to an experimental public school for gifted children (which he disliked, partly because he was required to study tap dancing there). He left the school soon after, when his parents moved from Manhattan to Riverdale in the Bronx, and was enrolled in a public school that he did not like either. "There were bullies and I was physically somewhat terrorized. Besides, a teacher there wanted me to repeat the third grade because my handwriting was so bad. My parents found this unreasonable so I was sent to Fieldston—a progressive private school." By this time he was also doing impressive original musical compositions that prompted a professional musician's offer to take Minsky on full-time as a prodigy, a notion that did not appeal to his parents.

Robert Oppenheimer had graduated from Fieldston in 1921, but even in Minsky's day his presence at the school was fresh in the minds of some of the teachers. "If you did anything astonishing at Fieldston," Minsky remembers, "somebody would say 'Oh you're another Oppenheimer.' At the time I had no idea what that meant. But I had a great science teacher at Fieldston, Herbert Zim. Later on he wrote the dinosaur books for Golden Books and was on the staff of the Museum of Natural History. He lives in Florida now and I call him up every once in awhile to chat." At Fieldston, Minsky became interested in both electronics and organic chemistry. He remembers:

I had been reading chemistry books and so I thought it would be nice to make some chemicals. In particular I had read about ethyl mercaptan, which intrigued me because it was said to be the worst smelling thing per gram. I went to Zim and told him that I wanted to make some. He said, "Sure—how do you plan to do it?" We talked about it for awhile and he convinced me that if we were going to be thorough we should first make the ethanol by fermenting and distilling grain from which we were to make ethyl chloride. In fact I did make the ethyl chloride, which promptly disappeared. It is about the most volatile thing there is. I think that Zim had fooled me into making this synthesis knowing that the product would evaporate before I actually got to make that awful mercaptan. I remember being sort of mad and I decided that chemistry was harder than it looked on paper because when you synthesize something it can just disappear.

He also recalls learning about positive and negative numbers. "I thought to myself that is very nice, but maybe there are three kinds of numbers—*a, b,* and *c.* I tried for days to find a number system with three bases that looked like arithmetic. Many years later I realized that there isn't one. At the time I didn't have the courage to add a fourth base number. That works and gives you the complex number system. There was no one around to talk to about these things and I lacked any kind of map or vision that there were a lot of different kinds of mathematics." Minsky also began to build radios and other electrical apparatus including a giant spark gap electric discharge machine that generated six-foot-long spark discharges. Once when fooling around with a radio, he was asked by an adult how the volume control worked. Minsky explained that it controlled the amount of electricity that went into the speaker and then asked the adult how *he* thought it worked. "He told me that he thought that there was some kind of little pillow and that when you turn the knob it puts the pillow over the speaker. I found that very shocking; not because the adult was ignorant of how it worked, but because here we are wandering around in this world with people who look sort of similar and it just astounded me that someone who looked somewhat similar to me could have such a different idea."

Minsky graduated from eighth grade at Fieldston in 1941, three years after the Bronx High School of Science had been created to attract and train budding scientific geniuses. (It has done just that over the years. For example, two of the three 1979 Nobel laureates in physics, Steven Weinberg and Sheldon Glashow, turn out to have been classmates at Science. In the company of Gerald Feinberg, now the chairman of the physics department at Columbia, they taught themselves quantum mechanics.) For Minsky, going to Science was a liberating experience. He recalls:

The other kids were people you could discuss your most elaborate ideas with and nobody would be condescending. Talking to people in the outside world was always a pain because they would say, "Don't be so serious...relax." I used to hate people saying "relax." I was a very hyperactive child, always zipping from one place to the next and doing things very fast. This seemed to bother most adults. But no one at Science felt that way. When a little later I got first to Andover and then to Harvard I was appalled and continually astonished at how relaxing and how much easier they were than Science. I keep running across people I knew at Science such as Russell Kirsch, a computer pioneer now at the Bureau of Standards, and Anthony Oettinger, who started the computer science department at Harvard. He was one of the first people to get a computer to learn something and to use them [computers] for language translation. Frank Rosenblatt was also one of my classmates at Science.

(Rosenblatt eventually joined the staff of the Cornell Aeronautical Laboratory, where he invented the so-called Perceptron. In the early 1960s, the Perceptron—of which more later—became the paradigm of artificial intelligence machines for a whole generation of young computer scientists. Rosenblatt was tragically drowned in a sailing accident in 1971. Just prior to Rosenblatt's death Minsky, in collaboration with Seymour Papert, wrote an entire book on the Perceptron demonstrating the limitations of the machine. It is one of the classical works in the field.)

Minsky's parents sent him to Andover for his senior year, reasoning that it would be easier for him to get into college as an Andover graduate than as a graduate of the Bronx High School of Science. It is difficult now to imagine any university not accepting someone with Minsky's gifts, whatever his academic background. His year at Andover left Minsky with mixed feelings, because he found he could not concentrate on science. On the other hand, he took an extraordinary English class with the poet Dudley Fitts that to some extent made up for the deemphasis on science. It was now 1945 and Minsky was seventeen. The war was on, and, thinking he would be drafted anyway, he enlisted in the navy. He had been told that if he enlisted in a particular navy program he would be sent to electronics school.

Everybody was a bit suspicious about it, since we felt that you couldn't trust the government in something like this. But it turned out to be true and I was sent to Chicago to start my training. There were about a hundred and twenty people in my company. About half of them seemed rather weird and somewhat scary to me. They were the regular recruits from the Midwest and places like that. I could hardly understand what they said and they certainly couldn't understand what I was talking about. But about forty of them were enrolled in the same sort of electronics program that I was. After we completed basic training, which involved shooting rifles and antiaircraft guns, we were going to be sent to radar school. There were about three or four people in my company who were really remarkable, a mathematician, John Wermer, an astronomer, James Parker, and a young musicologist named David Fuller, all now professors at distinguished universities. Fuller had been at Harvard for a year and was an organist. He took my music very seriously. By this time I had sort of drafted out a piano concerto which Fuller played for me and said I should finish. But I never did. Our little group was a strange kind of mini-Harvard in the middle of the navy. Everything was very unrealistic. I practiced shooting down planes on an antiaircraft simulator. I held the base record. I "shot down" a hundred and twenty planes in a row. I realized later I had memorized the training tape and knew in advance exactly where each plane would appear. But I must have some odd skill in marksmanship. Many years later my wife and I were in New Mexico on a trip. We came across some kids shooting at things with a rifle. I asked them if I could try it and I hit everything. It seems that I have some kind of highly developed skill for which I have no explanation. . . of shooting at things.

Before Minsky had a chance to try out his marksmanship in earnest, the war ended. "There really wasn't anything for us to do so we just spent a couple of months chatting until we were discharged in time for me to go to Harvard as a freshman." For Minsky, Harvard was a revelation; a sort of intellectual garden salad,

a whole universe of things to do. The only thing I was worried about was English, because there was a required English course.

The thing I had always disliked most of all in school was writing. I could never think of anything to write about...now I love to write. But they had a test which, if you passed, could get you out of the required course. I passed and it was one of the best things that happened to me. I felt that now I would not have to do the one thing I hadn't liked in high school...Dudley Fitts at Andover...always discouraged one from trying to write anything fancy. In this test [at Harvard] we were supposed to interpret a couple of passages from Dostoyevsky, and I just explained what they were about in a perfectly straightforward way. Apparently whoever was reading all those things was tired of reading the long ones the students were doing and he passed me.

I took freshman physics and advanced calculus. I had learned elementary calculus at Andover. I was nominally a physics major but I took courses in sociology and psychology. I got interested in neurology. Around the end of high school I started thinking about thinking. One of the things that got me started was wondering why it was so hard to learn mathematics. You read this thing and take an hour a page and still it doesn't make sense. Then, suddenly, it becomes trivial. I began to wonder about the learning process and about learning machines and I invented some reinforcement theories. I came across the theories of Skinner, which I thought were terrible because they were an attempt to fit curves to behavior without any internal ideas. Up until this time I had been almost pathologically uninterested in how minds work. I wasn't at all good at guessing how people felt. I think that I was generally insensitive, almost intentionally insensitive, to people's feelings and thoughts. I was only interested in what I was doing. But in my freshman year I began to get interested in psychological issues. After I had done some reading in neurology I talked a professor of biology—a man named Welsh—into letting me do some laboratory work on my own. For some reason he gave me a huge room with a lot of equipment all to myself.

Welsh informed Minsky that the problem of how the nerves in a crayfish claw work was unsolved.

I became an expert at dissecting crayfish. At one point I had a crayfish claw mounted on an apparatus in such a way that I could operate the individual nerves. I could get the several-jointed claw to reach down and pick up a pencil and wave it around. I am not sure that what I was doing had much scientific value, although I did learn which nerve fibers had to be excited to inhibit the effects of another fiber so that the claw would open. And it did get me interested in robotic instrumentation, something that I have now returned to. I am trying to build better micromanipulators for surgery and the like. There hasn't been much progress in that field for decades and I am determined to make some.

When not doing physics or working on his crayfish, Minsky began "hanging around" the psychology laboratory, then located in the basement of Memorial Hall.

The people down in that basement fascinated me. There were Skinner and his people. While the theory they were working with was of no interest to me, they *had* been able to optimize the training of animals to get them to do things in a shorter time and with less reward than anyone else. Clearly there was something in their technique that should be understood. At the other end of the basement there were people who were also called "psychologists" and who were totally removed from the sort of thing that Skinner did. There was a man, for example, who was trying to show that the sensitivity of the ear was a power law rather than a logarithmic one. I could never make any sense of why that was so important, and still can't; presumably both are false. But in the middle of the basement were some young assistant professors who were new kinds of people. There was the young George Miller, now at Princeton, with whom I spent lots of time and who was trying to make some mathematical theories of psychology. [Miller remembers Minsky as "wandering from department to department dissatisfied with all of them—the sure sign of a good student. Minsky taught me more than I taught him."] Too there was J. C. R. Licklider, with whom I later worked. He ran a wonderful seminar at that time, mostly of graduate students with a few undergraduates. It was a whole universe in that basement, but the thing that affected me the most was the geometry of it, and the fact that it was underground and away from the world. On the west there were the behaviorists who were trying to understand behavior without a theory; on the east there were the physiological psychologists who were trying to understand some little bit of the nervous system without any picture of the rest. And in the middle there were these new people who were trying to make little theories that might have something to do with language and learning and the like but weren't getting much of anywhere. Even farther underground there was Georg von Békèsy. He was in the subbasement. He didn't bother anyone, but just worked on the *real* problem of how the ear functions. [In 1961, von Békèsy became the first physicist to win a Nobel Prize for medicine for his work on the ear.]

What bothered me the most about it were the graduate students who were trying to learn from these people. They would gather in the middle of the basement and argue about one doctrine or another; the politics of the situation and the merits of the different schools...they never seemed to have any good ideas. There was something terrifying about this clash of two different worlds—the physiological and behavioral. There were no psychoanalytically oriented people around them. If there had been, the situation would have been worse, not better. I couldn't fathom how these people could live down there arguing about personalities, with no methodology, no ideas of what to do, and no real theories of what is happening deep inside the mind.

I tried to make up one. I imagined that the brain was made up of neurons—little relays—and each of them had a probability attached to it that would govern whether the neuron would conduct an electric pulse—a scheme that is known technically now as a stochastic neural network. I tried to explain Skinner's results by finding some plausible way for a reward sensor to change the probabilities to favor learning. It turned out that a man in Montreal named Donald Hebb had come up with a similar theory, but at the time—luckily or unluckily—I didn't know of his work, which he soon after described in a seminal book, *The Organization of Behavior,* published in 1949.

So I had a laboratory in the psychology department and one in the biology department and I was doing experimental work in the physics department—where I was nominally majoring—mostly on physical optics. They had some wonderful old instruments like prisms and a little brass thing on which one could do the Millikan oil drop experiment. [This was an experiment that the American physicist Robert A. Millikan carried out in 1909 to measure the charge of the electron.]

My grades were fairly low. I had taken a number of courses with a very excellent composer named Irving Fine. He usually gave me C's or D's but kept encouraging me to come back. He was a tremendously honest man. I think the problem was that I am basically an improviser. I may be one of the handful of people in the world who can occasionally produce an entire three-voice fugue in satisfactory form the first time. I can't do it the second time and I can't really write it down as a score, although I tried very hard to learn to write scores. During most of this time I didn't care very much what would happen to me in the future, but then I began to worry about graduate school. I thought that what I would do would be to write a nice undergraduate thesis to make up for my grades. I discovered that at Harvard you couldn't do an undergraduate thesis in physics so I switched to the mathematics department, where you *could* do a thesis. This was not a problem, since I had taken enough mathematics courses to qualify as a math major.

Early in college, Minsky had the good fortune to encounter someone who recognized his potential abilities as a mathematician—Andrew Gleason. Gleason was then a legendary figure in the mathematics department. Only six years older than Minsky, he already was recognized as one of the premier problem solvers in mathematics in the world. I remember him well as coach of the Harvard team of mathematicians who competed in the Putnam Competition—a national contest for undergraduate mathematicians—which he himself had won three times while at Yale. He had the ability to solve almost any well-formulated mathematics problem almost instantly. Minsky took part in the Putnam and placed in the top ten. Gleason had served in the navy during the war— in cryptoanalysis—and afterwards was awarded a Junior Fellowship at Harvard, which allowed unlimited freedom for a small number of creative people in various fields. Gleason made a tremendous impression on Minsky. "I couldn't understand," Minsky said "how anyone that age could know so much mathematics. But the most remarkable thing about him was his plan. Once when we were talking I asked him what he was doing. He told me that he was going to solve Hilbert's fifth problem."

In 1900 the German mathematician David Hilbert, generally regarded as the greatest mathematician of the twentieth century, delivered a paper entitled "Mathematical Problems" to the Second International Conference of Mathematicians in Paris. He presented a list of what he believed to be the ten most important unsolved problems in mathematics. The full Hilbert list consisted of twenty-three problems. Hilbert's list has all but defined mathematics for much of this century. Many of the problems have now been solved, and at least one which falls into Gödel's category of formally undecidable mathematical propositions, has been shown to be insoluble in principle. The sixth problem, "To axiomatise those physical sciences in which mathematics plays an important role," is probably too vague to have a real solution. Most of the remaining problems have opened up entirely new fields of mathematics. In his lecture Hilbert said, "This conviction of the solvability of any mathematical problem is a strong incentive in our work; it beckons us: *this is the problem, find its solution. You can find it by pure thinking since in mathematics there is no Ignorabimus.*" Hilbert's fifth problem was a deep conjecture in group theory. (In mathematics, a group is a collection of abstract objects that can be combined by some operation to make a sort of multiplication table.) In 1934, John von Neumann had given a preliminary solution to the fifth problem—a partial solution for a limited class of groups. Minsky vividly recalls learning about Gleason's plan in 1946, his freshman year:

First I managed to understand what the [fifth] problem was. Then I asked Gleason how he was going to solve it. Gleason said that...his plan...consisted of three steps, each of which he thought would take him three years to work out....Well, it took him only six years, with Deane Montgomery and Leo Zippin contributing part of the proof. But here I was a sophmore talking to this man who was only slightly older than I was and he was talking about these plans. I couldn't understand how anyone that age could understand the subject well enough to have such a plan and to have an estimate of the difficulties in filling in each of the steps. Now that I am older I still can't understand it. But for the first time Gleason gave me the realization that mathematics was a landscape with discernible canyons and mountain passes and things like that. In high school I had seen mathematics as simply a bunch of skills which were fun to master, but I had never thought of it as a journey and a universe to explore. No one else I knew at that time had that vision either.

Inspired by Gleason, Minsky began work on an original problem in topology that arose from the ideas of the great early twentieth-century Dutch mathematician L. E. J. Brouwer. Brouwer proved the first of what are known as fixed point theorems. Imagine that one attempts to rearrange the surface of an ordinary sphere by taking each point on it and moving it somewhere else on the sphere. This is what mathematicians would call a "mapping" of the surface of the sphere onto itself. Under very general assumptions, Brouwer managed to show that in any such mapping there would be *at least* one point that would necessarily remain fixed. An example of such a fixed point theorem is the rigid rotation of the sphere—of the surface of the earth, for example. In this case there are *two* fixed points, the north and south poles around which the rotation takes place. But Brouwer's result applies to almost any kind of mapping; a rotation is just a special case. Over the years, mathematicians have generalized this theorem in all sorts of surprising ways. At the time that Minsky began his thesis, a Japanese mathematician at Yale named Kakutani had proved a very strange version of a fixed point theorem. To illustrate it, suppose we have a function like the temperature which is defined on the surface of a sphere—for example, the earth. Then there must be at least three points that lie on the vertices of an equilateral triangle at which the values of the temperature are identical. "It was a rather surprising result," Minsky said, "but it bothered me. I thought that it might be true for other triangles, and perhaps for other geometric figures as well. First I managed to prove it for three of the four points on a square and then I tried it for three points on a pentagon. This required going into a space of a higher dimension. So I went into this higher dimension for a couple of months, living and breathing my problem. Finally, using the topology of knots in this dimension, I came out with a proof. I wrote it up and gave it to Gleason. He read it and said 'You are a mathematician.' " Sometime later, Minsky showed his proof to Freeman Dyson who, in what Minsky considers an amazingly ingenious piece of mathematics, generalized the result to four points lying at the vertices of a square made out of great circles—circles that are part of an equator—on the sphere.

When I asked Minsky if he had published his proof, he replied:

No, at the time I was influenced by the example of my father. When he made a surgical discovery he would take six or seven years to write it up, correcting it and doing many more operations to make sure that he had been right. I felt that a successful scientist might publish three or four real discoveries in his lifetime and not load up the airwaves with partial results. I still feel that way. I don't like to take some little discovery and make a whole paper out of it. When I make some little discovery, either I forget about it or wait until I have several that fit together before I write them up. In any case, at the time Gleason said "You are a mathematician and now you should go to Princeton." At first I felt rejected. I was perfectly happy at Harvard and I didn't see why I should go somewhere else. But Gleason insisted that it would be wrong for me to stay in one place. So I appeared at Princeton in the mathematics department the next year.

The graduate mathematics department at Princeton was another perfect world. It was like a club. They admitted only a handful of students each year, mostly by invitation. It was run by Solomon Lefschetz. He was a man who didn't care about anything except quality. There were no exams. Once I got a look at my transcript. The graduate school required grades. Instead of the usual grades I was used to, there were fifteen or twenty A's, many of them in courses I had never taken. Lefshetz felt that either one was a mathematician or one wasn't and it didn't matter how much mathematics one actually knew. For the next two years I hung around a kind of common room that Lefshetz had created for the graduate students, where people came to play go or chess. For awhile I studied topology, but then I ran into a young graduate student in physics named Dean Edmonds who was a whiz at electronics. We began to build vacuum tube circuits that did all sorts of things.

As an undergraduate, Minsky had begun to imagine building an electronic machine that could learn.

I told Edmonds that I thought it might not be too hard to build. The one I then envisioned would have to have had a lot of memory circuits. There would be electronic "neurons" connected by "synapses" that would control when the neurons fired. The synapses would have various probabilities for conducting. But to reinforce "success" one would have to have a way of changing these probabilities. So there would have to be loops and cycles in the circuits so that the machine could remember traces of its past and adjust its behavior. I thought that if I could ever build such a machine I might get it to learn to run mazes through its electronics—like rats or something. I didn't think it would be very intelligent—at least yet. I thought it would work pretty well with about forty neurons. Edmonds and I worked out some circuits so that we could, at least in principle, realize each of these neurons with just six vacuum tubes and a motor.

Minsky told George Miller at Harvard about the prospective design. "He said, 'Why don't [you] just try it?' He had a lot of faith in me, which I appreciated. Somehow he managed to get a couple of thousands dollars from the Office of Naval Research and in the summer of 1951 Dean Edmonds and I came to Harvard and built [the machine]. It had three hundred tubes and a lot of motors. It needed some gears and clutches which we machined ourselves."

Minsky's machine, which was what I saw in the Memorial Hall basement, was certainly one of the first, if not *the* first, electronic learning machine. In addition to its neurons and synapses and its internal memory loops, many of the networks were wired at random so that it was impossible in advance to predict what it would do. A "rat" would be created at some point in the network and then it would set out to learn a path to some desired end point. First it would proceed randomly and then correct choices were reinforced. There was an arrangement of lights so that one could actually follow the progress of the rat—or rats. Minsky noted,

It turned out that because of an electronic accident in our design you could put two or three rats in the same maze and follow them all. The rats actually interacted with each other. If one of them found a good path the others would tend to follow it. We sort of quit science for awhile to watch the machine. We were amazed that it would have several activities going on in its little nervous system. Because of the random wiring, it had a sort of fail-safe characteristic about it. If one of the neurons wasn't working, it wouldn't make much of a difference. With three hundred tubes and the thousands of connections we had soldered, there would usually be something wrong somewhere. In those days even a radio set with twenty tubes tended to fail a lot. I don't think that we ever debugged our machine completely. But it didn't matter. By having this crazy random design it was almost sure to work, no matter how you built it.

(The machine remained in the basement of Memorial Hall for a few years until eventually it was carted off to Dartmouth, by some students, where it seems to have disappeared. Minsky returned to Princeton to work on his doctoral thesis.)

Minsky explains his Harvard machine as "basically Skinnerean."

Skinner, with whom I talked a great deal while I was building it, was never much interested in it. I *did* help him on some of his experiments with pigeons. The unrewarded behavior of my machine was, more or less, random. This limited its learning abilities. It could never formulate a plan. The next idea I had, which I worked on theoretically for my thesis, was to give the network a second memory, which remembered what the stimulus had been *after* a response. This enabled one to bring in the idea of prediction. If the machine, or animal, is confronted with a new situation it can search its memory to see what would happen if it reacted in certain ways. If there is an unpleasant association with a certain stimulus, for example, then the machine could choose a different response. I had the naïve idea that if one could build a big enough network with enough of these memory loops, then it might get lucky and acquire the ability to envision things in its head. This became a field of study later. It was called "self-organizing random networks."

Even today I still get letters from young students here and

there who say, Why are you people trying to program intelligence? Why don't you try to find a way to build a nervous system that will just spontaneously create it? Finally I decided that this was either a bad idea or else it would take thousands or millions of neurons to make it work and I couldn't afford to try to build a machine like that.

I asked Minsky why it had not occurred to him to use a computer to simulate his machine. I knew that von Neumann's computer, which served as the prototype for so many of the present-day computers, had been completed and was operating at The Institute for Advanced Study in Princeton in 1952. Minsky answered,

I knew a little bit about computers. I had even taken a course with Howard Aiken [one of the first electronic computer designers] at Harvard on the logical design of computers. But Aiken's machine only had a few hundred memory registers and even von Neumann's machine only had a thousand. On the one hand, I was afraid of the complexity of these machines, and on the other hand, I thought that they weren't big enough to do anything interesting in the way of learning. In any case, I did my doctoral thesis on self-organizing networks. A couple of my fellow graduate students—Lloyd Shapley, the astronomer Harlow Shapley's son, and John Nash—helped out with a few points and occasionally I talked to von Neumann. He was on my thesis committee along with A. W. Tucker and J. W. Tukey. Later, Tucker told me that he had gone to von Neumann and said "This seems like very interesting work, but I can't evaluate it. I don't know whether it should really be called mathematics." Von Neumann replied, "Well, if it isn't now, it will be someday—let's encourage it." So I got my degree.

This was in 1954, two years after Minsky had gotten married. "I hadn't made any plans about what to do after I got my degree, but some intriguing people came along and said that they were starting a new kind of department at Tufts, which was to be called Systems Analysis...if I came, I could do anything I wanted to. I wanted to come back to Boston, so I joined them for awhile. But soon after Gleason came to me and said that I should be a Junior Fellow at Harvard. He helped to arrange that. He nominated me and he was supported by Claude Shannon, Warren McCulloch, and Norbert Wiener. So I spent the next three years as a Junior Fellow—there were about thirty of us, sort of one from each field: thirty gifted children."

I recall having encountered Minsky late one night in 1954 in the library of the Jefferson Physics Laboratory. When he saw me, he looked up from his book and muttered, "One microlumen per square yard." A "lumen" is an archaic unit of light flux and a microlumen is an infinitesimal amount of light, and, in any event, his sibylline pronouncement made no sense to me. I asked him what he was doing and he said "I am grinding lenses." He later told me that while he was thinking about the next steps to take in artificial intelligence, he had been spending his time designing a new optical microscope with a resolving power about one and a half times better than any previously designed optical microscope. He patented it, but never did anything with the patent, which has since expired. The real event during those years, though, occurred not at Harvard but at Dartmouth.

In her book, *Machines Who Think,* Pamela McCorduck describes the genesis of what was officially called The Dartmouth Summer Research Project on Artificial Intelligence. Early in 1956, Minsky—along with John McCarthy, then a professor of mathematics at Dartmouth, Nathaniel Rochester, then manager of information research at the IBM laboratories in Poughkeepsie, New York, and Claude Shannon, for whom Minsky had worked in the summer of 1952 at the Bell laboratories—submitted a proposal to the

Rockefeller Foundation for a conference on what McCarthy had called artificial intelligence, the belief that "every aspect of learning or any other feature of intelligence" could be simulated. The conference was funded in the amount of $7,500 by the Rockefeller Foundation and lasted for two months during the summer of 1956. The several participants have different recollections of the conference's significance, and Minsky told me a few of the things that struck him:

My friend Nat Rochester had programmed a neural network model—I think he got the idea from Hebb's book and not from me—on an early IBM 701 computer. His model had several hundred "neurons" all connected to each other in some terrible way. I think it was his hope that if you gave the network some simultaneous stimuli it would develop some neurons that were sensitive to this coincidence. I don't think he had anything specific in mind but was trying to discover correlations: something that could have been of profound importance. Nat would run the machine for a long time and then print out pages of data showing the state of the neural net. When he came to Dartmouth he brought with him a cubic foot of these printouts. He said, "I am trying to see if anything is happening but I can't see anything." He had at one point even rented an old drill-hall and taped the printouts to the wall so he could step back and see the whole picture. But if one didn't know what to look for one might miss any evidence of self-organization of these nets even if it took place. I think that that is what I had been worried about when I decided not to use computers to study some of the ideas connected with my thesis.

The other thing that Minsky told me that struck him at Dartmouth has, by now, become one of great legends in the field of artificial intelligence. It is the sequence of events that culminated in 1959, when for the first time

Herbert Gelernter used a computer—the IBM 704—to prove a theorem in geometry.

I had heard or read so many variants of this story that I was especially interested to hear Minsky's recollection. Sometime in the late spring of 1956, Minsky became interested in the idea of using computers to prove the geometric theorems in Euclid. (At about this same time a very powerful group at the RAND Corporation in Santa Monica, consisting of Allen Newell, J. C. Shaw, and Herbert Simon, had conceived of a general method—called Logic Theorist—to solve logic problems with computers. Newell and Simon reported on their work at the Dartmouth conference and out of it came a new generation of computer programming languages. I will come back to this in chapter 3 when I describe the evolution of these languages.) During the spring, Minsky began to reread Euclid's *Elements*. He told me,

If you look through Euclid's books, you find that he proves hundreds of theorems. All you have to do is to approach that with a viewpoint. I said to myself, "there are really only a small number of types of theorems. There are theorems about proving that angles are equal. There are theorems about circles intersecting. There are theorems about areas and so forth." Next I focused on the different ways he proves, for example, that certain angles are equal. One way is to show that the angles are in congruent triangles. I sketched all of this out on a few pieces of paper. I didn't have a computer, so I simulated one on paper. I wrote out a flow chart of how the theorem-proving program would work and some of the geometric knowledge it would have to have. Then I tried to pretend I was a computer obeying instructions without understanding them. To "simulate" a program like this, one has to reduce one's intelligence to a very primitive level and most people are unable to do this without a lot of practice. I had to give my "computer" alternate methods in case the first one failed, so I constructed a small program. I decided to try out my program on one of Euclid's first theorems, which is to prove that the base angles of an isosceles triangle are equal. I started working on that and after a few hours—this was during the conference—I nearly jumped out of my chair.

To understand Minsky's excitement, let me draw an isosceles triangle.

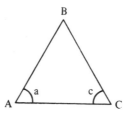

We are given that the line segments *AB* and *BC* are equal. The problem is to show that the base angles *a* and *c* are equal. To prove this, one has to show that the angles *a* and *c* are in congruent triangles. Minsky recalls saying to himself,

Now I have to show that *AB* is equal to something. But I am given that *AB* is equal to *BC*. Well, for heaven's sake, that's part of it. Now what about *BC*? Well, that's equal to *AB*. Now what about *CA*? But that is equal to *AC*. I almost jumped out of my chair. I hadn't known about this proof. It is not the one given in Euclid in which he constructs two new triangles by dropping a perpendicular from *B* to *AC,* although it was discovered by Pappus. It is sometimes credited to Frederick the Great. I thought that my program would have to go down a long logical search. But, basically, it was too dumb. A human—Euclid, for example—might have said that before we prove two triangles are congruent we have to make sure that there *are* two triangles. But my "machine" was perfectly willing to accept the idea that *BAC* and *BCA are* two triangles whereas a human feels it's sort of degenerate to give two names to the same object. A human would say, I don't have two houses because my house has a front door and a back door. So this proof comes from the fact that the machine doesn't understand what a triangle is in the many deep ways that a human being does—the deep ways that might inhibit you from making this identification. All it knows is the logical definition of the relationship among various lines that are called triangle.

For me, the rest of the summer was a bit of a shambles for the following reason. I said that it was too easy. The first method I gave to my "computer" worked right off. I am now going to try it on another simple problem. The next [time] I tried it...I couldn't prove the theorem at all—it was to show that if the bisectors of a triangle are equal, then the triangle is an isosceles. In fact, I never found a nice proof until finally I met a fellow from China at Harvard. He had studied geometry...in China and knew the proof right off. But Nat Rochester had been very impressed by my first proof. When he went back to IBM he recruited Gelernter, who was a physicist interested in programming. Gelernter finally invented a computer language which he called FLPL [and] which stood for FORTRAN LIST Processing Language, which generalized the ideas of Newell, Shaw, and Simon, and put them into FORTRAN, the IBM programming language. It never had a chance to become very popular because it was soon superseded by John McCarthy's invention of an even more powerful computer language—LISP.

By 1960 Gelernter had gotten his program to work, and he gave it the job of proving any way it saw fit that the base angles of an isosceles triangle are equal. The machine found Pappus's proof.

2

About

Intelligent

Machines

A FEW YEARS AGO, Marvin Minsky made a remark that many people, especially those who believe that thought—intelligence—can never be mechanized, found deeply troubling. Minsky said, "The brain happens to be a meat machine." Minsky has a fairly low tolerance for what he considers to be nonsense. The idea that it is somehow impossible to understand the mind he regards as nonsense. Nor does he believe that simply by annotating its component parts will we understand it. With nearly a century of brain surgery behind us, we still do not know where memory is located in the brain, or even how many memory locations there are, or by what mechanism the information in our memories is stored and recovered. During my series of interviews with Minsky about his life and work he remarked, "I think that intelligence does not emerge from a handful of very beautiful principles—like physics. It emerges from perhaps a hundred fundamentally different kinds of mechanisms that have to interact just right. So, even if it took only four years to understand each of them, it might take *four hundred* years to unscramble the whole thing."

In prescribing four hundred years to unscramble the mechanisms of thought, Minsky certainly is being more cautious than Isaac Newton's great contemporary, Gottfried Wilhelm Leibniz. Three hundred years ago, Leibniz proposed to find a formalization of all of thought and in this way to make all reasoning as exact as "Arithmetic and Geometry." He thought that this would take five years at most. As he wrote, "It will not require much more work than we see being spent on a good many procedures and on a good many encyclopedias, as they call them. I believe that a number of chosen men can complete the task within five years; within two years they will exhibit the common doctrines of life, that is, metaphysics and morals, in an irrefutable calculus."

Leibniz made a partially successful attempt to make an algebraic calculus of Aristotle's propositional logic. He wrote the proposition "All A are B" in the form A/B and "All B are C" in the form B/C. Thus, he combined the two in the formula $A/B \cdot B/C$, and by canceling out the common B he derived A/C or "All A are C," which is the fundamental law of the Aristotelian syllogism. The calculus was not completed until the self-taught English mathematician George Boole published his celebrated book, *An Investigation of the Laws of Thought, on Which Are Founded the Mathematical Theories of Logic and Probability,* in 1854. To construct his calculus, Boole had to invent a new form of algebra. He denoted by "*1*" the set that contained everything and by "*0*" the set that contained nothing. If x is a set then Boole called *1-x* the set that contained everything that was not in x. He called the union of two sets *xy*—for example, the set of all males and the set of people who live in New York—which, in this case, stands for the set of all males who live in New York. He observed that in his calculus the set of all males who are males would take the form $x^2 = x$, which he rewrote as $x(1-x) = 0$, which is Aristotle's Law of the excluded Middle—one is a male or one is not a male. Boole's work had many obscurities and loopholes that were cleared up by his successors.

What is of interest to us is that in the 1880s Boole's calculus was partially translated into an equivalent set of electric circuits. This may have been the first attempt to design an electronic machine that could carry out deductive reasoning. Some of its features are described in a fascinating essay, "Logic, Biology and Automata—Some Historical Reflections," by Arthur W. Burks, a professor in the Department of Computer and Communication Sciences at the University of Michigan. Burks, an associate of John von Neumann, edited von Neumann's *The Theory of Self-Reproducing Automata,* published in 1966, nine years after von Neumann's death at the age of fifty-four. In 1886, the American philosopher and logician Charles Sanders Peirce wrote to one of his students, Alan Marquand,

I think electricity would be the best thing to rely on. Let *A, B, C,* be the three keys or other points where the circuit may be open or closed. [Peirce drew two battery operated circuit diagrams to illustrate his point.] As in Figure 1 there is a circuit only if *all* are closed; in Figure 2 there is a circuit if *any one* is closed. This is like multiplication and addition in logic.

Marquand drew up a design for the logic machine, indicating that the switches would have been telephone relays, but the machine was never built.

Burks conjectures, no doubt correctly, that Peirce had been inspired by the work of Charles Babbage. Babbage is one of the truly singular figures in modern science. Born the son of a banker in Devonshire in 1792, he inherited a considerable fortune that he ultimately exhausted on the financing of his scientific experiments. He was a polymathic genius and inventor who also contrived the notion that the Post Office charge a flat rate for mail deliveries irrespective of the distance traveled by the letter. He also invented the cowcatcher for trains and the first speedometer. A very temperamental man, he constantly carried on futile and enervating battles with his contemporaries. Early on in his life, Babbage decided to dedicate himself to the manufacture of machines that could relieve people of the drudgery of computation. The first, completed in 1822—indeed, the only one that actually computed something—he called the Difference Engine. With the Difference Engine, Babbage could numerically evaluate, to six decimal places, polynomials such as $x^2 + x + 41$—one of Babbage's favorite examples. Since most functions can be approximated by polynomials, this might have been the beginning of a highly useful and practical program of numerical analysis. Babbage, however, was a visionary whose main interest was in the machines he could *imagine* building rather than in the ones he could actually build.

Soon after building the Difference Engine, Babbage tried to make a more accurate version of it, a device that would produce results to an accuracy of twenty decimal places. The best electronic pocket computers now work to an accuracy of something like *nine* decimal places, so it is not surprising that Babbage never completed this machine. In fact, by 1833 he had lost all interest in it and was busy trying to design what would have been the first general purpose computer. The Difference Engine was a specialized device that was to use the method of so-called finite differences to compute polynomials. The new machine, the Analytical Engine, was meant to carry out any conceivable string of arithmetic operations and thus to solve any arithmetic problem for which one could devise an algorithm—a program. Babbage thought that his device would work on steam and would turn a vast array of gears and cranks. He hoped the machine would be able to perform about sixty additions a minute.

(At the present time, the most rapid solid-state computer, a machine known as the CYBER 205, made by the Control Data Corporation, has a cycle time—the basic unit of time which determines the speed of successive computer operations—of about twelve-billionths of a second. The cycle times of computers in common use are between thirty- and fifty-billionths of a second and the next generation of computers is expected to operate with cycle times of one-billionth of a second. Incidentally one may well wonder if there is any limit in principle as to how fast a computing machine can process information. In fact, there does appear to be such a limit and it was derived in an article entitled "Energy Cost of Information Transfer" written by the American-born Israeli physicist, Jacob D. Bekenstein. The basic idea is that all transmission of information requires energy. For example, the electrical signals in a computer transport electromagnetic energy from one part of the machine to another. It turns out there there is a theoretical minimum amount of energy required for a given amount of information transmitted; this energy will necessarily heat the machine. Bekenstein is considering machines that are microscopic in size in order to avoid the limitations that are presented by the fact that signals can never propagate faster than the speed of light. Indeed, if the rate of the machine operations is made too fast, such a machine simply will burn itself up. By looking at the details, Bekenstein finds that the fastest possible machine could carry out about 10^{15} operations a second, which is about a million times faster than the computers now being developed.)

Hence, like many visionaries, Babbage underestimated the power of his own vision. What he *did do* was to analyze the component structure of such a computing machine. Babbage realized that his machine would have to consist of three basic elements. It would have to have a memory that Babbage called the "store," which was to consist of columns of wheels, each engraved with ten digits. A modern machine uses a hierarchy of memories. Information is stored in a binary code—a "yes–no" or a "1–0" code that is physically realized by the presence or absence of a small number of electrons at a certain location in a transistor. Such a piece of information, as has been mentioned, is called a "bit." Typically these locations have a size somewhat larger than a human blood cell and they are packed together in "chips." The entire chip has an area of a few square millimeters and can hold about sixteen thousand bits of information. (The densest memory chips now available will hold 65,536 bits, that is, 2^{16} bits.) The machine can read any memory location in about 200-billionths of a second. Such a memory chip costs about five dollars. This part of the memory is called the "random access memory" (RAM) of the machine, since any storage location is always accessible to the machine in the course of its operating cycle. In addition, the machine has an external memory available to it on call with an almost unlimited storage capacity. Nowadays, information in these external memories is stored on thin circular discs that resemble phonograph records. There are two common types. The so-called floppy disc is made of a thin sheet of Mylar plastic coated with iron oxide. Typically, such a disc has a diameter of about eight inches and can hold twenty million bits of information. Floppy discs are read by a magnetic head that touches their surface so they are subject to wear. The second type of disc is made of aluminum. It can be as large as fourteen inches in diameter and can hold billions of bits. Such a disc can spin at 3,000 revolutions per minute, and at this enormous speed a layer of air is set up between the head and the disc to prevent wear. The memories can be read out in times between ten- and one hundred-thousandths of a second—much slower than the internal memory. The key to efficient machine operation is to have the information in the central memory available when it is needed. Babbage thought that his store should hold about a thousand 50-digit numbers or about 100,000 bits. The largest modern machines use internal memories of a few million bits.

The next component of Babbage's machine was the "mill"—what would now be known as the central processor—where the arithmetic operations were to be carried out. As I mentioned, he thought he might achieve a speed of about one addition per second. With the cycle times that now seem achievable, the next generation of machines should be able to do about a billion operations per second. (There are computers in which the entire central processor is on a single chip.) Finally, Babbage realized that he would have to get information in and out of the machine. In short, he would have to be able to program his computer.

At this stage, Babbage met a remarkable collaborator, Ada Augusta, the Countess of Lovelace. Lady Lovelace, "the only daughter of the house and heart" of the poet Byron, was born in 1815. Like her father, she died at the age of thirty-six and is buried next to him in Newstead in Nottinghamshire. Byron had separated from Ada's mother, Annabella Millbanke, when the child was a month old, and for the rest of her life Ada did not see him. As a young girl, she had been taken to see Babbage's Difference Engine. According to a witness, "young as she was [she] understood its working and saw the great beauty of the invention." Much of what we know about Babbage's Analytical Engine comes from the writings of Lady Lovelace. As even Babbage agreed, they were clearer than his own. Babbage did not build the machine in his lifetime, but he left detailed enough drawings so that after his death in 1871, his son was able to supervise at least the construction of the mill with its printer, which would have been used to print out the results of the arithmetic operations. Some years ago, IBM had working models of the Difference Engine and the Analytical Engine built for display.

To program his machine, Babbage intended to take over an invention of J. M. Jacquard of Lyons. In 1801, Jacquard made the first successful, fully automated weaving loom. He used punch cards—cards with holes punched in them—to produce patterns. If one of the rods in the loom mechanism encountered a hole, it would pass through; otherwise, it could not. An elaborate pattern could be woven automatically. Indeed, Babbage had a portrait of Jacquard himself woven with the aid of 24,000 punch cards. Babbage wanted to use a similar arrangement to instruct his machine, and Lady Lovelace was moved to write, "We may say most aptly that the Analytical Engine *weaves algebraic patterns* just as the Jacquard-loom weaves flowers and leaves." Babbage had a remarkable feeling for the specifics of programming. He thought of using an external memory to store mathematical tables. For instance, if a certain logarithm were needed, the machine was to ring a bell and display a card that supplied the operator with it. Babbage also had the foresight to realize that the machine could probably arrive at logarithms much faster using a built-in subroutine, as it is now called, than could the operator looking them up in a table. Indeed, this is done now. Babbage also understood that the machine would have to have the capacity to modify its program as it went along, since what it would do next might essentially depend on what it had done previously. To effect this, Babbage invented a rudimentary form of what is now known as stored programming. In its modern version—usually attributed to von Neumann—numbers in the machine's memory may be read by the machine as numbers or instructions, depending on the context. Hence, since the machine acts on these numerical registers, it can modify its own program. Babbage proposed that his numerical registers would have an extra place, which, instead of designating a number, would activate the next set of instructions if the result of a certain subtraction were, for example, negative.

In one of her writings, Lady Lovelace issued a sort of edict on the limitations of computers. At least, it is often quoted in that spirit:

> The Analytical Engine has no pretensions whatever to originate anything. It can do whatever we *know how to order* it to perform. It can *follow* analysis; but it has no power of *anticipating* any analytical relations or truths. Its province is to assist us in making *available* what we are already acquainted with.

I have now come to believe that what is true in this statement is essentially trivial and that what is profound in it is untrue or, at least, highly misleading. Certainly computers need to be programmed and in this trivial sense the machine "can do [only] whatever we *know how to order* it to perform." But the programs that are now in use in the most sophisticated parts of artificial intelligence are at the limit of the ability of the human programmer to keep track of them—to keep all the details straight.

One of Minsky's students, Terry Winograd, wrote an operational program, which I will discuss later, that consisted of more than a *quarter of a million* words. As a result of this experience, Winograd and another student, Daniel Bobrow, have gone to the Xerox laboratories in Palo Alto, where for several years they have been working on automatic systems for organizing and keeping track of very large computer programs—programs that humans can no longer monitor. Moreover, because of the abilities of the machines to function conditionally and, with the new programming languages, to adjoin new pieces to their own programs and thus make the programs iterate on themselves, what will happen in the end simply cannot be predicted. The route that the machines will take cannot be predicted. While it may be possible in principle to make the machine print out the steps it followed in a certain algorithm, it is reaching the point where in a practical sense it is, in effect, impossible. Is this the point where it is appropriate to attribute "intelligence" to the machine? Perhaps this is only a matter of semantics. Many of us would be tempted to say that in principle all programs can be unraveled and that the "mechanical" nature of the programs, if that is what it is, can be explained. If people like Minsky are right, then so can the workings of the human mind.

In 1961 Minsky published a monumental critical review of the field of artificial intelligence, "Steps Toward Artificial Intelligence." It contains a bibliography with six hundred references, essentially all the significant papers that had been published on the subject. In his article, Minsky discussed the cited papers with all but six of their authors.

For several years the article served to define the field, and it has since been reprinted in a collection edited by Edward A. Feigenbaum and Julian Feldman, *Computers and Thought*. In it he wrote,

In all of this discussion we have not come to grips with anything we can isolate as "intelligence." We have discussed only heuristics, shortcuts and classification techniques. Is there something missing? I am confident that sooner or later [Minsky's prediction has now been amply realized] we will be able to assemble programs of great problem solving ability from complex combinations of heuristic devices—multiple optimizers, pattern-recognition tricks, planning algebras, and the like. In no one of these will we find the seat of intelligence. Should we ask what intelligence "really is"? My own view is that this is more of an aesthetic question, or one of sense of dignity, than a technical matter! To me "intelligence" seems to denote little more than the complex of performances which we happen to respect, but do not understand. So it is, usually, with the question of "depth" in mathematics. Once the proof of a theorem is really understood its content seems to become trivial. (Still there may remain a sense of wonder about how the proof was discovered.)...Programmers, too, know that there is never any "heart" in a program. There are high level routines in each program, but all they do is dictate that "if such and such, then transfer to such and such a subroutine." And when we look at the low-level subroutines, which "actually do the work," we find senseless loops and sequences of trivial operations, merely carrying out the dictates of their superiors. The intelligence in such a system seems to be as intangible as becomes the meaning of a single common word when it is thoughtfully pronounced over and over again.

We should not let our inability to discern a locus of intelligence lead us to conclude that programmed computers cannot think. For it may be so with *man,* as with *machine,* that when we understand finally the structure and program, the feeling of mystery (and self-approbation) will weaken.

The modern era in computation began in 1937, when Howard Aiken at Harvard and George R. Stibitz of the Bell laboratories, with associated engineers, began the design and construction of electromechanical computers based on Babbage's conception and using telephone relay switches. In a long letter that Dr. Stibitz wrote to me nearly twenty years ago, he pointed out that as early as 1939 he had built a small computer called the Complex Computer that used binary arithmetic. It seems to have been the first machine to have done so. Exhibited in the fall of 1940 at a meeting of the American Mathematical Society at Dartmouth, the machine was operated from New York City over the telegraph lines and thus was also a forerunner of the sort of remote controlled data processing that is now common. Dr. Stibitz wrote, "One of the interested people in the audience who pushed keys in Hanover, New Hampshire, and got back answers from New York was Norbert Weiner."

Like Stibitz, Howard Aiken began his career as a physicist. Balking at the tedious labor of evaluating the equations in his Ph.D. thesis, he began to design a machine that would do it for him. In 1939, he got support from IBM, and with a small group of IBM engineers he began constructing his machine at Harvard. Many years ago, Dr. Aiken told me that it was not until three years after he had begun to work on computers that he came across Babbage's work. In fact, Dr. Aiken said, "If Babbage had lived seventy-five years later I would have been out of a job." Aiken's machine, the Mark I, was completed in 1944. It had a central memory that consisted of seventy-two counters, each of which could store one twenty-three-digit number and its sign, plus or minus. The machine worked in decimals, and it also had sixty registers that functioned as an external memory where constants could be stored. It took about six seconds to do a multiplication and about twelve to do a division. By the time it was completed, it had already become obsolete, because in May of 1943 work had begun on the first truly electronic computer: the ENIAC—Electronic Numerical Integrator and Calculator. Herman H. Goldstine, one of the ENIAC's creators, has written the most complete account now available of the calculator, *The Computer from Pascal to von Neumann*. But he was prevented from giving a definitive history by patent litigation that has been going on since the late 1940s. In July of 1942 Goldstine, then a young mathematician, was drafted into the army and sent to the Ballistic Research Laboratory at the Aberdeen Proving Ground in Maryland to work on the computation of firing tables for artillery pieces. He soon discovered that this required the computation of about three thousand trajectories for each type of gun, and that with the crude methods then available for this type of calculation thirty days would have to be spent on each table. As Goldstine wrote, "These estimates reveal a situation that was unsupportable both because the volume of work was too large and, perhaps more importantly, because the work had to be done very promptly to avoid delays in putting weapons into the hands of the troops in the field." In the fall, Goldstine met John Mauchly, a physicist at the University of Pennsylvania who, in collaboration with a brilliant engineer, J. Presper Eckert, of the Moore School of Electrical Engineering at the University of Pennsylvania, had begun to design a purely electronic computer. By April of 1943, Army Ordnance had agreed to back a joint Aberdeen-Moore School project. It took three years to build the computer, which was moved from the Moore School to Aberdeen in 1947 where it ran until October of 1955.

The ENIAC was certainly the most complex electronic device that had ever been built. To get some idea of it, one has only to read Arthur Burks's report: "In addition to its 18,000 vacuum tubes the ENIAC contained about 70,000 resistors, 10,000 capacitors and 6,000 switches. It was a hundred feet long, 10 feet high and 3 deep. In operation it consumed 140 kilowatts of power." It was basically a decimal machine that could handle ten-digit numbers with their signs. Its internal memory could hold only twenty "words," that is, twenty ten-digit numbers. Each multiplication took about three-thousandths of a second and each division about three-hundredths of a second. This was a gain in time of a factor of several hundred over the relay machines like Aiken's, something that is easily understood when one realizes that a relay is a macroscopic object with a mass of at least a gram and thus has a good deal of inertia that prevents it from being opened and closed rapidly. The electrons in a vacuum tube or transistor, on the other hand, have masses of about 10^{-27} grams and so their switches operate almost instantaneously.

In the summer of 1944, the ENIAC project got a remarkable new "recruit," von Neumann. Goldstine met von Neumann, whom he had known previously by reputation only, on a railroad platform in Aberdeen. Goldstine struck up a conversation with von Neumann and, as Goldstine writes in *The Computer from Pascal to von Neumann,* "When it became clear to von Neumann that I was concerned with the development of an electronic computer capable of 333 multiplications per second, the whole atmosphere of our conversation changed from one of relaxed good humor to one more like the oral examination for the doctor's degree in mathematics." Von Neumann visited the ENIAC project in August, and from that time on computers and automata and their relation to the human mind became a dominant theme in his life work.

This is not the place to review in detail von Neumann's contributions to computing machines. In essence, he spelled out the logical structure of the machines—the real implementation of Babbage's program. This work was published in a series of monumental reports written in collaboration with Burks, Goldstine, and others. Their ideas were put into practice in a landmark computer that von Neumann, Goldstine, and several others helped design and build at the Institute for Advanced Study in Princeton, and that went into operation in 1952. The machine was widely copied and the copies were copied; the original is in the Smithsonian Institution. What concerns us here is the connection that von Neumann perceived between this work and what is now called artificial intelligence. As Goldstine confirms, von Neumann was profoundly affected by a paper, written in 1943 by Warren McCulloch and Walter Pitts, called "A Logical Calculus of the Ideas Immanent in Nervous Activity." In some sense this is the seminal paper in the field of artificial intelligence, and it was due to von Neumann's interest that it became widely known as early as it did. It is also a perfect example of the fact that a profound but partially incorrect paper in science can have a vastly greater impact than a correct but less meaningful paper. Indeed, after reading the paper von Neumann used its notation for much of his subsequent work in automata theory.

Warren McCulloch, who died in 1969, was asked as a freshman at Haverford College in 1918 how he was going to spend his life. He answered, "I have no idea, but there is one question I would like to answer: What is a number, that a man may know it, and a man that he may know a number?" His interlocutor, who was a Quaker, replied "Friend, thee will be busy as long as thee lives." After receiving his graduate degree in psychology from Columbia, he transferred into the medical school there. He served his internship at Bellevue Hospital and then specialized in the study of epilepsy and head injuries. After some years at Yale, where he studied neurophysiology, he went to the University of Illinois, where he directed the Laboratory for Basic Research in the Department of Psychiatry. In 1952 he became a member of the staff of the Research Laboratory of Electronics at M.I.T. and remained at M.I.T. for the rest of his life. In her book *Machines Who Think,* Pamela McCorduck has given a biographical sketch of McCulloch in which she points out that he was a gifted poet. I was struck by the following sample of his poetry, written when he was a junior at Haverford.

Appointments
November 16, 1919
(His Birthday)

Yesterday:

       Christ thought for me in the morning
       Nietzsche in the afternoon

Today:

       Their appointments are at the same hour

Tomorrow:

       I shall think for myself all day long.
       That is why I am rubbing my hands.

A highly idiosyncratic and original figure, McCulloch certainly spent the rest of his life thinking for himself. He was not a mathematician, which is undoubtedly why he joined forces with Walter Pitts, who was; and they published their first paper when Pitts was seventeen. Forced to drop out of high school by his father, who wanted him to go to work, Pitts ran away from home and finally ended up in Chicago. McCulloch used to tell the story of young

Pitts spending a lot of time in the park near the University of Chicago, carrying on philosophical conversations with a man he knew only as Bert. Bert turned out to be Bertrand Russell, who spent the academic year 1938-39 as a visiting professor of philosophy at the University of Chicago. According to McCulloch, Russell suggested that Pitts read a book by Rudolf Carnap, a noted logician and philosopher of science who was at Chicago and who used to attend Russell's seminar. Pitts read the book and then visited Carnap to point out a mistake in it. I cannot find this tale in Ronald Clark's detailed biography of Russell, although the chronology certainly fits. It was in Chicago that McCulloch came to work with Pitts who then became his student at Illinois.

Their great paper of 1943 is difficult reading. In fact, the part entitled "Nets With Circles," which attempted to deal with how neural networks might learn and evolve, is certainly wrong. Minsky read the paper while still an undergraduate. Recently he told me,

I encountered their paper rather early and had understood as much of it as I could. George Miller, who was then an assistant professor at Harvard and was interested in mathematical psychology couldn't understand the second half of it, although he understood the first half perfectly. So I worked on it very hard and, finally, I reassured him by saying that I thought the notation was inconsistent and the definitions weren't correct. There couldn't be things with exactly those definitions. I believe that McCulloch was dazzled by Pitts, who was then about sixteen and a mathematical prodigy. Later I attempted to have some conversations with Pitts [who came to M.I.T. with McCulloch] about it but he would never discuss it. I concluded that Pitts [who died in 1960] was on the track of a theory which he never got. He was bluffing and McCulloch had been somewhat taken in by it. I reassured Miller that if he couldn't understand it, it wasn't his fault. It wasn't all there. It took a lot of courage for me to decide that it wasn't all there.

Nonetheless, the question remains, Why were the McCulloch-Pitts paper and its sequels the dominant influence on Minsky and his contemporaries as they tried to begin to understand intelligence?

To answer this, it is necessary to describe something of the physiology of the nervous system. Early in this century, through the work of Santiago Ramón y Cajal and others, it was established that in the brain there are about ten billion discrete nerve cells called neurons. Each neuron possesses up to two hundred thousand synapses—entry ports— through which ions can flow. There is also one axon for each neuron—a fiber that can carry away pulses of ions released when the neuron fires—when it releases an ion pulse. A given neuron may fire as often as about a thousand times a second. A neuron has a *firing threshold*. If the impulses it receives are greater than a certain critical value, it will fire; otherwise, it will not. (Diseased neurons may fire spontaneously and are not controlled by the input information.) Some inputs can be negative—inhibitory— and others positive, but what counts is whether the sum of these inputs exceeds the critical firing threshold. The pulse a neuron fires can split if the axon branches and thus it can feed inputs into several of its neighbors. The speed of the pulse can vary from one meter per second for thin axons to a hundred and fifty meters a second for thick ones. The question that McCulloch and Pitts tried to answer was, What can such a neural network do?

To deal with this, they replaced the real neural network with a fictitious, or idealized, network in which the neurons were sort of black boxes subject to five properties—axioms. (A related set of axioms had been given several years earlier by the mathematician-biologist N. Rashevsky of the University of Chicago.) McCulloch and Pitts listed their axioms as follows:

1. The activity of a neuron is an "all-or-none" process. [A neuron does, or does not, fire.]
2. A certain fixed number of synapses must be excited within the period of latent addition in order to excite a neuron at any time and this number is independent of previous activity and position of the neuron. [The neuron has a certain fixed firing threshold and this must be achieved for it to fire.]
3. The only significant delay within the nervous system is synaptic delay. [The speed with which pulses propagate in the axons is so great that, effectively, the cycle time of the network is the time it takes for a neuron to fire and then return to its normal unexcited state, which is about one-thousandth of a second.]
4. The activity of any inhibitory synapse absolutely prevents excitation of the neuron at that time. [At the time McCulloch and Pitts wrote their paper it was believed that an inhibitory impulse was absolute. Now we know that they sum with the rest of the synaptic input. This is one of the elements in their paper that required reworking.]
5. The structure of the net does not change with time.

This last axiom presumably means that the components of this idealized net are assumed to be immortal. In reality, one of the striking features of the nerve cells is that they die and are not replaced. In the course of our lifetime, we lose about 10 percent of our neurons. Nonetheless, we continue to function, unlike for example, a radio, which ceases to operate if a transistor is removed. At a conference on information storage and neural control in 1962, McCulloch commented on this. After a lecture, when asked about dead or injured neurons, he replied, "I have not seen my own cerebellum, but I have seen that of many a man my age. I am over fifty, and I expect that at least 10 percent of the Purkinje cells [or Purkyne cells, named after the nineteenth-century Czech physiologist Jan Evangelista Purkyne, who first observed these nerve cells in the cerebellum] in my cerebellum are replaced by nice holes at my age, but I can still touch my nose. It is incredible how little brain has to be left in order for it to function.''

Under the influence of the McCulloch-Pitts paper, von Neumann initiated a profound study of how to organize a reliable automaton—for example, a neural network—from unreliable components. Von Neumann realized that one of the keys was to build redundancy into the system, which means having two, or several, components that can take over for each other if something goes wrong. He also had the notion of hooking systems together so that they could monitor each other. He gave the following concrete example. Suppose one has three identical machines, each of which can make a long calculation, for example, a million steps long with one chance in a hundred of making an error somewhere. Of course, it would be intolerable because none of the machines would ever complete the whole calculation correctly. However, if the machines were to proceed so that when two of them disagree they would be required to take the word of the third machine and then proceed, this reduces the chance of error from one in a hundred to one in thirty-three million. Von Neumann speculated that the central nervous system must have some sort of redundancy built into it—probably all sorts of redundancies—and now we know that this is certainly the case. A reflection of it is the fact that memory does not seem to be located in the brain in any single place. Some people have speculated that *each* neuron has the entire memory built into it. This seems to be unnecessary redundance, especially since, as Minsky has pointed out to me, an analysis by Claude Shannon shows that if the memory—or memories, since there may be more than one kind—are copied in a small number of widely separated places in the brain, then even if half the brain were removed, a substantial part of the memory would be left. Morever, it is probably true that some of the memories can be deduced from the others, that is, that what was lost can be partially reconstructed. Since evolution usually follows the most efficient path, one imagines that something like this has happened.

Von Neumann's ideas have been put into practice in the design of computers. Indeed, they have become central in the new generation of machines. As I have pointed out, the memories in these machines are packed into tiny chips made of "bits," where bits are the presence or absence of a relatively few electrons at some site in a semiconductor. These electrons can be displaced by the residual radioactivity in the ceramic package in which the chips are encapsulated or even by cosmic rays. This can change a "1" to a "0" or vice versa, which ultimately can change and ruin an entire program. The machine can monitor potential changes making checks on what it has stored to see that nothing has been altered. This requires a still larger memory in the machine with more potential for error. But the process can be kept within acceptable bounds.

Before I describe what the McCulloch-Pitts network cannot do, I will describe what it *does* do. To put the matter in a crude way, the network can function as a computer. In a more refined sense, in any proposition in a logical system—such as the one found in Whitehead and Russell's *Principia Mathematica,* one finds a configuration of neurons that in its joint activity is equivalent to this proposition. We saw this when we discussed how Charles

Sanders Peirce proposed to use an electrical network to do Boolean algebra. The McCulloch-Pitts paper contains a page of arcane drawings exemplifying how to do this in increasingly complex cases, and they purport to give a general proof that I, at least, found so elliptical as to be impossible to follow. Subsequent workers have filled in the details. There is another way to state their result, and McCulloch and Pitts give a brief reference to it. Their neural net is equivalent to a Turing machine, or partially equivalent to a Turing machine. Since, as I will explain, a Turing machine can compute anything that most people would call computable, their net can compute almost anything.

Alan Mathison Turing was born in London in 1912. He died, probably suicidally, in 1954. After von Neumann, I would say that Turing was the most influential thinker on the subject of the logic of automata in this century. Ironically, his most important work was done in the 1930s, when computers did not exist. He created them in his mind and made an enormously profound analysis of what such a machine could do in principle. His idealized machine bears the same abstract resemblance to a real computer as the neural network of McCulloch and Pitts does to a real brain. The Turing machine consists of an infinitely long tape divided into equal squares. The tape is made infinitely long so that it will not run out of room to do its work. Minsky told me that it was the length of the tape that kept him away from Turing machines at first. He was less interested in the possibilities of abstract models of a computer than in what real computers could do—until in the mid 1950s he realized that the number of internal states in a real computer is so huge that a Turing machine with an infinite tape is a good approximation of it. To understand this, let us take a specific example. Suppose one has a computer with

16,000 memory registers and that each register holds 8 bits—otherwise known as a byte—which is the typical size for a modest home computer. Then how many possible distinct configurations or "states" of this memory are there? With 8 bits one can make 2^8, or 256, different bytes. When one doubles the number of memory registers, one squares the number of possible memory states; and when one triples the number of registers, one cubes the number of states and so forth. So in this example, the number of memory states is $2^{128,000}$. To get some feeling for this incredibly large number, there are something like 2^{190} particles in the sun or 2^{60} seconds since the universe began. And this is only the number of possible memory states in a modest hobby computer. The number of such states in a real computer is almost unthinkably larger than this, which explains why a Turing machine with an infinite tape is a good idealization of a real computer.

The squares of the Turing machine tape are either blank or marked with a slash (- ⁄). One may imagine that there is a movable arrow that can point to any given square. The machine language contains just four "words" or four different possible types of instruction. We may call them L, R, *, and / . They mean, respectively:

1. L—move the arrow one step to the left
2. R—move one step to the right
3. *—erase the slash if there is one
4. /—print a slash if there isn't one

The machine begins with its arrow pointing at one of the squares and there is some sequence of dashes and blanks on the tape. An instruction takes the form of, for example, "Move one step to the right, and if that square is blank then repeat this instruction," (which would get the machine to move two steps to the right), "or if it is not blank then go to the next instruction." In this way, a program is built up that resembles a computer program. It is not difficult to write programs for the usual arithmetic operations—addition, multiplication, and so on—in this somewhat clumsy language, if a number is simply represented by an equivalent number of slashed squares. One must simply write these programs carefully and prevent the machine from simply moving over blank squares forever. In fact, there is a very deep theorem lurking here that closely resembles Gödel's theorem in mathematical logic. Suppose one has written some general program. Can one state in advance whether or not the machine can carry it out in a finite number of steps? Known as the "halting problem," the theorem states that, in general, this question cannot be decided. No algorithm exists to determine whether an arbitrary program can be carried out in a finite number of steps. The computing machine version of Gödel's result is that in a mathematically consistent, formal system there must necessarily exist statements that cannot be proven within the language of the system.

Turing proved—and it came as a considerable surprise—that there existed what is now known as a "universal Turing machine," or a machine that could calculate anything that any Turing machine could compute. This means that, in a certain deep sense, there is only one computer. The details concerning how various individual Turing machines are constructed is irrelevant. For many years, it was felt that such a universal machine would necessarily have to be incredibly complex, with millions or at least thousands of instructions to define it. A few years ago, Minsky devised a construction that uses only twenty-eight instructions. He holds the record for building the simplest conceptual universal computer. We can now state McCulloch's and Pitt's results in the following way: Anything that their network can compute can also be computed by a universal Turing machine. Conversely, their network can compute anything that a Turing machine can compute. (In their paper McCulloch and Pitts were vague in describing how one would attach the tapes and scanners to the neural network in order to turn it into a Turing machine; but their general intuition was certainly correct.) Their results inspired von Neumann to write a few years after the McCulloch-Pitts paper appeared: "Anything that can be exhaustively and unambiguously described, anything that can be completely and unambiguously put into words, is *ipso facto* realizable by a suitable finite neural network...."

The McCulloch-Pitts paper was attractive to young people, because it was clear that even on its own terms it was not a complete piece of work. In the section "Nets With Circles," McCulloch and Pitts covered cycles of neurons that closed back on themselves. They wanted to allow for the possibility of setting up circuits that could "continue reverberating" around the network "for an indefinite period of time." They hoped to account for the memory of events that had taken place in the network in the distant past. To this day, their successors have been trying to make sense of this part of the paper. On a deep level, the McCulloch-Pitts paper did not give a clue as to how the *real* brain is organized to do anything. As Minsky said to me recently, "Their network was both too modular and not modular enough." In other words, the unit acted like one large module without any clue as to how things are organized into the functional units that one thinks must be present, given what the brain actually does. A perfect example of this gap in understanding is our present concept of vision. When asked how we see, most people answer that light passes through the optical lens in the front of the eye to impinge on the retina, which is the actual organ that is stimulated by light signals. The retina is commonly thought to be something like a television screen, where the optical images are flashed. The trouble with this explanation of vision can be encapsulated in the question: Who is watching the television screen? Clearly, somehow the physical image on the retina gets transformed into symbolic information in the brain. We can experience this ourselves by looking at those optical paradoxes that seem to be a blur of lines and colors but that suddenly turn into Abraham Lincoln. How often have we failed to recognize someone because he was out of context? Now, thanks to experiments on cats by people like David Hubel and Torsten Wiesel at Harvard, one can at least follow the pathway that this information processing takes in the brain. (A good description of this work and the questions it raises is given in Douglas Hofstadter's *Gödel, Escher, Bach: an Eternal Golden Braid*.)

The neurons in the retina fire at a regular rate until they are stimulated by light. When stimulated, they may change their rate of firing—either faster or slower—but only if there is a contrast in the illumination of neighboring areas of the retina. Uniform illumination of the retina does not change the firing rates. We are very sensitive to patterns with sharp contrasts in illumination. We readily detect edges, and this constitutes the first level of pattern formation; it is two-dimensional, since the retina is essentially a planar surface. The signals from the retina are collected and propagate to a volume in the mid-brain containing what are known as lateral geniculate neurons. As Hofstadter observes, there is something rather odd about this development in the sense that the two-dimensional retinal information is mapped into a three-dimensional network of neurons. Why this mapping with its change in dimension takes place is not clear—perhaps to heighten the

69

articulation of the light and dark contrast. From here the pattern information moves to the back of the brain to the visual cortex. It is interesting that *this* neural network in which visual information becomes part of our conscious recognition, is as far away from our eyes as it is possible for brain cells to be. While much is known about the anatomy of the visual cortex and the columns of neurons that form it, essentially nothing is known about how the recognition process occurs. Are there individual neurons so complex that they can recognize lines and enable us to say, "Oh yes, that is Abraham Lincoln?" Or is it the organization of groups of neurons that is important? Again and again, when one tries to correlate some mental process like cognition or memory with some bit of neuronal hardware, one comes up against a wall. The complex of problems this poses is certainly one of the most fundamental in modern biology. No answers to this set of problems is found in McCulloch and Pitts.

In the years following the McCulloch-Pitts paper the field of artificial intelligence has developed along two broad lines. The first is usually referred to as robotics—construction of machines that perform various behavior. Robotics was a very popular enterprise in the artificial intelligence community until a few years ago, when people appeared to lose interest in it. Minsky told me that it has been enjoying a revival very recently. Indeed, major industrial companies are now trying to locate and hire all the experts in robot construction who are available to make machines for use in high-technology manufacturing. The second line of development in artificial intelligence one might call programming—the design of programs to be used by computers to carry out more and more complex problem-solving tasks. The two areas have often overlapped. For example, the M.I.T. group has attached robots to their computer and has pioneered developments in computer hardware in order to be able to develop more sophisticated programs.

Minsky has been involved in both developments directly or indirectly. He is particularly fond of electronic gadgets and has put any number of them together, including a sophisticated new computer of his own. However, as he once said, "I don't like programming much so I have never written a big, messy artificial intelligence program. I have all sorts of blocks when I try to write them—like thinking of what to name things and remembering what I did yesterday." Nonetheless, over the years he has supervised a series of brilliant students and younger colleagues constructing some of the most complex computer programs ever assembled.

Since I am sort of detached from the specifics I have always felt free to think about the grand scheme, which at the time seemed impossible until some brilliant student showed up—usually three or four years later—and did it. Sometimes after they have done it I wonder what I had to do with it. I guess I provide the atmosphere and push them into looking deeper by asking questions. Sometimes students come to me and say, "That was a great idea you had. It really worked." I may not even remember having had the idea. I guess students have just as much of an inferiority complex as I do. If something unexpected happens they are liable to think I told them to do it, while I am liable to think that it was *their* idea. I have never published a joint paper with a student and most of them have gone on to do important original things on their own. I have always enjoyed collaborating with people. It is a fantastic experience. It's not that two people working together are twice as smart, but rather that one never gets stuck. If I work by myself I tend to pursue an idea—good or bad—in some fanatical direction without seeing that some slight change will make it much better. Another person can say "Why are you doing it that way?" and force me to rethink what I am doing. I don't see why I can't do that for my-self—but I can't.

The first of Minsky's collaborators was Oliver Selfridge. Selfridge had a small group at the Lincoln Laboratory at M.I.T.—this laboratory evolved from the Radiation Laboratory at M.I.T., where radar was developed during the war—that Minsky joined in 1958 after completing three years as a Junior Fellow at Harvard. Like Minsky, Selfridge also had a great fondness for electronic devices. Indeed, while working for Selfridge, Minsky invented a device that could identify the pitch of a voice.

It was a mess of electronics and a microphone, and if you sang to it it would tell you whether you were singing B-flat or C or whatever. It was a nice gadget that worked by its first computing four different upper estimates of the pitch and then there was a second gadget that would pick the lowest of these estimates. It had a lot of parts including some flip-flops [electronic devices that could operate in one of two stable modes]. I ordered about fifty of them from the stockroom at M.I.T. They had been de-signed by some engineers at Lincoln. The flip-flops were so popular in our lab that these fellows quit to form their own com-pany to make them. I don't think that at the time they had any plans to actually make computers—to compete with IBM. They thought that designing computer modules—laboratory devices that could be used to develop computers—would be a profitable thing for them to do. But for a trade show one of them, Ben Gurley, cooked up an arrangement of modules that *was* a com-puter. He connected a few hundred of them together and con-nected the whole thing to an oscilloscope so that one could see what they were doing. I think that it took about three months for Gurley to put it together. It made a tremendous hit at the show and some people wanted to buy it.

This became the first of the so-called PDP (for program data processor) computers. The company—the Digital

Equipment Corporation, whose president Kenneth Olsen, was one of the original Lincoln engineers—is now one of the largest computer manufacturers in the world. PDP computers are widely used for complex scientific applications, such as the pattern recognition process used to analyze events in the collisions among elementary particles that take place in the large accelerators and which are revealed in bubble chamber photographs. (The PDP-10 computer at Carnegie-Mellon is the world champion backgammon player.)

With Selfridge, who had once been a roommate of Walter Pitts, Minsky worked on some generalizations of the neural network models. In 1958 he was asked to join the mathematics department at M.I.T. as an assistant professor. He joined the group that included John McCarthy who, like Minsky, is widely regarded as one of the seminal figures in the field of artificial intelligence and computer science. Minsky and McCarthy had been graduate students together at Princeton, and Minsky recalls that McCarthy wrote a very impressive twenty-page thesis and then "disappeared" to join the Dartmouth mathematics department faculty, many of whose members had recently retired. The university built a whole new department dedicated to modern pursuits, hiring John Kemeny (later and until recently the president of Dartmouth), whose interests have always included artificial intelligence and computers, McCarthy, and others. The group invented BASIC (for Beginner's All-purpose Symbolic Instruction Code), the language designed especially for computers with very small memories of the type that they thought might be available to students. Virtually every home computer now sold uses BASIC. Incidentally, no computer language is patentable.

In 1956, using the phrase aparently for the first time, McCarthy and others organized the M.I.T. conference in "artificial intelligence." Minsky met McCarthy there, and the two men became reacquainted in 1957 when McCarthy came to M.I.T., where he remained for four years. (He is now at Stanford University.) From 1957 through 1962, McCarthy originated or completed some developments in computer science that have been a fundamental part of the field ever since, such as what is now known universally as time sharing. Minsky explained the general idea to me:

The idea of time sharing was to arrange things so that many people could use a computer at the same time rather than what had been the traditional way in which the computer processed one job after another. In those days it usually took a day or two for the computer to do your job. The reason that the old system was so painful was because most of the programs one wrote would inevitably fail because of some clerical error. Typically, a small program might take five or ten attempts to make it work, because there are so many possible ways to make mistakes. This meant that three weeks could elapse before you could even try your original idea. Then, very likely, that idea would be wrong—if you were doing anything interesting. So people became used to the notion that it would take six months to make and debug a really interesting program. So the idea of time sharing was to make the computer switch very quickly from one job to another. At first it doesn't sound very complicated, but it turns out that there are some real problems. The credit for solving them goes in part to McCarthy and in part to an English group that was working at the University of London.

One of the problems was the hardware. If you are running several jobs on a computer then you have to have some way of changing the things in the computer memory. To do this we developed a high-speed way of transferring things in and out of the computer memory into a magnetic drum. This required some engineering because if the computer spent too much time doing that then it became uneconomical. One of the things we had to develop was a way of writing on one part of the drum while the computer could read from another part. This cut the time down by half. Then we needed something that we called memory protection. One had to arrange things so that if there were several pieces of different people's programs in the computer, one piece could not damage another one by, say, erasing it from the main memory. We introduced what we called protection registers to prevent this from happening. Without them the various users would have interacted with each other in ways that they least expected.

One of the most interesting aspects of all of this was that for a long time we couldn't convince the computer manufacturers that what we were doing was important. They thought, so to say, that time sharing was a waste of time. I think that many of them were confused between what is called time sharing and what is called multiprocessing, which means having different parts of the computer running different parts of someone's program at the same time—which is totally different from the idea of many people sharing the same computer nearly simultaneously with each user getting a fraction of a second on the machine. IBM, for example, was working on a system in which while a program was being run another one was being written on tape and a third one was being prepared. This was not what we had in mind. We wanted, say, a hundred users to be able to make use of the hardware at once. It took several years before we got a computer manufacturer to take this seriously. Finally, we got the Digital Equipment Company to supply the hardware, and in collaboration with them we used their first little computer—the PDP-1—as the time-sharing prototype. We debugged it in our laboratory along with their engineers. Then we decided to make it work on our big IBM machine. It worked so beautifully that on the basis of it, M.I.T. got three million dollars a year for a long time from the Advanced Research Project Administration of the Defense Department for research in computer science.

Using time sharing, it is now possible to hook up one's home computer by telephone to one of the big computers that uses the system, and to run any problem one can think of from one's living room.

McCarthy's other interest during this period will take us deeply into the heart of artificial intelligence. It concerned the development of computer languages—the languages that have made the activities of these machines less and less distinguishable from the activities of our own brains.

3

Programming
Intelligence

AS A STUDENT in the 1940s, Marvin Minsky remembers thinking to himself that there appeared to be only three interesting problems in the world—at least in the world of science:

> Genetics seemed to be pretty interesting because nobody knew how it worked yet. But I wasn't sure that it was profound. The problems of physics seemed profound and solvable. It might have been nice to have done that. But the problem of intelligence seemed hopelessly profound. I can't remember considering anything else worth doing.

It is far from clear what is meant by the problem of intelligence or the attempt to discover how intelligence works. In fact, it is not entirely clear what a solution to this problem would consist of. But one possible goal might be to design a machine, something that everyone would agree was a *machine*—whose output could not be distinguished from that of an entity, a human being—whom everyone would agree was intelligent. This is the basic idea of what is known as "Turing's game," named after the British logician and computer scientist Alan Turing. He imagined concealing both a person and a machine and then—by a series of typewritten exchanges, for example—testing whether a third party who communicated with both of them could tell one from the other. By "machine," Turing and most of his successors surely meant some sort of general purpose computer.

When in the fall of 1944 John von Neumann was first shown the ENIAC computer—the world's first electronic computer—he immediately began to refer to its vacuum tubes, which were then being used to execute logical functions, as "neurons." He spent the rest of his life trying to complete the analogy between some sort of computer and the human mind, hardly imagining in 1944 that within thirty-five years computers substantially more powerful than the ENIAC would become household appliances. If I were to single out two reasons for the proliferation of computers, they would be the invention of the transistor and the development of computing languages so close to English that even young children have little trouble in learning to use them. What is called *the* transistor was invented in 1948 by physicists John Bardeen, Walter H. Brattain, and William Shockley of the Bell laboratories. They were awarded the Nobel Prize in physics for this work in 1956. In fact, there is more than one type of transistor, and properly speaking they invented what is called the bipolar transistor.

The material of choice for making transistors is silicon—a common crystalline substance. The trick in making a transistor is to deliberately introduce an impurity into the silicon crystal, known as "doping" the crystal. Two basic types of impurities are introduced, the so-called *n*-types and *p*-types. Here *n* and *p,* for reasons to be explained, stand for negative and positive. Suppose, for example, that the silicon is doped with phosphorous. The electronic structure of phosphorous is such that it contains an extra electron that cannot be fitted into the interatomic bonds between the phosphorous and one silicon atom. If a small voltage is now applied across the doped crystal, this electron—and any others created by any additional phosphorous impurity atoms that have been implanted—will move, making a current of negative charges. (The charge of an electron is, by convention, taken as negative.) This is the *n*-type of doping. On the other hand, if an element like boron is inserted in the silicon lattice an electron deficiency is created—what is known as a hole. If a voltage is applied, an electron from another atom will move to fill in the hole and this will leave another hole. The progression of holes cannot be distinguished, in its effects, from a current of *positive* charge—hence the name *p*-type. Transistor components are sandwiches of *n*-type and *p*-type doped crystals. Let us consider two examples, both of which fall under the general category of what is called a semiconductor.

The simplest form of transistor is made of adjacent regions of *n*-type and *p*-type materials—for example, a block of *n*-type adjoined to a block of *p*-type. If a voltage of a suitable sign is applied across the entire device, it will make the holes and electrons flow across the junction between the two regions in opposite directions so that a net current is produced in the device. On the other hand, if the polarity of the voltage is reversed *no* current will flow across the junction. The device can function in a circuit as what was known as a diode, although that term, which arose from the name given to the corresponding element in a vacuum tube circuit, is now archaic. To go from a diode to what is conventionally called a transistor, one adjoins a third doped region to the diode. Thus, one may have, for example, three adjacent regions, *n-p-n,* with the *p*-region sandwiched between the two *n*-regions. This arrangement can

79

be made to function like what was known in the vacuum tube days as a triode, a tube that could be used to amplify weak signals received by a radio antenna, for example. By applying a suitable voltage to the *p*-region of this transistor, one can control the current that flows between the two *n*-regions and produce amplification effects just like those in the vacuum tube, with the great advantage that a fraction of the power is used. (Transistor circuits run "cold.")

In 1954, the first transistor radio—the Regency—appeared on the market. It was not, as it happened, a financial success. By 1959, the first so-called integrated circuit had been developed in the United States by the Fairchild Semiconductor Company. The idea here is to use a single chip of silicon, which is then doped in whatever surface regions are needed to make the different circuit components. In turn, the components are connected by conducting materials such as aluminum. By the very early 1960s logic circuits were being put together from these components. In fact, in 1961, the Digital Equipment Company designed the first minicomputer here, and in 1963—first in Great Britain and then here—the first electronic pocket calculators with semiconductor components were being manufactured, although it was not until the 1970s that mass production brought the costs down to something like what they are now. In an introduction to a collection of articles in the September 1977 issue of *Scientific American* on microelectronics, Robert N. Noyce, one of the pioneers in the field, described what this has meant:

An individual integrated circuit on a chip perhaps a quarter of an inch square now can embrace more electronic elements than the most complex piece of electronic equipment that could be built in 1950. Today's microcomputer, at a cost of perhaps $300, has more computing capacity than the first large electronic computer, ENIAC. It is twenty times faster, has a larger memory, consumes the power of a light bulb rather than that of a locomotive, occupies 1/30,000 the volume, and costs 1/10,000 as much. It is available by mail order or at your local hobby shop.

By themselves, developments in computer hardware would not account for the ubiquity of computers in contemporary life. Concurrent with this technology is a steady—even spectacular—evolution in how we communicate with the machines. To get a feeling for this it is useful to consider a concrete example described in detail in Herman Goldstine's *The Computer from Pascal to von Neumann.* Goldstine helped to design both the ENIAC and the von Neumann computer at the Institute for Advanced Study in Princeton, which went into service in 1952. The Institute machine had a basic vocabulary of twenty-nine instructions, each coded in a ten-bit, or binary digit, expression. A register known as "the accumulator" functioned like a sort of scratch pad. Numbers could be brought in and out of it and operated on in various ways. The instruction "clear the accumulator"—that is, erase what is on the pad—was, to take an example, written as the binary digit 1111001010. Each location in the machine's memory had an "address" that was also coded by a ten-digit binary expression. This meant that there were 2^{10} or 1024 possible addresses. One could then say that the machine could address 1024 "words" of memory. (The meaning of the word "word" in the computer business has changed over time, but some years ago the industry standardized the definition to mean an eight-bit expression. This allows for 2^8 or 256 distinct "words" or "bytes" as they are now called.) Hence a typical "machine language" phrase on the Institute machine might be 00000010101111001010, meaning "clear the accumulator and replace what had been stored in it by whatever number was located in the address 0000001010." A program written in this language would consist of a sequence of these machine language phrases. It is obvious from even this trivial example that a long enough program written out this way would be all but impossible to follow, except perhaps by a trained mathematician. It is also clear that if this situation had not drastically changed, very few people would have learned to program computers.

By the early 1950s, the first attempts to create modern programming languages were underway. These early attempts and the ones that followed have centered around an understanding of what one does—the steps one follows—in actually trying to solve a problem. Consequently, workers in the field examined the logic of problem solving more and more deeply. In the beginning, the concentration was on the relatively simple steps that one follows when one wants to do fundamental arithmetic problems like finding the square root of a number. It became clear that certain subroutines come into play over and over again. Once these were identified, one could make a code—a compiler—that would translate them into machine language automatically, every time they were needed in a computation. J. Halcombe Laning and Neal Zierler at M.I.T. and, independently, Heinz Rutishauser of the *Eidgenössische Techniche Hochschule* in Zurich—Einstein's alma mater—made the first attempts to do this. Their work did not gain wide acceptance, and it was really the development of FORTRAN (for formula translator) in 1954 by a group led by John Backus of IBM that made computers widely accessible. Many years ago I had the opportunity of discussing the development of FORTRAN with John Backus. He told me that he and his group proceeded more or less by trial and error. Some member of the group would suggest a subroutine—a phrase—and then they would translate it into machine language to see what would happen. They were constantly surprised by what the machine did. Sometimes a set of machine instructions did not seem to arise from any specific FORTRAN phrase and sometimes a FORTRAN phrase did not give rise to any machine instructions at all. When the system was fairly well advanced they began to race their FORTRAN programs against machine language programs produced for the same job by a human programmer, using a stopwatch to see which program was faster. It took them two and a half years to complete FORTRAN, which was finally released in 1957. The translating program consisted of over 25,000 lines of machine language instruction.

In a recent article in *Scientific American* on programming languages, Jerome A. Feldman of the University of Rochester noted that at the present time in the United States alone there are more than 150 of these languages used for various purposes. For simple numerical computations, most of these languages work about equally well, and in fact BASIC (for beginner's all-purpose symbolic instruction code), which was developed in 1964 by the group at Dartmouth and is the language of choice for all small home computers, will do about anything that most people want to do with such a computer. (What most people seem to want to do with these computers is to play games on them and for this the programs come in packages.) But where the differences begin to be felt, and where FORTRAN and BASIC simply are not sophisticated enough, are in the incredibly complex programs needed in the field of artificial intelligence. So far I have discussed two levels of computer language abstraction—machine language and compilers. An intermediate level—assemblers—was developed even before the compilers, and it is worth discussing assembly-language instruction for a moment to show the difference between it and, for example, FORTRAN. In writing an assembly-language instruction, instead of using a string of binary digits that might get the machine to add two numbers one can simply use ADD in the program, which would get translated into machine language. FORTRAN is one step up in sophistication. To take a specific example, it often arises in a computation that a second step will depend on the alternative possible results of the first step. If in one case a number is larger than another, one may want to do one mathematical operation in that case and in the opposite case another. This can be signaled in a FORTRAN program by the instruction IF followed by instructions as to what to do in either of the two alternate cases—a marvelous simplification if one knows in advance that there *are* two cases. In a chess-playing program, however, the number of cases one might like to examine will depend on the position of the pieces on the board, which cannot be predicted in advance. Here, one would like some way for the machine to be able to reflect on what it is doing before it proceeds. For this purpose, in the late 1950s a new class of languages was developed that Douglas Hofstadter, in *Gödel, Escher, Bach,* has labeled "interpreters." The instructions in these languages interact *creatively* with the machine. As Minsky explained it to me,

In the ordinary programming languages like FORTRAN or BASIC you have to do a lot of hard, and sometimes impossible, things to get the program even started. For example, you must state in advance that in the computer memory certain locations are going to be used for certain specific things. You have to know in advance that it is, say, going to use 265 storage cells in its memory for something, and where these locations will be. A typical program is made up of a lot of different processes and in ordinary programs you must say in advance how each of these processes is to get the information from the others and where it is to store it. These are called "declarations" and "storage allocations." Therefore, the programmer must know in advance what things there will be. So you can't get a FORTRAN program to do something that is essentially new. If you don't know in advance what the program will do you can't make storage allocations for it. In these new languages the program system automatically creates space for new things as the program creates them. It does not treat its memory as being in any particular place but rather in one long string, and when it needs a new location it just takes it off the beginning of the string. When it discovers that some part of the program is not being used it automatically puts it at the end of the string where it can be used again if it is needed. The machine manipulates symbols and not merely numbers. It is much closer to using a natural language."

As Hofstadter has put it, the new languages create "pathways" as the program proceeds. One remarkable feature of these new languages—known generically as list processing languages—is that they can be used to design new languages. A list processing program can be designed to read and write list processing programs and so generate new programs of essentially limitless complexity.

The development of the list processing languages derived from attempts to carry out two of the classical problems in artificial intelligence: the use of machines to play games like chess or checkers and the use of them to prove theorems in mathematics or mathematical logic. Since more people are familiar with chess and checkers than they are with mathematical logic, I will start there, though many of the programming ideas are the same in the two domains. The first significant modern paper on chess-playing machines was written in 1949 by Claude Shannon, Minsky's predecessor as the Donner Professor in the Department of Electrical Engineering at M.I.T. (Shannon, now retired, still lives in Boston. Minsky informed me that, among his other skills, he can juggle while riding a unicycle.) The basic element in Shannon's analysis, and in all other analyses that lead to chess programs including the commercially available chess-playing machines, are "branching logic trees." First let us consider the naïve tree. Suppose one is playing white. Counting all the pieces, we see that on any next move allowed by the rules there will be a choice of about thirty moves. (Obviously, the number will change depending on the state of the game, but thirty is an average number.) To each of these moves, the opponent has then about thirty replies. Hence in two moves, if all possibilities were to be considered, we would have to consider 30 x 30 or about 1,000 alternatives. This would be tolerable for a machine. But Shannon showed that if we kept it up and were to produce all possible continuations and all possible replies, there would be something like 10^{120} in a typical game. To get some idea of what this absurd number means, suppose we had a computer that could process these continuations at a rate of one per billionth of a second. It would take 10^{111} seconds to run the entire tree. (The universe is only 10^{17} seconds old.) In checkers, one is somewhat better off, since there are "only" about 10^{40} continuations, which at the same rate would take 10^{21} centuries...that is, 10^{30} *seconds* to consider. The human player escapes this trap by considering only a minute fraction of the branches of the tree of continuations following from any given move—and so must the computer. Brute computational force simply will not work. While Shannon did not actually write a computer program, he suggested a framework for writing such programs. One would first choose a "depth"—for instance, two or three moves—to which one would analyze all acceptable moves and their responses. Next, by criteria to be specified, one would evaluate the position at the end of each of these configurations. One would then choose the move that lead to the best final configuration. To get an idea of how to evaluate such a continuation, suppose we are in a position where there are three acceptable moves. In one of them, white finds himself in a position that will lead to a draw if black makes *his* best move. In the second, white loses if black does what he is supposed to do, and in the third, white will win if black does something stupid but will lose if black does something intelligent. In this case Shannon's procedure (known in game theory as "mini-maxing," since white must consider his best, or maximum, case, and black's best, or white's minimum, case) would call for white to make the first move, which would guarantee a draw. In reality matters are rarely this cut and dried. More complicated criteria, such as material mobility, king defense, and area control have to be introduced and given numerical weights in the mini-maxing calculation. In 1951 Alan Turing developed a program to carry out Shannon's scheme. He did not have a computer to try it on so it was tried in a game, with the two players simulating computers. The weaker player lost. In 1956 it was tried on the MANIAC-1 computer at Los Alamos, a relatively small and slow machine for which the game was simplified through use of a 6 x 6-inch board rather than the standard 8 x 8-inch board. It beat a weak player. The first real chess-playing machine program was constructed by Alex Bernstein in 1957. It selected seven plausible moves, which it examined to a two-move depth. It was coded in machine language, and it played what was described as "passable amateur chess." It ran on the IBM 704 computer, which could execute about 42,000 operations a second, whereas the MANIAC-1 was capable of only about 11,000 operations a second.

In 1955, a group at the RAND Corporation consisting of Allen Newell, J. C. Shaw, and Herbert Simon began work on a chess program. (Newell and Simon are now at Carnegie-Mellon. Simon was awarded the Nobel Prize in Economics in 1978.) As they later wrote, "Although our own work on chess started in 1955, it took a prolonged vacation in which we were developing programs that discover proofs for theorems in symbolic logic. In a fundamental sense, proving theorems and playing chess involve the same problem: reasoning with heuristics that select fruitful paths of exploration in a space of possibilities that grows exponentially. The same dilemmas of speed versus selection and uniformity versus sophistication exist in both problem domains." During the "vacation" they invented what they called the Logic Theorist. This was a scheme designed to prove the sort of theorems in symbolic logic that are found, for example, in the *Principia Mathematica* of Russell and Whitehead. First, they had to code the language of symbolic logic—phrases like "(*p* implies not-*p*) implies not *p*"—or, symbolically,

$$(p \supset \sim p) \supset \sim p$$

into machine language. This enabled them to code the five axioms of the logic in the *Principia* for the machine, along with the rules of inference. The machine would then be given a theorem to prove and would undertake a search among the axioms to locate the most appropriate first step. In the more complicated cases it was allowed to search among theorems it had previously proved, in order to find the one that was most relevant to the case at hand. Then, using the rules of inference, it would try to find a proof of the theorem. Here again, brute force will not work. While there are methods that will produce any proof in symbolic logic, these, Newell, Shaw, and Simon noted, can take "thousands of years" of computing time. There is an analogy to be drawn here to chess, which is also a determinate game. An exhaustive search of the tree will always produce a win, or at least a draw, but would take an almost infinite time to carry out the move. Finding an efficient set of heuristics—simplifying tactics—is *the* problem both for humans and machines. A brute force heuristic would be to start from the theorem and see by working backwards if first it follows in one step from the axioms. If not, try two steps, and so on. One often sees this method used in student papers. Unless the student or the machine is lucky, the results rapidly run away exponentially. The student and the machine are much better off to start from the known axioms or theorems and to work forward by a series of methods suggested by experience. There is no completely formal way to codify this procedure for all of mathematics. If there were, mathematics could be done by anybody with enough patience. So, criteria for these searches have to be formulated. This is true even in those branches of mathematics where proof procedures can be codified, since these procedures are so inefficient that they amount to trying out all the possibilities—a hopeless proposition in practice. If the machine proceeds in steps that are too small, it may not see where it is going and may get stuck on some plateau where it wanders indefinitely. The precise way to maximize the efficiency of these searches is one of the major problems in artificial intelligence. As Newell, Shaw, and Simon state in their paper, "Empirical Explorations with the Logic Theory Machine: A Case Study in Heuristics,"

The reasons why problems are problems is that the original set of possible solutions given to the problem-solver can be very large, the actual solutions can be dispersed very widely and rarely throughout it, and the cost of obtaining each new element and of testing it can be very expensive. Thus the problem-solver is not really "given" the set of possible solutions; instead he is given some process for generating the elements of that set in some order. This generator has properties of its own, not usually specified in stating the problem; *e.g.* there is associated with it a certain cost per element produced, it may be possible to change the order in which it produces the elements, and so on. Likewise the verification test has costs and times associated with it. The problem can be solved if these costs are not too large in relation to the time and computing power available for solution.

The Logic Theorist was run on the JOHNNIAC computer named, over his objections, after von Neumann at RAND and was able to supply proofs of some fairly complex theorems while it failed to supply others. To program the JOHNNIAC for this purpose, Newell, Shaw, and Simon invented what they called IPL's (for information processing languages), that were the forerunners of the list-processing languages discussed earlier. In 1958 they coded their chess program in this language for the JOHNNIAC and described its performance as "good in spots." Before commenting on the present status of the chess- and checker-playing programs, I should note that in 1960 John McCarthy, then Minsky's colleague at M.I.T., made a profound analysis of the theory of computation, which led him to invent the language LISP (for list processor). This language enables one to carry out automatically all of the procedures of the IPL languages of Newell, Shaw, and Simon. (The flexible uses of memory and so on, described earlier, are all done automatically in LISP.) Almost all of the present work in artificial intelligence done on computers—with an exception I will discuss shortly—is now done using LISP. As Minsky put it recently,

LISP is used for developing programs that are too hard to develop in other languages. A person could write a chess program in LISP in a few days that might take two or three months in some other language. Once it is written in LISP one might be able to translate it back into, for example, FORTRAN, or one might not, in any practical sense. Some of the LISP programs we use are so complicated that they have never been translated back into the other languages.

One feature of LISP has prevented its use in constructing the most successful of the present-day chess machines. It requires something like ten to thirty times as much time to run on the computer as does the best available chess-playing programs that are written directly, and very painfully, in machine language. Since tournament chess has a time limit, the very "smart" LISP programs are not the most effective at winning. They presumably will be when the next generation of even faster computers is unleashed. Chess players who compete in tournaments are given a numerical point rating. At the present time the median rating of all the United States tournament players on this scale is 1,500. Anatoly Karpov, the world champion, is rated at 2,700. The best machine program at the moment—Belle, which was developed by Ken Thompson and Joe Condon of the Bell laboratories—is rated at about 2,200. The commercially available microcomputer chess-playing machines that sell for somewhere between one and three hundred dollars have a rating of about 1,000. They can be set to play at various levels, but at the higher levels they take an eternity to decide on a hard move. In general, these programs do not really mimic what a human chess master does. The human chess master can take in the general structure of a position, more or less at a glance, and can then focus on analyzing a very limited number (three or four) of continuations to depths that vary greatly depending on the position.

To give a famous example, when Bobby Fischer was

thirteen he played a tournament game against the American master Donald Byrne, a game that some people have called the greatest chess game played in this century. In the seventeenth move, for reasons apparent at the time to no one but Fischer, he sacrificed his queen. The resulting combination was so profound that it was not until fourteen moves later that the mate, which Fischer must have seen from the beginning, was executed. This game convinced many people that it was only a matter of time before he became the chess champion of the world. It would be fascinating to replay the game with Belle taking Fischer's role to see if by using *its* methods, which appear to be quite different, it also would have found this mate. It seems unlikely. Nonetheless, Belle plays chess better than all but 5 percent of American tournament chess players, and there is every reason to believe that in the near future, it or some variant will beat all of them. (The ability of machines to beat us at many of our own games—to say nothing of many other activities we call "intellectual"—raises what many people think is the fundamental dilemma of artificial intelligence. What are we to make of this? Will it help us to understand ourselves? Will we always be different from the machines in some essential way, and if so, what is it?)

Ever since the 1950s, checker-playing programs have been the province of Arthur L. Samuel, formerly of IBM and now at Stanford University. For years, Samuel ran checkers programs on each generation of new IBM computers being factory tested. It has even been suggested—half facetiously—that the logic of these machines was designed to facilitate the representation of a checkerboard. But in 1977 Samuel's best program was finally defeated by Paaslow, a program designed by Eric C. Jensen and Tom R. Truscott of Duke University. The claim is that there are now only ten checkers players in the world who can beat

Paaslow. But in a recent letter to *Scientific American,* Marion Tinsley, the world checkers champion, said of the machine programs, "I have seen games played by most of them, including six games played by the Duke program. They all play at the very weak amateur level. The programs may indeed consider a lot of moves and positions, but one thing is certain. They do not see much!..." Mr. Tinsley is apparently scheduled to play Paaslow for money and we shall see.

In the course of our discussions of game-playing machines Minsky told me a remarkable story about one of the early chess-playing programs. To fully appreciate the cast of characters, I will briefly review a bit of the early history of the development of the Artificial Intelligence Laboratory at M.I.T. When Minsky became an assistant professor in the mathematics department at M.I.T. in 1958, he joined John McCarthy there. Both Claude Shannon and Warren McCulloch were there but neither of them, although they were deeply interested in artificial intelligence, took much interest in computers specifically. Hence in the late 1950s there was no field of artificial intelligence at M.I.T. However, M.I.T. has always had, as one might imagine, an undergraduate population with a fascination for high technology...any technology. Indeed, when Minsky arrived, a celebrated model railroad club existed where, as Minsky recalled, "undergraduates did all sorts of interesting kinds of switching and engineering building. They had a fabulous, almost legendary, layout of model trains running around at various levels with complicated and interesting automatic controls that the students used to work on all the time." M.I.T. gradually acquired some surplus computers from the Lincoln Laboratory. Needless to say, these same students soon gravitated to the computers, inventing, among other things, a game called "space wars," which may have been the first of the kind of computer games that everyone seems to be playing now. It had artificial gravity and simulated the gravitational attraction of the planets and star fields, so that rocket ships had the right dynamics. The students worked on computer programming day and night; indeed, there were no courses then at M.I.T in which one could discuss and write programs on the same level of sophistication as these students were doing on their own. A number of them simply dropped out of school, and when Minsky and McCarthy began to get funding for their research they hired these dropouts or "hackers" as they are often called.

Minsky gave me a somewhat extended definition of a hacker.

It refers to a person who understands computer systems so well that he can make them do things—almost anything he wants them to do. You don't have to call a service man if you can find a good systems hacker. The skills these people develop are very impressive. They can go to a strange computer and type at it for awhile and figure out how to add a new feature, or fix a bug, without understanding very much about the rest of the system. They are like comparative biologists. They know so much about the various ways things can be done that they can figure out the situation at hand from fewer clues than most people think is possible. They find ways to do things in a program with fewer instructions than other people—something we call a hack. Sometimes they would work for days to make a program just one instruction shorter—for example, by making the machine instructions do two things at once— a property that had not been sufficiently appreciated. Now this sort of thing has been replaced by a respectable new branch of mathematics which is called complexity theory—the theory of why it takes longer to compute some things than others.

In 1965, the Artificial Laboratory got a PDP-6 computer

from the Digital Equipment Company. It has now somewhat broken down but can't be got rid of because it is attached umbilically, in a manner of speaking, to the PDP-10
computer that is the main computer now in use in the laboratory. (Originally, the hackers wired the PDP-6 to the bigger machine so that they could use the smaller machine
when they needed extra space to run a big program. The little machine eventually ceased functioning). As Minsky said,
"Now it's rather old and its printed circuit cards have pretty
much deteriorated. First we used to fix it every week or so,
but finally it got too hard to fix. It turns out that if you let a
number of bugs accumulate in a machine it gets progressive-
ly more difficult to fix, since you can't run diagnostic programs on it to locate its bugs. After a while it got to the
point that no program would run on it. Nobody has used it
for several years and now it is hopeless."

I asked Minsky why they simply could not remove it. He
remarked, somewhat wistfully, "We can't remove it
because no one understands all of the little wires that go
between the two machines. We're sort of stuck with it as a
monument. We simply can't afford to devote a whole person for many months to try to understand the relations
between the two machines. The hackers put in various
things that they were careful not to tell anyone about and
which I didn't want to know about because then I would
be responsible for them."

Sometime in the middle 1960s Richard Greenblatt, one
of the hackers, programmed the then viable PDP-6 to play
chess. Greenblatt was so good at programming that he was
able to write his program directly in machine language,
which enabled it to run faster. The machine, which reached
the 1500 level, was entered in various tournaments in the
novice class and won several of them. The little gold
trophies still sit on its chassis. Greenblatt's program was

supposed to select the seven best moves according to the limited criteria it had available in any situation and then explore these in more depth. For a year or so Greenblatt assumed that this was what the machine had been doing. One of Greenblatt's important innovations in the laboratory was the invention of what Minsky called "parasite programs" that would run while the main program was running and make summaries of what the big program was doing. In this case, after each move, the program would print out a very elaborate analysis of what moves had been considered and why the machine had chosen to make the moves it did. When Greenblatt used his program to examine the PDP-6's chess-playing program, he discovered to his astonishment that while the machine had been playing fairly decent chess it had not been following his procedure. Because of some programming error the machine was actually considering the six best moves along with the *worst* possible move. Remarkably, this did not show up for almost a year, the reason being that the program was running at more than one level. After the initial selection of moves it would begin to examine these with more care. It quickly realized that the worst move led to disaster and it instantly rejected it. As Minsky commented,

No such move ever gets up to the surface to be played, since the other six moves it considered were always better. So here you had a sort of demon inside the machine—a sort of self-destructive impulse of the worst kind, but it was always censored before it reached the machine's consciousness. This demon was always considering the worst. There are probably lots of people who are always doing that too and who hardly ever do the worst thing they can think of. For me, the interesting question that this raised was that if you had some large complex program how would you ever be able to detect such a demon? In a business program, which does not have the kind of heuristics that Greenblatt built in for his chess program, such a bug would be detected very quickly since some customer would get an incredibly large or small bill. But in our programs, for all we know, the machine may be wasting its time in some fissure of its mind and this might never get to the surface. Arthur Samuel once told me about an even more bizarre bug than Greenblatt's that one of his checkers programs had. It had a sign wrong somewhere and it would play to try to *give away* its pieces—it tried to get them captured. But, nonetheless, it was playing very good checkers. Samuel's only explanation, and many checkers players confirmed this, was that the strategy for giving away checkers—for *forcing* your opponent to take them—is almost the same as the strategy for winning checkers. It requires the same kind of control over the situation—everything is tit for tat and very carefully balanced. Here the means have very little to do with the ends—the means are to get control of the board, while the end is very remote. The brain also has a lot of bad thoughts that get censored by the good ones. It's only in Freudian slips—as Freud would say—that one can see that a person is considering some horrible thought as well. The person himself may not even be aware of it on a conscious level. But a little error information can leak out in a moment of confusion.

The vast majority of the contemporary workers in the field of artificial intelligence have identified their activity with the construction of increasingly more complex programs for computers. This activity is certainly a justifiable and productive one, considering what has been achieved. But it may also be misleading. This point was made in a recent article by Francis Crick in *Scientific American* called "Thinking about the Brain." He writes,

The advent of larger, faster and cheaper computers, a development that is far from reaching its end, has given us some feeling for what can be achieved by rapid computation. Unfortunately the analogy between the computer and the brain, although it is useful in some ways, is apt to be misleading. In a computer information is processed at a rapid pulse rate and serially. In the brain the rate is much lower, but the information can be handled on millions of channels in parallel. The components of a modern computer are very reliable, but removing one or two of them can upset an entire computation. [In both of these matters Crick may be underestimating some of the possibilities of the computer, since at present there is an active effort to do parallel processing in the next generation of machines, and machines have error codes built into them to protect against alterations in, for example, their memories.] In comparison the neurons of the brain are somewhat unreliable, but the deletion of quite a few of them is unlikely to lead to any appreciable difference in behavior. A computer works on a strict binary code. [The binary aspect of the code is really incidental, and in principle a computer could use many different kinds of codes.] The brain seems to rely on less precise methods of signaling. Against this it probably adjusts the number and efficiency of its synapses in complex and subtle ways to adapt its operation to experience. Hence it is not surprising to find that although a computer can accurately and rapidly do long and intricate arithmetical calculations, a task at which human beings are poor, human beings can recognize patterns in ways no contemporary computer can begin to approach.

While many workers in artificial intelligence might agree with this last statement, it is also only fair to say that computers, in conjunction with visual aids, as we shall see, are now able to do some rather remarkable feats of pattern recognition. The first machine that was able to do sophisticated pattern recognition was the so-called Perceptron. It has had an odd history in which Minsky has been deeply involved. For awhile it and the computer were considered to be the two paradigms for machine intelligence. The Perceptron was conceived in 1958 by the late Frank Rosenblatt. He and Minsky, as I have mentioned, had attended the Bronx High School of Science in New York at about the same time in the early 1940s. In 1959, Rosenblatt built the prototype version—the so-called Mark I—at the Cornell Aeronautical Laboratories. A few years later, I had the opportunity to discuss with him how it worked. The machine, he explained, was built in three levels. The first level consisted of a grid of photocells—four hundred of them—which were supposed to correspond to the light sensitive neurons in the retina. They received the primary optical stimuli. These in turn were connected to a group of components Rosenblatt called associator units, whose function was to collect the electrical impulses produced by the photocells. There were five hundred and twenty of them and each could have as many as forty connections to the photocells. These connections were made by randomly wiring the associators to the cells, because at the time it was believed that some, if not most of the "wiring" in the brain connecting one neuron to another was random. The argument for this was essentially one of complexity. From conception to birth we gain—grow—about 250,000 new neurons a minute until the total reaches the allotted 10 billion or more. How do they all know where to go in the brain and elsewhere, and what to connect up to when they get there? It was argued that if this wiring was largely random the neurons wouldn't have to know, since where an individual neuron went would not matter much. The result of a great deal of experimental work done in recent years seem to indicate that this is not, in fact, how things work. The connections *do* seem to be determined from an early stage of development and are specific both for various regions of the brain and even for specific neurons within these regions. How the information to specify all of this is processed so that the neurons do what they are supposed to do is a mystery. At the time Rosenblatt was building the

Perceptron it was thought that randomness was important and perhaps could account for the learning capacity—or part of it—of the brain.

On the third level of Rosenblatt's Perceptron were what he called response units. An associator—in analogy to a neuron—would produce a signal only if the stimuli it received were above a certain threshold, at which point it would signal the response units. The idea was to use this structure to recognize shapes. First the machine was shown, for instance, an illuminated *A*. Then the *A* was deformed—or moved—and shown once again to the machine. If it did not respond in the same way as when it had recognized the *A,* then part of its responses would presumably be "right" and some "wrong." By adjusting the electronics, the wrong responses could be suppressed and the claim was that after a finite number of these adjustments the machine would eventually learn to recognize these patterns.

Rosenblatt was an enormously persuasive man, and many people following his example began to work on building Perceptrons. Minsky was not among them. From his days as a graduate student, when he and a colleague built one of the earliest electronic learning machines, he had been aware of their limitations and had come to the conclusion that he would rather concentrate on finding the principles that will make a machine learn than on building machines and hoping that somehow they would work. He and Rosenblatt engaged in some heated debates at the time. Minsky described, in retrospect, what the issues were:

Rosenblatt made a very strong claim, which at first I didn't believe. He said that if the machine were physically capable of being wired up to recognize something then there would be a procedure for changing its responses so that eventually it will learn to carry out the recognition. He never proved it himself, but it turned out to be mathematically correct. I have a tremendous admiration for Rosenblatt for guessing this theorem, since it is very hard to prove. However, I started to worry about what it could not do. For example, it can tell E's from F's or 5's from 6's—things like that. But if there are disturbing stimuli near these figures that aren't correlated with them the recognition gets destroyed. The first workers in the field misled themselves by experimenting with examples that were too neat and clean. It would recognize a vertical line or a horizontal line by itself, but when you put in a varying background with slanted lines the machine would break down. They knew this, but they felt, incorrectly, that if you made the machine big enough—with even more wires and the rest—it would get better, whereas in fact it gets worse. It reminds me, in some ways, of a wonderful machine a teacher of mine, Licklider, made early in the 1950s. It could recognize the word "watermelon" no matter who said it in no matter what sentence. With a simple enough recognition problem almost anything will work with some reliability. But to this day there is no machine that can recognize arbitrary words if spoken by different people.

In 1963 Minsky began to work with his present collaborator Seymour Papert. Papert, born in South Africa, had gotten his Ph.D. in mathematics there. Deciding that he didn't know enough mathematics, he went to Cambridge University to get a *second* Ph.D. in mathematics. There he became interested in the question of learning and joined Jean Piaget as Piaget's associate in Geneva where he remained for several years. Inevitably, Papert also became interested in the Perceptron. Warren McCulloch learned about Papert and suggested that Minsky meet him. "Seymour visited M.I.T. in 1963," Minsky recalled, "and then stayed forever." With McCulloch's help he obtained first a position in the mathematics department and then with the Artificial Intelligence Group. In the middle 1960s, he and Minsky set out to kill the Perceptron or at least to settle its limitations, a task Minsky saw as a sort of social service they could perform for the artificial intelligence community. For two years they worked in various locations including the Everglades, where they went canoeing in the swamp "looking at strange animals" and proving various theorems. In 1969, they published *Perceptrons,* a book that pretty much exhausted the subject for the next decade, according to Minsky.

There had been several thousand papers published on perceptrons up to 1969, but our book put a stop to that. It had, in all modesty, some beautiful mathematics in it. It's really nineteenth-century mathematics which we got very good at by taking those trips and so forth. As we went on, more and more questions got generated; so we worked on them and finally we solved almost all of them. As a result, when the book came out, it got some rave reviews. People said, "Now computer science has some fundamentally new mathematics of its own. These people have taken this apparently qualitative problem and made a really elegant theory that is going to stand." The trouble was that the book was *too* good. We really spent one year too much on it. We finished off all of the easy conjectures—so that no beginner could do anything. We didn't leave anything for students to do. We got too greedy. As a result, ten years went by without another significant paper on the subject. It's a fact about the sociology of science that the people who should work in a field like this are the students and graduate students. If we had given some of these problems to students they would have gotten as good at it as we were since there was nothing special about what we did except to work together for several years. Furthermore, I now believe that the book was an "overkill" in another way. What we showed, fundamentally, came down to the fact that a perception can't put things together that are visually nonlocal.

Here Minsky took a spoon and put it behind a bowl.

This looks like a spoon to you even though you don't see the whole thing—just the handle and a little part of the other end.

102

The Perceptron is not able to put things together like that; but neither can we without resorting to some additional algorithms. In fact while I was writing chapter 13 of the book it began to dawn on me that for certain purposes the Perceptron was actually very good. I realized that all you needed in principle to make one were a couple of molecules and a membrane. So, after being irritated with Rosenblatt for overclaiming and diverting all those people along a false path, I started to realize that for what you get out of it—the kind of recognition it can do—that it is such a simple machine that it would be astonishing if nature did not make use of it somewhere. It may be that one of the best things a neuron can have is a tiny Perceptron since you get so much from it for so little. You can't get one big Perceptron to do very much, but, for some things, it remains one of the most elegant and simple learning devices I know of.

From 1961 to the present Minsky has supervised around twenty doctoral theses on his own—over half of the present faculty of the M.I.T. Artificial Intelligence Laboratory are former Minsky students—and another half-dozen or so with Seymour Papert or Claude Shannon. In addition, he has done a great deal of research with the hackers and, somehow, along the way he found time to solve a classical problem in symbolic logic that had been outstanding since it was first posed in 1921 by the American logician Emil Post. This last led Minsky to the construction of the simplest theoretical universal computer that has been found so far—a so-called Turing machine—and in 1967 he published *Computation: Finite and Infinite Machines,* still a standard reference book. Before turning to the subjects of his students' theses—which will take us into the heart of the recent developments in artificial intelligence—it is interesting to note how his work was financed, since it involves a relatively little known aspect of the funding of certain scientific projects in this country.

When computers first began to make their appearance in this country in the 1950s, they were so expensive that they remained for a time the province of giant corporations like IBM, Sperry Rand, or RCA, or of the large military-related government laboratories like Los Alamos or the RAND Corporation—the former being financed by the then Atomic Energy Commission and the latter by the Air Force. The Princeton Institute for Advanced Study computer project, one of the few then being carried out in an educational institution, was jointly financed by RCA, the Atomic Energy Commission, the Office of Naval Research, and Army Ordnance. No one—or at least very few people—imagined that within a few decades almost every major university would have a large computer and a computer science department. A great deal of the funding for pure science in this country now comes from the National Science Foundation, whose budget is spread across all of the sciences and includes a small fraction for computer science. Within the Defense Department, a not very public agency called the Advanced Research Projects Agency (ARPA) has as its mission to finance high technology that might eventually have some application to the military. This agency has sometimes interpreted as its function to detect technological weaknesses in American science and to attempt to fill these gaps. In the early 1960s, ARPA began to fund pure research in universities in computer science, and over half the money spent in this field has come from ARPA. Around 1963, following the work of John McCarthy and his collaborators at M.I.T. on time sharing, something called Project MAC was initiated. MAC, which stands for both "machine aided cognition" and "multiple access computers," existed on an ARPA-funded budget of about three million dollars a year, of which about a million dollars went to the Artificial Intelligence Group, directed by Minsky. "In the first years we spent this money on hardware and students," Minsky told me, "but by the tenth year we were making our own hardware so we spent nearly all of the money on faculty and students. We assembled the most powerful and well human-engineered computer support system in the world—bar none." At least some of the students were the dropouts who became systems engineers; others were "refugees" from other fields like mathematics and physics. From the beginning it was Minsky's goal to use this enormous pool of talent to learn what computers could be made to do in solving nonarithmetic problems—in short, to make these machines intelligent.

The first problem Minsky and his students attacked was to attempt to program a computer to do freshman calculus. To appreciate what they wanted to do, it is essential to understand the distinction between this enterprise and what the traditional way had been of using computers to solve calculus problems. Computers had always been used to study calculus problems. Typically in calculus, one is confronted with a so-called differential equation—an equation like Newton's second law of motion—which relates a force to an acceleration. The acceleration is what is called the second derivative of a position variable, which is considered a function of time. A derivative or differential is the slope of a curve taken at each point along the curve. One wants an expression that gives the position at each point in time. To find this from the equation, one integrates the equation—a procedure that Newton invented—which amounts to finding the area under a curve if one knows its slope at every point. This can be done numerically to essentially any accuracy if one is given the curve. Numerical integration was one of the first things computers were used for. Prior to their advent it was also done by hand on desk calculators, and in fact I spent many months in 1954 doing around seventy numerical integrals for my Ph.D. thesis—a somewhat fatuous but not totally unpleasant task once I got started on it. A computer could now do the whole thing in a couple of minutes.

There is a large class of functions that can be integrated exactly. In freshman calculus, one is taught a certain number of algorithms for integrating almost any simple function in closed form. When confronted with a new problem, one searches around in one's head, or the calculus book, for a procedure that looks like it can be made to work. Then, one tries to mutilate the expression so as to make it fit one of these algorithms. It was this process that Minsky's student James Slagle codified in his SAINT (for Symbolic Automatic INTegrator) in 1961. The machine, an IBM 7090, was given twenty-six standard forms—certain elementary integrals—and eighteen simple algorithms, a varied and complex group of solvable integrals. By comparison, "A Short Table of Integrals" by B. O. Peirce—a standard simple integral table—has over a hundred pages of integrals with about seven to a page. SAINT would take its problem, given in the language of elementary functions that had to be defined as well, and begin a search procedure among its algorithms. If the problem was too hard it would break it up into simpler ones. If the problem could not be done in closed form the computer would try and then quit. When first tested, the IBM 7090 (a dinosaur by modern standards) was given eight-six integrals to evaluate, all solvable by M.I.T. freshmen. It did eighty-four out of eighty-six at speeds comparable to an M.I.T. freshman if not faster. Many it did in less than a minute. Two integrals were beyond it. At the time, Slagle's program, written in LISP, was regarded as a landmark breakthrough in getting a computer to do symbolic manipulation. Shortly after, two more of Minsky's students, William Martin and Joel Moses, building

106

on Slagle's work, began designing a program that in its present form can do any symbolic manipulation that a working physicist or engineer would be called on to do. It is called MACSYMA (for project mac symbolic mathematician). Comparable systems are available now in some of the other major computer centers. Today, some of the algebraic computations that physicists run into would take thousands of pages to work out. They are beyond the point where one would have a great deal of confidence in the answer even if one could find it. Such calculations can be done automatically on MACSYMA, which has become a standard reference in many theoretical physics papers. It is possible to tie into this system by telephone; for better or for worse, one can get one's algebra done by dialing a number. As yet, these machines have not actually thought up a good physics problem.

The next kind of problem that Minsky attacked with a student, Thomas Evans, was to get the machine to reason by analogy. In this case, a few pictures are worth no end of words. Following, I have given a sample of the kind of problem the machine was supposed to solve. These problems were of the form A is to B as C is to D_1 or D_2 and so on, and I have illustrated a typical one from Evans's thesis. The reader may enjoy figuring which is the best solution, and the reasoning process that led to it.

The first thing that came to mind when I saw these drawings was, How did they get the computer to deal with them? Did it *look* at them? "No," Minsky explained, "the trouble with computer vision programs in those days was that they were always full of bugs. We really didn't know how to make them work reliably. It would have taken us a year to get one that worked and then nobody would have really cared. Evans developed a little language for describing line figures and this was typed into the machine."

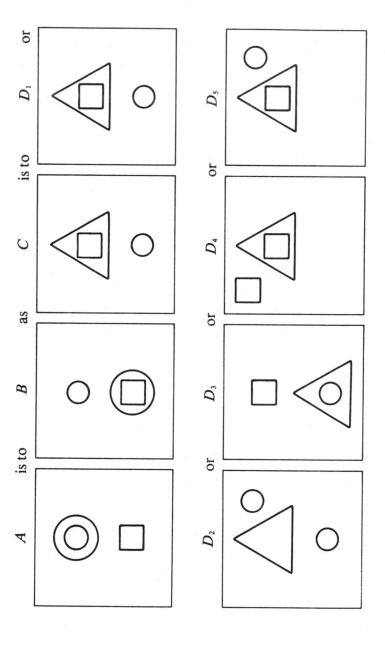

Something like this was also being done by Gelernter, who, as it has been discussed, had used such programs to prove simple geometrical theorems. In both of these efforts the new list-processing languages were essential and Evans wrote his program in LISP. The advantage of using LISP is that if one defines two symbols, S and T, one can create a third, related symbol, L. In this way one can code the proposition that the two points, S, and T, define a line, L. This is all the computer has to know about what a line is; namely, that a line is defined by two symbols called points. Likewise, a line and point define a plane, and so on. From a mathematical point of view these objects are an abstract set of relationships, although of course we attach many other common-sense meanings to them (which may help, or sometimes hinder, *our* thinking about them—but they are irrelevant to the logical structure). "Nowhere," Minsky noted, "does the machine 'really' know what a line is, but I believe that, for us, there is nothing that 'really' knows what a line is either—except that our visual system identifies certain inputs with 'lineness.' It is the web of order among these inputs that makes them unique. And even if they are not unique one pretends to know what a line is anyway."

Once the machine had some figures coded into its memory, it would proceed to compare them, using such criteria as big and small, inside and outside, left and right, and so on. It would attempt to see what operations were necessary to transform one drawing into the other. The specification of inside and outside is rather interesting. It is done using a method invented in the nineteenth century. To take an example, imagine one is somewhere inside a circle and draws a line from where he is due north. This line will intersect the circle once as it goes through it. On the other hand, if one is below the circle and *outside* it and draws a line north, the line either will not intersect the circle at all or it will intersect it twice. There are nuances but, in general, this procedure shows that one is *inside* a closed curve if there is an odd number of crossings and *outside* if there is an even number. In the case at hand, the machine would note that one of the differences between A and B is that the circle has been moved down to encase the small figure, the square. After completing the comparisons of A and B, the machine would next compare A with C. In this case, it would note that both have big figures above that encase a small figure. Now the machine would try to find the best D, in this case D_3, where the big figure has once again moved to encase the small one below it. To enable the machine to make such comparisons, Evans wrote what was certainly one of the most complex computer programs ever written to that date: thirty pages of LISP instructions. The IBM 7090 had a memory of 32,000 words, each of 36 bits—about a million bits of memory. At that time memory cost about a dollar a bit, so the memory alone cost about a million dollars. Memory is now about a twentieth of a cent per bit, so a comparable memory would cost about five hundred dollars today. Evans's program used essentially every bit in the machine's memory and was able to have the machine do about as well on the tests as an intelligent high school student.

Apart from the specific results of the program, what intrigued Minsky were the reactions to it.

It irritated some people a lot. Rudolph Arnheim, who was a Gestalt psychologist, wrote an article in which he said that what the machine did was a bizarre travesty of what people really do. He felt that what *they* [people] do involves "intuitions" and Gestalt abilities to see form. He was typical of a lot of people who felt that if you could program something then the machine is not "really" doing it—that it really doesn't have a sense of

110

analogy. *I* think that what it showed was that once one comes to grips with "intuitions" they turn into a lot of other things. I was convinced that the way the thing worked was pretty lifelike. Until one finds a logic for the kind of thing that Evans's program did, it looks like "intuition"—but that is really superficial. What we had done was to find a logic for this kind of problem solving. What we never did was to use a lot of statistical psychology to learn what some "average" person does when solving these problems. For a long time I had a rule in my laboratory that no psychological data were allowed. I had read a lot of that when I was in college and I felt that one couldn't learn very much by averaging a lot of people's responses; what you had to do was something like what Freud did. Tom Evans and I asked *ourselves,* in depth, what we did to solve problems like this and that seemed to work out pretty well.

During the period when Evans was finishing his work, Minsky and his colleagues were involved in two other kinds of projects—computer linguistics and robotics. I will begin with the linguistics. One of the earliest nonnumerical applications tried on computers was language translation. It was not a notable success, in part because not enough was known about syntax, and in part because of the inherent ambiguity of words. Simple word-by-word translation leads to absurdities. For example, one often cannot tell a noun from a verb without an understanding of the contextual meaning; something that at the time seemed beyond the capacity of computers. Minsky told me that in his view the mathematical theories of syntax of Chomsky and others, while it made tremendous progress in its domain, actually distracted the linguist from the problems of meaning and reference, which is what was holding up machine translation. "The artificial intelligence community worked on semantic processing," he said, "all by itself without the help, or hindrance, of the linguists—at least until much later."

Work in the 1960s resulted in two M.I.T. student theses that have become widely known. In 1964, a student from the mathematics department named Bertram Raphael did a thesis in which a machine was programmed to make decisions, in a limited domain, about the meaning of words within a context. This is taken from Raphael's thesis; for example, one could proceed to give the machine a sequence of statements of the form

"Every boy is a person."
"A finger is part of a hand."
"There are two hands on each person."

and then ask

"How many fingers does John have?"

Up to this point the word "John" has not been defined in the program and the word "have" is ambiguous if one goes by its dictionary definition. The word "had" in the sentences "John had his dinner," "John was had for dinner," and "We had John to dinner" means quite different things. But when confronted with something like this Raphael's program does not break down and the machine responds, literally.

"The above sentence is ambiguous. But I assume 'has' means 'has as parts.' "

It then goes on to ask
"How many fingers per hand?"

It is told that "John is a boy" and that each hand has five fingers. It is then asked once again how many fingers John

112

has, to which it now replies "ten." A few sentences later in the program Raphael asked the machine

"Who is president of the United States?"

to which it replied

"Statement form not recognized."

Minsky commented that Raphael's program was particularly interesting "because it could tolerate contradictions. If you told it that John had nine fingers it would not break down. It would try to build a sort of hierarchy of knowledge around this fact. In other words, given any situation, it would look for the most specific information it had about it and attempt to use it." I will return later to describe some of the recent programs that combine both vision and language.

I turn now to what in the 1960s was probably the most spectacular program combining language and mathematics. It was developed by another of Minsky's students, Daniel Bobrow, who named it the STUDENT program. To keep the mathematics relatively simple Bobrow chose to work with high-school algebra problems—basically word problems, since once the words have been translated into equations, all that is left is the solution of two, or possibly three, simultaneous algebraic equations, and solving such equations is absolutely trivial work for a computer. Following is an example, taken from Bobrow's thesis, of what the program was able to deal with. (The reader may enjoy trying this one. I once had an office full of distinguished theoretical physicists working on it at several blackboards.)

"Mary is twice as old as Ann was when Mary was as old as Ann is now. If Mary is 24 years old, how old is Ann?"

This one is perhaps a little too hair-raising to illustrate how the program works, so let us take a much simpler example, also from Bobrow's thesis:

"The gas consumption of my car is 15 miles per gallon. The distance between Boston and New York is 250 miles. What is the number of gallons of gas used on a trip between New York and Boston?"

In dealing with a problem like this the machine may well have an advantage over a high-school student, or any of the rest of us. We get distracted by a whole web of connections and associations that keep us from abstracting what is relevant to solving the problem, *"Why* am I going to Boston?" "Why am I driving my car?" and so forth. The machine, on the other hand, is programmed to make the assumption that every sentence is an equation. It ignores grammatical nuances. The machine is given a certain set of functional category words such as "is," which often corresponds to an equal sign in an equation, or the word "per," which indicates division. Other than that it doesn't know what most words mean. So whenever it comes to an unfamiliar phrase it gives it a label like X or Y. It begins linking up these phrases by realizing that each sentence represents an equation and that the number of equations and unknowns must be equal. In this way it finally reduces the problem to a set of algebraic equations it can solve.

The program is driven by the semantics to analyze the syntax. If there are two phrases that are not identical it will see how many words they have in common, giving priority to the function words like mile. The result of all this was a program that, on the surface at least, not only could manipulate words syntactically but understood, at least in a shallow way, what it was doing. It does not know what gas is or what gallons are but it knows that if it takes miles per gallon and multiplies by gallons it will find the total distance. It can wander through a little of this common-sense logic and solve algebra problems that students find hard because they get balled up in the understanding of how the words work.

I am much more interested in something like this than I am in one of those large performances in which a machine beats, for example, a chess master. In something like Bobrow's or Raphael's programs one has cases where the skills required appear rather obscure, but which can nonetheless be analyzed. In some sense, the performance of the machine here is childish; but this impresses me more than when it does calculus, which takes a kind of expertise that I think is fundamentally easy. What children do requires the integration of many different kinds of knowledge and when I see a machine that can do something like that—that impresses me the most.

While Minsky has always had a great fondness for robots, he came to the conclusion rather early in the game that, from the point of view of laboratory experiments, making robots mobile was more trouble than it was worth:

I thought that there were enough problems in trying to understand hands and eyes, and so forth, without getting into any extra irrelevant engineering. My friends at the Stanford Research Institute decided to make their first robot mobile against my advice. They called it Shakey and it was. It required a lot of engineering maintenance since it kept shaking around and pulling out its cables and causing its camera to malfunction because of vibrations. This may have kept them from concentrating on other things.

In 1962 a joint student of Minsky and Claude Shannon named Henry Ernst, made the laboratory's first computer-controlled robot. It was a mechanical arm with a shoulder, an elbow and a gripper like the kind of arms that are used to manipulate radioactive materials remotely. The arm was firmly attached to a wall and manipulated by several motors that were in turn controlled by the PDP-1 computer. The robot's universe of discourse consisted of boxes and blocks placed on a table. It had photocells in the fingertips of its gripper. The hand would come down until it was nearly in contact with the surface of the table and then its program would tell it to stop, at which point it would begin to move sideways until it came into contact with either a block or a box. It could tell the difference between the two objects by measuring size; if the object was less than three inches long it was a block, and otherwise it was a box. The program then would direct the arm to pick up the block, for instance, and put it into the box. In this way the robot could find all the blocks on a table and put them into a box. Minsky recalls:

It was sort of eerie to watch. Actually the program was way ahead of its time. I don't know if we appreciated then how advanced it was. It could deal with the unexpected. If something happened it didn't expect, it would jump to another part of its program. If you moved the box in the middle of things, that wouldn't bother it much. It would just go and look for it. If you moved a block it would go and find another one. If you put a ball on the table it would try to verify that it was a block.

Not long afterwards Minsky was asked by Stanley Kubrick to act as consultant on Kubrick's film *2001*. Minsky recalls,

He asked me to look over his plans to see if anything in the script was impossible. I don't think anything is impossible with computers, although I doubt if we will have anything as smart as HAL by the year 2001. In any case, I gave Kubrick a sketch of how the mechanical hands on the space pod might work. When I saw them in the film, I was terribly impressed and wondered how they managed to do so much better than we could in our laboratory. The hands moved so smoothly and accurately when they opened the spaceship doors. Later I found that the arm was attached to the doorknob which was turned by someone from the other side.

By the mid-1960s, the Artificial Intelligence Laboratory had moved to its present quarters, a modern multistoried structure overlooking Technology Square—just across from the main campus at M.I.T. Originally located on the eighth and ninth floors, it now sprawls over parts of three floors. The ninth floor was the domain of the hackers; it was where the machines were. On the eighth floor Minsky, Seymour Papert (who had just joined the group), and others had their offices. Aside from destroying the Perceptron, Minsky and Papert worked on the problem of vision. This ultimately produced two quite different types of programs. While Minsky and a group of hackers including Gerald Sussman, William Gosper, Jack Holloway, Richard Greenblatt, Thomas Knight, and others tried to program a computer to "see," Papert and his student Terry Winograd, who is now a professor at Stanford, produced a system called SHRDLU. The name is taken from an old code used by linotype operators in which the phrase "ETAOIN SHRDLU" marked a typographical error. SHRDLU was so complicated that Winograd himself had difficulty keeping track of it, and no one else was ever able to understand it fully. (Sussman, by the way, was a freshman when he began working on computer vision, and because of his energy Minsky put him in charge of the project. He *did* get his degrees and is now a professor at M.I.T.) To make a seeing computer Minsky adapted some television cameras. The most accurate one that he found had been invented in the early 1930s by Philo Farnsworth and it was still being manufactured by ITT. He ordered one and managed to get it working, but it had a number of bugs. It kept blurring. He called up the company and was told that the best thing to do was to talk with Farnsworth himself. Minsky did, and Farnsworth instantly diagnosed the problem, and Minsky was able to fix it. He then attached the camera to the PDP-6 computer. The idea was to associate this camera with an arm, so that in the end one would be able to tell the computer's arm to pick up various objects that the eye had identified and located. The arm was then to do various things with the objects. In the course of working at this, Minsky designed and built a mechanical arm with a shoulder, a wrist, and three elbows. It could reach around a corner and pick up a small person.

The project turned out to be much more difficult than anyone had imagined. In the first place, it developed that the eye preferred to focus on the shadows of objects rather than on the objects themselves. When *that* problem got sorted out, it developed if one of the lights was moved the robot once again got confused and furthermore if they used *shiny* cubes the robot went for reflections. So on the eighth floor a student named David Waltz, now a professor at the University of Illinois, developed a new optical theory of shadows and edges to eliminate most of these problems. Minsky and Papert also found that conventional programming techniques were not adequate. They began to try to invent programs that were not centralized but had parts—hetarechies—that were semi-independent but could call on each other for assistance. Eventually these notions grew into something that they called "The Society Theory of the Mind," in which they conjectured that intelligence emerges from the interactions of many small systems operating within an evolving administrative structure. The final visual computer program was put together by one of the hackers, William Gosper. Whenever the machine was turned on, the hand would first wave around until the eye found it. As Minsky said, "It would hold its hand in front of its eye and move it a little bit to see if it really was itself." The eye had to locate itself in the coordinate system of the hand. Despite all the problems, they were able to get the arm to catch a ball when Greenblatt attached a grocer's cornucopia to the hand so that the ball would not fall out. And, by 1970, when the money for the project ran out, they had been able to show the computer a simple structure, like a bridge made of blocks, and the machine would build a duplicate on its own. While this is not yet a realization of von Neumann's program to make robots that can copy themselves, it is as close as anyone has come.

Within a limited domain, SHRDLU is a computer program that is almost able to play Turing's game. Turing's idealized computer was meant to be polymathic. It could discuss Dickens and Shakespeare as well as love and war. SHRDLU's world, on the other hand, consists of boxes, cubes, and pyramids of various colors. To avoid the complications of robotics, these are not realized, as they were in the hacker's program, in terms of actual blocks. Rather, they are represented in three dimensions on a television screen. Even this much display is more for the benefit of the people running the program than for the machine—the machine in this case being a PDP-10 that had about a quarter of a million words in its memory, all of which were needed. SHRDLU does all of its communication in the symbolic language appropriate to its world. It can respond to commands like "Find a block which is bigger than the one you are holding and put it into the box," or "Will you please stack up both of the red blocks and either a green cube or a pyramid?" When it receives such a request an "arm," symbolized by a line on the television screen, moves around and carries it out. The programming language—in this case PLANNER, which in turn is translated into LISP—does not have arithmetic words in it. One can ask it to describe what it has done and why. One can ask "Can a pyramid be supported by a block?" and it will say "yes," or "Can the table pick up blocks?" and it will say "no." It is sensitive to ambiguities. If one asks it to pick up a block, and there are several, it will ask, "which block?" and SHRDLU can even learn to some extent. If asked to build a steeple it replies, "I don't know the word 'steeple.'" Then you could say to it, "A steeple is a stack containing at least two cubes and a pyramid." It *does* know what a stack is. Then SHRDLU will build a steeple and even figure out where the pyramid goes since nothing can be on top of a pyramid. (A full SHRDLU dialogue is given in Douglas Hofstadter's book *Gödel, Escher, Bach,* and a complete description of the system can be found in an article by Terry Winograd in the book *Understanding Natural Language.*) SHRDLU has limitations even within its limited context. As Hofstadter puts it, "It cannot handle 'hazy' language." If one asks it, for example, "How many blocks go on top of each other to make a steeple?" the phrase "go on top of each other," which despite its paradoxical character makes sense to us, is too imprecise to be understood by the machine. We use phrases like this all the time in our language—it gives it metaphorical richness—without being conscious of how peculiar they are when analyzed logically.

The SHRDLU program does not make any clear separation between semantics and syntax. As Winograd writes:

Our program does not operate by first parsing a sentence, then doing semantic analysis, and finally by using deduction to produce a response. These three activities go on concurrently throughout the understanding of a sentence. As soon as a piece of syntactic structure begins to take shape, a semantic program is called to see whether it might make sense, and the resultant answer can direct the parsing. In deciding whether it makes sense, the semantic routine may call deductive processes and ask questions about the real world [of boxes and pyramids]. As an example, in the sentence "Put the blue pyramid on the block in the box," the parser first comes up with "the blue pyramid on the block" as a candidate for the noun group. At this point the semantic analysis is done, and since "the" is definite a check is made in the data base for the object being referred to. When no such object is found, the parsing is redirected to find the noun group "the blue pyramid." It will then go on to find "on the block in the box" as a single phrase indicating a location.... Thus there is a continuing interplay between the different sorts of analysis, with the results of one affecting the others."

What are we to make of SHRDLU and its successor programs—such as Raj Reddy's HEARSAY program at Carnegie-Mellon, which is beginning to understand speech on a limited basis? Do these programs bring us closer to understanding how our minds work, or are they too "mechanistic"—too "scientific," whatever that might mean—to give us any fundamental insights? Perhaps what they show us is that the closer we get to making machine models of ourselves the less we understand the functioning of the machines. These are issues that Minsky and I discussed at length. We also reflected over whether the fact that we are beginning to learn to communicate with machines might help us communicate with each other, or whether, instead, our sense of alienation from the machines will grow, as machines increasingly perform in domains we have traditionally reserved for ourselves? In this respect, it is interesting to recall that the Luddites—bands of masked rioters who first appeared in Great Britain in 1811—were organized as a reaction to the introduction of machines that wove cloth. (The Luddites tried to destroy the machines). It is also interesting that the model for Charles Babbage and Lady Lovelace's modern idea of computer programming was the cloth-weaving Jacquard loom.

What would it mean to *understand* the mind? Since we really don't know, we might turn the question around, and ask in light of what we *do* know what such an understanding is *unlikely* to resemble? It is difficult to imagine that it will consist of an enumeration of the component parts. Even if we had a diagram containing every one of the billions of neurons in the human mind and the billions of interconnections, it would stare at us as mutely as the grains of sand in a desert. For that matter, this is how a high-resolution microscope photograph of a silicon computer chip appears to most of us. Such a photograph is not really of the component parts if by "components" we mean the atoms and molecules. These have been organized on the chip into functional units—memory, logic circuits, and so on—that can be understood and described. People, like Minsky and others working in this field, believe that in time the functional parts of the brain will be identified and their function described in some language we can understand. They admit that at least in principle it is possible that no such description exists, or not in any single form of language that would enable us to understand the entire picture in a unified sense. Of one thing the present workers in the field seem sure: that the description, whatever it is, will not be like the great unifying descriptions in physics in which a single equation or a few equations can be derived from what appear to be almost self-evident principles, and which describe and predict vast realms of phenomena. If the artificial intelligence programs are a clue, the more lifelike they become, the more they resist simple description in mathematical terms. Will the ultimate description, if there is one, resemble a machine, and in particular a computer? Here we are confronted with a rather odd situation. The nervous system of living organisms has been evolving, at least on Earth, for over three billion years, while the computer has been evolving for a little over a century. In fact, the computer's "Cambrian explosion" took place a mere forty years ago. We simply do not yet know what computers can be made to do, and until this is clearer, we cannot be sure what the final comparisons may be.

In the meantime, how should we view the machines we do have? This depends very much on who *we* are. Minsky and his colleagues, like Seymour Papert, see in the machines a great new opportunity for changing our methods of education—not because the machines can do arithmetic better than we can, for that was true even in my day, and if there had been any point to it I could perfectly well have been taught arithmetic on a Marchant calculator. Rather, as Minsky explained,

[It is] because the computer provides a more flexible experience than anything else a child is likely to encounter. With it a child can become an architect or an artist. Children can now be given resources for dealing with complex systems that no one has ever had before. That's one side of it. On the other side, dealing with a computer, at least as Papert and I see it, allows a child to have a whole new set of attitudes towards making mistakes, which we call finding "bugs." We have not been able to find any other word for it. It does not seem to get taught in schools where the concern is to teach the "truth." To really understand a mechanism, for example a piece of clockwork, what you have to understand is what would happen if there were, say, a tooth missing from a gear. In this case, part of the mechanism might spin very fast and set off a long chain of things which could result in the clock's smashing itself to bits. To understand

123

something like this you must know what happens if you make a perturbation around the normal behavior—the sort of thing physicists do in what they call perturbation theory. We call this kind of knowledge, knowledge about bugs. In the traditional way of looking at these things these encounters are looked on as mistakes—something to be avoided. Seymour wanted to develop a working place for a child in which it would be a positive achievement when a child can find the things that can go wrong. If you know enough of them you get close to something like the truth. This is what happens with children who use computers in the schoolroom environments that Seymour has set up and, in this, the computers are essential since their behavior is so flexible.

We hope that when a child does something that does not quite work out he will say, "Oh isn't it interesting that I came out with this peculiar result. What procedure in my head could have resulted in something like this?" The idea is that thinking is a process and if your thinking does something that you don't want it to do you should be able to say something microscopic and interesting about it and not something enveloping and evaluative about yourself as a person. The important thing in refining one's own thought is to try to depersonalize your interior; it may be all right to treat other people in a vague global way by having "attitudes" towards them but it is devastating if this is the way you treat yourself.

For purposes of helping children learn such things, Papert created the language, LOGO. As Minsky put it, "It is like a baby version of LISP. It has separate statements like FORTRAN or BASIC so it is easy for beginners to edit and manipulate. It has the usual arithmetic operations but it also allows one to manipulate sentences and build sophisticated structures and can even be used to write programs to write programs." One of the characteristics of LOGO is that it barely can be made to fit inside today's hobby computers. This is a particular source of irritation to Minsky. As he pointed out to me, these computers use BASIC, a language invented in 1964 at a time when memory was so expensive that the main concern was to make a language that could do something of interest on a computer with a very limited memory—say, a thousand words. Now memory has become so inexpensive that for very little additional cost the hobby computers will soon be equipped with enough memory to use a really powerful, and much simpler—because of its closeness to natural language—coding system. At the present time there is a kind of race going on among various computer companies, both here and abroad and especially in Japan, to see which company can make a personal computer that is both inexpensive and can address millions rather than merely thousands of words of memory. When this happens, anybody will be able to use the most expensive modern computer languages.

In the past few years Minsky's thoughts have ranged from the use of robotics both on Earth and in outer space—he thinks that with a relatively small amount of technical improvement in the robots, automatic factories in space would be feasible—to the development of the human mind and its ability to cope with paradoxes. On a recent visit with him we talked about mental development and logical paradoxes. Minsky said:

Children's innate learning mechanisms do not mature for a long time. For example, usually a child doesn't completely learn spatial perspective until he is about ten. If one is seated at a table with a six-year-old and there are several objects on the table and the child is asked to draw them not from the point of view of what he sees but from the point of view of someone who's sitting opposite him the child will get the perspective wrong. They won't begin to get this right until they are ten or twelve. I suspect that this is one of many examples where the computational ability for doing many things, while it may be built in from the beginning, is not dispensed to you until later in life. It is like memory.

125

Most of your memory capacity is, very likely, not available to you when you are a baby. If it were you might fill it up with childish nonsense. Probably the genetics is arranged to add computational features as you grow, whatever they are—push down stacks, interrupt programs—all kinds of things computer scientists talk about. The hardware for these things is probably built in, but it makes more sense not to give them right away to the infant. He has to learn to use each of the pieces of machinery reliably before he is given the next one. If he were given too many at once he would ruin them or make no use of them.

There is another side to this which occurred to me recently. I have often wondered why most people who learn a foreign language as an adult never learn to speak it without an accent. I made up a little theory about that. What is a mother trying to do when she talks with her baby? What is her goal? I don't think that it is to teach the baby English, or some other adult language. Her goal is to communicate with the baby—to find out what it wants and to talk it out of some silly demands that she can't satisfy. If she could really imitate the baby—speak its language without an accent—she would. But she can't. Children can learn to speak their parent's language without an accent but not vice versa. I suspect there is a gene that shuts off that learning mechanism when a child reaches sexual maturity. If not, parents would learn their children's language and language itself would not have developed. A tribe in which adults lost their ability to imitate language at sexual maturity would have an evolutionary advantage since it could develop a continous culture in which the communication between adult and child went in the right direction.

There is something else that is interesting about children, and that is their attitude towards logical paradoxes. I have often discussed Zeno's paradox with little kids. I ask them to try to walk halfway to a wall and the kids do it. Then I say, Now walk halfway from where you are now to the wall, and then I ask them, What would happen if you kept that up? Would you ever get to the wall? If the child appreciates the problem at all what happens is that he says, "That is a very funny joke" and he begins to laugh. This seems to me to be very significant. It reminds me of the Freudian theory of humor. Something that is funny represents a forbidden thought that gets past the censor. These logical paradoxes are cognitively traumatic experiences. They set up mental oscillations that are almost painful—like trying to see both sides of the liar paradox, "The sentence that you are now reading is false." These intellectual jokes reflect the same sort of threat to the intellect that sexy or sadistic jokes do to the emotions. The fact that we can laugh at them is very valuable. It enables us to get by with an inconsistent logic, by treating inconsistencies and paradoxes as thought patterns to avoid. The smart people don't just know the correct ways of thinking but also somewhere in their minds they know countless faulty thought patterns which could get them into trouble.

Minsky concluded:

To me this is the real implication of Gödel's theorem. It says that if you have a consistent mathematical system then it has some limitations. The price you pay for consistency is a certain restrictiveness. You get consistency by being unable to use certain kinds of reasoning. But there is no reason why a machine or a mathematician cannot use an inconsistent logical system to prove things like Gödel's theorem and even understand them just as Gödel did. I do not think that even Gödel would have insisted that he had a perfectly consistent system and never made a logical error, although, as far as I know, he never published one. If I am doing mathematical logic I take great pains to work within one of those logical systems that are believed to be foolproof. On the other hand...in every day life my behavior is quite different. The image that I have [of doing mathematics] is that it is like ice skating. If you live in a conscientious community which does not try to prohibit everything, then it will place red flags where the ice is thin, which tells you to be careful. When you are doing mathematics and you begin to discover that you are working with a function that has a peculiar behavior you begin to see red flags that tell you to be careful. When you come to a sentence that says it's false or you come to sentences that appear to be discussing things that resemble themselves you get nervous, just like people who are afraid of flying get nervous when they get near an airport. You say to yourself, as a mathematician, I am on thin ice now. My view of mathematical thinking is like Freud's view of everyday thinking. We have in our subconscious a number of little demons...or little parasites... and each of them is afraid of something. Right now I am working on the society of the mind theory. I believe that the way to realize intelligence is to have some parts of the mind that know certain things and other parts of the mind that know things about the first part. If you want to learn something, the most important thing to know is which part of your mind is good at learning that kind of thing. I am not looking so much for a unified general theory. I am looking for an administrative theory of how the mind can have enough parts and know enough about each of them to solve all the problems it confronts. I am interested in developing a set of ideas about different kinds of simple learning machines each one of whose main concerns is to learn what the others are good at. Eventually I hope to close the circle so that the whole thing can figure out how to make itself better. At least that is my fantasy.

Minsky's great predecessor, Warren McCulloch, when asked as a student how he was going to spend his life, replied that he was going to try to answer the question, What is a man that he may know a number? That was over a half-century ago. We still do not know the answer, but the question is still there, beckoning us like a beacon.

PART II

Science Observed

4

The Need to Know

IN the late summer of 1957, in the desert in Nevada, I witnessed the explosion of two atomic bombs. This was surely one of the most memorable experiences of my life, and recently I have been trying to reconstruct it in some detail. By writing to and talking with the few people who were there with me, I have managed to re-create much of it, but there are places where our memories don't agree. Mine is so graphic and so distinct that it is as if the events had happened yesterday. I cannot understand why the others don't recall them in the same way.

In 1957, I was finishing the last of two years as the "house theoretician" at the Harvard Cyclotron, an ancient machine, long since demolished, financed by the U. S. Navy. Although my job paid next to nothing by the standards of today's salaries for young Ph.D.'s—I had had my degree for just two years then—there were no clearly defined responsibilities except to do research and try to answer questions from the experimenters. Having come to physics rather late from the side of philosophy and mathematics, I really did not know much when I got the job, and during those two years I made up for as many gaps in my education as I could. The atmosphere was wonderfully stimulating, and altogether, it was one of the happiest times of my life.

Before moving on to a new job in the fall at the Institute for Advanced Study in Princeton, I had the summer free,

131

and I arranged to spend the time as an "intern" at Los Alamos Laboratory. There was no real way that I could be fitted into any of the existing programs in the lab, so I was assigned an office in the Theoretical Physics Division, where I worked with a colleague from Harvard now at M.I.T., Ken Johnson, on a recondite problem in pure physics that had been suggested to us by Francis Low, then a brilliant young theoretician who was at the time about to move from the University of Illinois to M.I.T., where both he and Johnson have had long and very distinguished careers. Low is now the provost at M.I.T.

I should try to describe the rather odd emotions I had then about nuclear weapons. To understand them one must have a feeling about how being at Los Alamos seemed to a young physicist. Los Alamos was then still very much a closed community. There were fences within fences. Much of the "temporary" construction used during the war was still standing, including the barrackslike housing project in which I lived. All of us who worked there had "Q-clearances," which were the highest clearances then given out by the Atomic Energy Commission. This meant—and it had been the policy of the laboratory from the days of its first director Robert Oppenheimer—that we had access to classified information on a "need-to-know" basis. In the work that I was doing with Johnson there was nothing classified that we needed to know, so I didn't learn any secrets. Low was working on fusion, and he and the other senior people were at that time fairly optimistic that it could be made to work for power production. Access to the fusion program was restricted, too, but Ken Johnson and I were allowed to attend some of the fusion seminars. For a young student, as I was, going to them gave me the feeling of being admitted to some sort of secret brotherhood—the brotherhood of people who needed to know. I don't recall any discussions of atomic weapons, but one had a sense of their presence. Indeed, I think some were stored near the lab in a cave surrounded by barbed wire and guarded by machine guns. As strange as this may now appear, the weapons represented a brooding and almost romantic presence. I, at least, lost sight of what they were and what they were for. They became symbols of the brotherhood of the need to know. Being part of the brotherhood gave me a somewhat superior feeling toward people—most people—who did not need to know. I do not think that this attitude was characteristic of most of the senior people, who had any real responsibility for the larger decisions, but I am trying to describe how things then seemed to me—the seduction of power.

In any case, when Francis Low announced one day that he was going to Nevada to see some atomic bomb tests, I decided that I would very much like to go along. There was absolutely no reason for my being there except curiosity. But this was also Low's reason for going. He promised that he would speak to Carson Mark, then the director of our division. He has now retired. In due time, I was told that I could go if I agreed to pay my expenses—the commercial flights and so on—since there was no reason to charge them to the laboratory. Thus it was that sometime in August, Low and I and Carson Mark left Los Alamos in a light plane that took us to Albuquerque, where we took a commercial flight to Las Vegas.

By the time we reached Las Vegas, it was about nine at night. A test had been scheduled for the following morning, but it had become customary for the people who were working at the test site to spend their free time in Las Vegas. Since the tests were scheduled just before dawn to insure the right light for photography, and since there was nothing for us to do at the site anyway, we joined some of the other people from Los Alamos to play blackjack in the casinos. Not long before my summer at Los Alamos it had been shown, mathematically, that blackjack is the only casino gambling game in which a successful strategy can actually be made. It is fairly complicated, and makes use of the fact that in casino blackjack the dealer is, in effect, an automaton who follows preset rules. In any event, the theoreticians at Los Alamos had developed the strategy empirically by playing thousands and thousands of hands on one of the computers in its off hours. (The same strategy had also been worked out independently by mathematical methods.) This had resulted in the preparation of a summary strategy card of which people going to the test site could get a copy. If one followed the rules one would be assured, at least, of losing one's money at the slowest possible rate. I have never enjoyed card games very much, but this one appealed to me as a mathematical exercise. I do not have any recollection of having won anything. Low remembers that he won about ten dollars. About 1:00 A.M., there was some prearranged signal in the casino, and we all left by automobile for the test site.

The site was located in Mercury, Nevada, about two hours by car from Las Vegas. We arrived there about 3:00 A.M. and went at once to some sort of central control building. There was a large room which had cots, and I remember talking to a meteorologist about the weather for the next morning and then dozing off for a couple of hours. Someone woke me up—perhaps it was Low—and, still in darkness, we went outside. We had been told that all of the Los Alamos bombs that summer had been named after famous scientists. (The bombs from the Livermore Laboratories in California had been named after mountains.) In fact, Carson Mark had told us that the following afternoon we would be able to go to a tower and visit "Galileo"—a bomb that was to be exploded later in the series. I suppose that I regarded the prospective explosion as some sort of fireworks display. Viewed now, from a perspective of twenty years, I find it difficult to understand how I felt then, but I am sure that I had not thought of bombs as weapons designed to kill people. I once had a long talk about atomic weapons with Stanley Kubrick after he had made *Doctor Strangelove*. He said that, in his view, most of the time we make a successful psychological denial of their existence. They become abstractions. They become something that we cannot think about, because we don't want to think about them. I had read a great deal about nuclear weapons and about Hiroshima, but I hadn't experienced anything. It was all words and pictures.

It was quite cold that morning. Carson Mark told us to face away from the blast and then, after it came, to count to ten. To look at the explosion before that would be to risk blindness. I think that we had some sort of smoked glass, and after ten we could turn around and look through the glass. There was a loudspeaker that reported on the time left before the blast: "T-minus ten minutes"—something like that. The last few seconds were counted off one by one. We had all turned away. At zero there was the flash. I counted and then turned around. The first thing I saw was a yellow-orange fireball that kept getting larger. As it grew, it turned more orange and then red. A mushroom-shaped cloud of glowing magenta began to rise over the desert where the explosion had been. My first thought was, "My God that is beautiful!" I wonder if any of the citizens of Pompeii said that to themselves in that first unguarded moment after the volcano erupted. It then struck me that there had been no sound. We were some ten miles away, and the light had gotten to us first. While I was thinking this, someone said "The shock wave!" and the next thing I remember was a rather painful click in my ears as the shock wave from the explosion passed by us. I do not have any recollection of any real sound. I didn't notice any—just this sudden pressure in my ears. By this time, the sun had risen almost as if it had been summoned by the explosion. The cloud had now turned into a leaden purple-black—a malignant mass of radioactive debris, pure and undiluted death. After looking at it for some time, I went inside.

I wanted to be alone with my thoughts and went back to get some sleep in the dormitory room I had been assigned. I had not really been to sleep for something like twenty-four hours, so when I woke up it was early afternoon. Low and I went to find Carson Mark, and he proposed that we take a tour of the test site. I have not retained a very clear impression of the test site as a whole. I remember that it was set in the scrub desert. There were a few hills around covered with yucca trees. Some tunnels had been dug into some of the hills for underground tests. Both Low and I remember the light. It was exceedingly bright and flat. I do not recall having seen any animals. There were a great many military people around. This was a time when soldiers were being used in maneuvers near the test explosions. People were in their shirt sleeves.

I have retained a very clear memory of "Galileo." The bomb was located on top of a metal tower perhaps a hundred feet high, about ten miles from the buildings. I had not expected to be allowed to see an unexploded bomb, and I made a remark to Low about "visiting the old gentleman in his tower" that Low still recalls. We drove to the tower by car. I recall that there was a crude elevator that took us most of the way up the tower to a platform. I also remember that Low and I climbed up some kind of metal ladder suspended in midair to get to the top of the tower. On that ladder I got a sudden feeling of acrophobia, of near panic that contributed to a growing feeling of uneasiness as we approached the bomb. "Galileo" looked like a slightly oversized cannister vacuum cleaner, with wires and cables leading from it. I also remember that there were pumps—perhaps vacuum pumps or a cooling system—that made rhythmic clicking sounds. There were a few men in the tower making adjustments of some sort on the bomb. I recall being told that both "Galileo" and the bomb we had seen explode in the morning were substantially more powerful than the two fission bombs that had actually been used in World War II. It was difficult to make any connection between this machinery we were looking at and a weapon of war. I had by this time been around complicated scientific equipment for several years and, on the scale of a cyclotron, for instance, the bomb did not look very impressive. After a while, we had seen what there was to see of "Galileo" and continued on with our tour.

As we drove around the site, I noticed that it had been divided up by zones with signs indicating levels of radioactivity, presumably corresponding to how long it was since the area had been used for an explosion. Working in the cyclotron had accustomed me to going into areas where there was radioactivity of one kind or another. I was not especially frightened of it—just cautious. There was no way to tell by looking which parts of the desert were relatively safe and which were not. While the areas had been marked off with signs, other than that there was no visible difference between one sere burned-off patch of desert and the next. Of the tower that had held the bomb we had seen exploded in the morning there was not a trace. It had been vaporized.

Then came an experience about which I and Francis Low remember different details. We do not necessarily disagree, but they have arranged themselves differently in our minds. It is so vivid to me that as I write this I can see the scene perfectly. I am sure that it happened as I remember it. Carson Mark took us to a low, concrete building somewhat separated from the rest. This was the building where the atomic bombs were assembled and stored. When we walked inside, I remember looking and recoiling toward the door. I also remember Low's telling me that if they exploded, being a little farther away was not going to make much difference. I have no idea how many of them there were: very likely enough to devastate a country. The center of an atomic bomb is a perfect sphere of uranium or plutonium. I believe it was called the "pit." The pits looked like shiny bowling balls. Around the pit was to be wrapped a high-explosive shell, carefully shaped, so that when it was ignited it would implode the pit inward simultaneously from all sides and thus assemble a "critical mass" to set off a chain reaction. In the building, we saw—and I am sure of this—a man filing on the high explosive that had been wrapped around a pit. Low remembers him as whittling on the explosives. Next to him there was a woman knitting. My thought at the time was that maybe she was his wife and that they had agreed she would be with him while he worked so that if it all went up they would go together. When I wrote recently and asked Carson Mark if he recalled this scene, he replied that he did not but he was quite sure that it could not have been a man and his wife since he did not remember any such couple in the testing activity. He thought that it might have been a secretary visiting from another area. Low does not remember the woman at all. But she was there. I also remember that I was given a pit to hold briefly. Although it was heavy, I was able to hold it. It was slightly warm to the touch, warmed by the radioactive metals inside. There was something so strange, both human and so inhuman, about this scene—I thought, is this the way the world ends?—that it made more of an impression on me than either of the explosions we saw. The next morning, a bomb named after a mountain—I think "Shasta"—was suspended in a balloon; when it exploded, it lit up and consumed an entire hillside of yucca trees.

There is an epilogue to all of this. In 1963, the United States and the Soviet Union signed a limited test-ban treaty. The signing of this treaty followed five years of debate, both within our government and with the Soviet Union. But in 1957, things seemed quite different. We were more naïve about these weapons than people can ever be in the future. I certainly was. I believed then that these above-ground tests were somehow essential for our national security, given the state of the Cold War. Therefore, when Adlai Stevenson, for whom I had voted in 1952, took the position in his election campaign of 1956 against Eisenhower that above-ground testing should be stopped, I thought that on this issue he was wrong. I simply had not understood the long-range implications of the open-air testing. It now appears that these tests have caused deadly illness, both in the soldiers who had been deployed to witness them—some as close as a mile from an explosion—and in the civilian population surrounding the site.

As it happened, at the end of that summer of 1957 I met Stevenson. I was then going out with a girl who lived near Chicago, and since Francis Low was driving to Boston I hitched a ride with him as far as Chicago and went to visit my friend, who was at home with her family. They knew Stevenson well, since he lived nearby. After listening to my description of the tests, they thought that Governor

Stevenson would be also interested and they took me to a party to meet him. After we were introduced, I began to tell him about the tests and the need for the tests. He listened for about five minutes and then simply got up and walked away without saying a word. I have never forgotten that. At the time I was enormously embarrassed, and when I think of it now I am embarrassed still. But I now think I understand why he walked away. He must have seen in me a young man made foolish by his proximity to absolute power—the absolute power of an atomic bomb. He was right. Proximity to absolute power can make fools of any of us.

Epilogue:

When I was trying to reconstruct these events, which took place nearly twenty-five years ago, there was something that I now find that I left out. I did recall vaguely that there had been some sort of military presence in the desert, but I could not remember its purpose, if ever I knew it. Recently I came across a book—*Atomic Soldiers* by Howard L. Rosenberg—which explains what Francis Low and I witnessed at Los Alamos. The explosion on August 31 of "Smokey"—a forty-two-kiloton bomb— more than the combined power of the two bombs that fell on Hiroshima and Nagasaki, and the explosion of the eleven-kiloton "Galileo" on September 2, were the last above-ground tests in the United States that were accompanied by troop maneuvers. Indeed, about three thousand troops were stationed within three miles of the places where these bombs were exploded, and soon after, the soldiers were moved to within a few hundred yards of ground zero. This was done, apparently, in an attempt to determine how soldiers would perform, psychologically and otherwise, under the conditions of atomic warfare. It is difficult to understand in retrospect how a maneuver like this could ever have made sense to anybody. At the present time, several of these former soldiers are attempting to sue the government for disability compensations. What appears to be an anomalously large number of them have developed what may be radiation induced illnesses. The disposition of these suits is still undecided.

5

I Am This Whole World: Erwin Schrödinger

THERE IS a parlor game often played by my colleagues in physics. It consists of trying to decide whether the physicists of the extraordinary generation that produced the modern quantum theory, in the late twenties, were intrinsically more gifted than our present generation or whether they simply had the good fortune to be at the height of their creative powers (for physicists, with some notable exceptions, this lies between the ages of twenty-five and thirty-five) at a time when there was a state of acute and total crisis in physics—a crisis brought about by the fact that existing physics simply did not account for what was known about the atom. In brief, if our generation had been alive at that time, could we have invented the quantum theory?

It is a question that will never be answered. But there is no doubt that the group of men who *did* invent the theory was absolutely remarkable. There were Max Planck and Einstein (it was Planck who invented the notion of the quantum—the idea that energy was always emitted and absorbed in distinct units, or quanta, and not continuously like water flowing from a tap—and it was Einstein who first understood the real significance of Planck's work and extended it to explain a variety of mysteries about matter and radiation), who did their important work before 1925. The list also includes Niels Bohr, who conceived the theory that the orbits of electrons around atoms were quantized (electrons, according to the Bohr theory, can move only in special elliptical paths—"Bohr orbits"—around the nucleus and not in any path, as the older physics would have predicted); Prince Louis de Broglie, a French aristocrat who conjectured in his doctoral thesis that both light and matter had particle and wave aspects; Werner Heisenberg, who made the first breakthrough that led to the mathematical formulation of the quantum theory, from which the Bohr orbits can be derived, and whose "uncertainty relations" set the limitations on measurements of atomic systems; P. A. M. Dirac, who made basic contributions to the mathematics of the theory and who showed how it could be reconciled with Einstein's theory of relativity; Wolfgang Pauli, whose "exclusion principle" led to an explanation of why there is a periodic table of chemical elements; Max Born and Pascual Jordan, who contributed to the interpretation of the theory; and, finally, Erwin Schrödinger, whose Schrödinger Equation is in many ways the basic equation of the quantum theory, and is to the new physics what Newton's laws of motion were to the physics that went before it.

While Heisenberg, Pauli, and Dirac were all in their early twenties when they did their work, de Broglie and Bohr were older, as was Schrödinger, who was born in Vienna in 1887. In 1926, he published the paper in which his equation was formulated. Oddly, just a few years before, he had decided to give up physics altogether for philosophy. Philipp Frank, who had been a classmate of Schrödinger's in

Vienna, once told me that just before Schrödinger began his work on the quantum theory he had been working on a psychological theory of color perception. Schrödinger himself writes in the preface of his last book, *My View of the World,* published posthumously (he died in 1961),

> In 1918, when I was thirty-one, I had good reason to expect a chair of theoretical physics at Czernowitz.... I was prepared to do a good job lecturing on theoretical physics...but for the rest, to devote myself to philosophy, being deeply imbued at the time with the writings of Spinoza, Schopenhauer, Ernst Mach, Richard Semon, and Richard Avenarius. My guardian angel intervened: Czernowitz soon no longer belonged to Austria. So nothing came of it. I had to stick to theoretical physics, and, to my astonishment, something occasionally emerged from it.

The early quantum theoreticians were a small group, mainly Europeans, who knew each other well. There was among them a sense of collaborating on one of the most important discoveries in the history of physics. In his *Science and the Common Understanding,* Robert Oppenheimer wrote,

> Our understanding of atomic physics, of what we call the quantum theory of atomic systems, had its origins at the turn of the century and its great synthesis and resolutions in the nineteen-twenties. It was a heroic time. It was not the doing of any one man; it involved the collaboration of scores of scientists from many different lands, though from first to last the deeply creative and subtle and critical spirit of Niels Bohr guided, restrained, deepened, and finally transmuted the enterprise. It was a period of patient work in the laboratory, of crucial experiments and daring action, of many false starts and many untenable conjectures. It was a time of earnest correspondence and hurried conjectures, of debate, criticism, and brilliant mathematical improvisation. For those who participated, it was a time of creation; there was terror as well as exaltation in their new insight. It will probably not be recorded very completely as his-

tory. As history, its re-creation would call for an art as high as the story of Oedipus or the story of Cromwell, yet in a realm of action so remote from our common experience that it is unlikely to be known to any poet or any historian.

However, as the outlines of the theory became clearer, a sharp division of opinion arose as to the ultimate significance of it. Indeed, de Broglie, Einstein, and Schrödinger came to feel that even though the theory illuminated vast stretches of physics and chemistry ("All of chemistry and most of physics," Dirac wrote), there was fundamentally something unsatisfactory about it. The basic problem that troubled them was that the theory abandons causation of the kind that had been the goal of the classical physics of Newton and his successors: In the quantum theory, one cannot ask what one single electron in a single atom will do at a given time; the theory only describes the most probable behavior of an electron in a large collection of electrons. The theory is fundamentally statistical and deals solely with probabilities. The Schrödinger Equation enables one to work out the mathematical expressions for these probabilities and to determine how the probabilities will change in time, but according to the accepted interpretation it does not provide a step-by-step description of the motion of, for example, a single electron in an atom, in the way that Newtonian mechanics predicts the trajectory of a planet moving around the sun.

To most physicists, these limitations are a fundamental limitation, in principle, on the type of information that can be gathered by carrying out measurements of atomic systems. These limitations, which were first analyzed by Heisenberg and Bohr, are summarized in the Heisenberg uncertainty relations, which state, generally speaking, that the very process of making most measurements of an atomic system disturbs the system's behavior so greatly that it is put into a state qualitatively different from the one it was in before the measurement. (For example, to measure the position of an electron in an atom, one must illuminate the electron with light of very short wavelength. This light carries so much momentum that the process of illuminating the electron knocks it clear out of the atom, so a second measurement of the position of the electron in the atom is impossible. "We murder to dissect," as Wordsworth wrote.) The observer—or, really, his measuring apparatus—has an essential influence on the observed. The physicists who have objected to the quantum theory feel that this limitation indicates the incompleteness of the theory and that there must exist a deeper explanation that would yield the same universal agreement with experiment that the quantum theory does but that would allow a completely deterministic description of atomic events. Naturally, the burden of finding such a theory rests upon those who feel that it must exist; so far, despite the repeated efforts of people like de Broglie, Einstein, and Schrödinger, no such theory has been forthcoming.

Schrödinger, who was a brilliant writer of both scientific texts and popular scientific essays, summarized his distaste for the quantum theory in an essay entitled "Are There Quantum Jumps?" published in 1952:

I have been trying to produce a mood that makes one wonder what parts of contemporary science will still be of interest to more than historians two thousand years hence. There have been ingenious constructs of the human mind that gave an exceedingly accurate description of observed facts and have yet lost all interest except to historians. I am thinking of the theory of epicycles. [This theory was used, especially by the Alexandrian astronomer Ptolemy, to account for the extremely complicated planetary motions that had been observed; it postulated that they were compounded of innumerable simple circular motions. Reduced to the simplest terms, a planet was presumed to move in a small circle around a point that moved in a large circle around the earth rather than moving in elliptical orbits around the sun.] I confess to the heretical view that their modern counterpart in physical theory are the quantum jumps.

In his introduction to *My View of the World,* Schrödinger puts his belief even more strongly:

> There is one complaint which I shall not escape. Not a word is said here of acausality, wave mechanics, indeterminacy relations, complementarity, an expanding universe, continuous creation, etc. Why doesn't he talk about what he knows instead of trespassing on the professional philosopher's preserves? *Ne sutor supra crepidam.* On this I can cheerfully justify myself: because I do not think that these things have as much connection as is currently supposed with a philosophical view of the world.

There is a story that after Schrödinger lectured in the twenties at the Institute of Theoretical Physics in Copenhagen, (where Bohr was teaching), a vigorous debate took place on the implications of his equation, in the course of which Schrödinger remarked that if he had known that the whole thing would be taken so seriously he never would have invented it in the first place.

Schrödinger was too great a scientist not to recognize the significance of the all but universal success of the quantum theory—it accounts not only for "all of chemistry and most of physics" but even for astronomy; it can be used, for example, to make very precise computations of the energy generated in the nuclear reactions that go on in the sun and other stars. Indeed, Schrödinger's popular masterpiece *What Is Life?* deals with the impact of quantum ideas on biology and above all on the molecular processes that underlie the laws of heredity. The two striking features of the hereditary mechanism are its stability and its changeability—the existence of mutations, which allow for the evolution of a biological species. The characteristics that are inherited by a child from its mother and father are all contained in several large organic molecules—the genes. Genes are maintained at a fairly high temperature, 98 °F, in the human body, which means that they are subject to constant thermal agitation. The question is how does this molecule retain its identity through generation after generation. Schrödinger states the problem brilliantly:

> Let me throw the truly amazing situation into relief once again. Several members of the Habsburg dynasty have a peculiar disfigurement of the lower lip ("Habsburger Lippe"). Its inheritance has been studied carefully and published, complete with historical portraits, by the Imperial Academy of Vienna, under the auspices of the family.... Fixing our attention on the portraits of a member of the family in the sixteenth century and of his descendant, living in the nineteenth, we may safely assume that the material gene structure responsible for the abnormal feature has been carried on from generation to generation through the centuries, faithfully reproduced at every one of the not very numerous cell divisions that lie between.... The gene has been kept at a temperature around 98 °F during all that time. How are we to understand that it has remained unperturbed by the disordering tendency of the heat motion for centuries?

According to the quantum theory, the stability of any chemical molecule has a natural explanation. The molecule is in a definite energy state. To go from one state to another the molecule must absorb just the right amount of energy. If too little energy is supplied, the molecule will not make the transition. This situation differs completely from that envisaged by classical physics, in which the change of state can be achieved by absorbing any energy. It can be shown that the thermal agitations that go on in the human body do not in general supply enough energy to cause such

148

a transition, but mutations can take place in those rare thermal processes in which enough energy is available to alter the gene.

What Is Life? was published in 1944. Since then the field of molecular biology has become one of the most active and exciting in all science. A good deal of what Schrödinger said is now dated. But the book has had an enormous influence on physicists and biologists in that it hints how the two disciplines join together at their base. Schrödinger, who received the Nobel Prize jointly with Dirac in 1933, succeeded Max Planck at the University of Berlin in 1927. When Hitler came to power, Schrödinger, although not a Jew, was deeply affected by the political climate. Philipp Frank has told me that Schrödinger attempted to intervene in a storm trooper raid on a Jewish ghetto and would have been beaten to death if one of the troopers, who had studied physics, had not recognized him as Germany's most recent Nobel Laureate and persuaded his colleagues to let him go. Shortly afterward, Schrödinger went to England, then back to Austria, then to Belgium, when Austria fell, and finally to the Dublin Institute for Advanced Studies, where he remained until he returned to Vienna in 1956. By the end of his life, he must have mastered as much general culture—scientific and nonscientific—as it is possible for any single person to absorb in this age of technical specialization. He read widely in several languages, and wrote perceptively about the relation between science and the humanities and about Greek science, in which he was particularly interested. He even wrote poetry, which, I am told, was extremely romantic. (The pictures of Schrödinger as a young man give him a Byronic look.) What kind of personal metaphysics would such a man derive from his reading and experience? In *My View of the World,* he leaves a partial answer.

My View of the World consists of two long essays—one written in 1925, just before the discovery of the Schrödinger Equation, and one written in 1960, just before his death. In both essays he reveals himself as a mystic deeply influenced by the philosophy of the Vedas. In 1925 he writes,

This life of yours which you are living is not merely a piece of the entire existence, but is in a certain sense the *whole;* only this whole is not so constituted that it can be surveyed in one single glance. This, as we know, is what the Brahmins express in that sacred, mystic formula which is yet really so simple and so clear: *Tat tvam asi,* this is you. Or, again, in such words as "I am in the east and in the west. I am below and above, *I am this whole world.*"

In the later essay he returns to this theme. He does not attempt to derive or justify his convictions with scientific argument. In fact, as he stresses in his preface, he feels that modern science, his own work included, is not relevant to the search for the underlying metaphysical and moral truths by which one lives. For him, they must be intuitively, almost mystically arrived at. He writes,

It is the vision of this truth (of which the individual is seldom conscious in his actions) which underlies all morally valuable activity. It brings a man of nobility not only to risk his life for an end which he recognizes or believes to be good but—in rare cases— to lay it down in full serenity, even when there is no prospect of saving his own person. It guides the hand of the well-doer—this pehaps even more rarely—when, without hope of future reward, he gives to relieve a stranger's suffering what he cannot spare without suffering himself.

In 1960, I had the chance to visit Schrödinger in Vienna. I was studying at the Boltzmann Institute for Theoretical Physics, whose director, Walter Thirring, is the son of

Hans Thirring, a distinguished Austrian physicist, also a classmate of Schrödinger. Schrödinger had been very ill and he rarely appeared at the Institute. But he enjoyed maintaining his contact with physics and the young physicists who were working under Walter Thirring. Thirring took a small group of us to visit Schrödinger. He lived in an old-fashioned Viennese apartment house, with a rickety elevator and dimly lit hallways. The Schrödinger living room-library was piled to the ceiling with books, and Schrödinger was in the process of writing the second of the two essays in *My View of the World*. Physically he was extremely frail, but his intellectual vigor was intact. He told us some of the lessons that modern scientists might learn from the Greeks. In particular, he stressed the recurrent theme of the writings of his later years—that modern science may be as far from revealing the underlying laws of the natural universe as was the science of ancient Greece. It was clear from watching and listening to him that the flame that illuminated his intellectual curiosity throughout his long life still burned brightly at the end of it.

6

Einstein and Company:
The Philosophy of Science

THE present generation of physicists has at best a casual interest in the philosophy of science. Biologists who have come close to unraveling what they call the "secret of life," computer specialists who believe they are dealing with models of cognition, or cosmologists who deal with the origins and destiny of the whole affair appear to be more philosophically-minded. This lack of philosophical concern on the part of my colleagues exists, in my opinion, because the present physics works so well. We have been living off the intellectual capital of the quantum theory for well over a half a century, and closer to a century in the case of relativity. The inventors of these theories were, by and large, philosophically sophisticated. While part of their sophistication was a result of their cultural backgrounds—a product of their European educations—it was due also to the fact that, in the course of making their discoveries, they felt the earth tremble beneath their feet. It was not just a luxury in those heroic days to analyze space and time and the processes of measurement; it was a professional necessity. The time to make discoveries of such magnitude will come again if, and when, any of these mighty theories falters and breaks down.

Einstein's interest in philosophy, which I will trace in some detail, became evident when he was in his twenties. Early in 1902, at about the time Einstein entered the Swiss National Patent Office in Bern as a technical expert third class, where he was hired to examine the technical feasibility of new inventions, he offered private physics lessons at the price of three Swiss francs per hour. What a way that would have been to learn the Maxwell equations—certainly a better one than to have learned them from Maxwell himself. One of Einstein's first students was a young Hungarian refugee named Maurice Solovine. The two soon were joined by another young man, Conrad Habicht. Together, they called themselves—ironically, considering the group's size and each member's generally modest financial resources—the Olympian Academy. Einstein, Solovine, and Habicht shared a desire to learn, and they decided to take up the study of philosophy. Solovine once described how he had been punished by the other two members of the academy for failing to appear at a scheduled reading of some of the works of the Scottish philosopher David Hume. Solovine had been seduced by a chamber music concert. It was his turn to provide dinner at his lodgings, and he left for his two comrades four hard-boiled eggs and a message with his landlady that he had been called away on urgent business. Solovine wrote,*

When they came for dinner and heard this story, they of course understood what had happened and (after finishing their meal) knowing that I detested tobacco in any form they proceeded to smoke furiously, Einstein with his pipe and Habicht

---

*See A. Einstein, *A Centenary Volume,* ed, A. P. French (Cambridge, Mass.: Harvard Press, 1970). This anecdote is given in a reminiscence by Solovine on p. 9*ff.*

with a big cigar. They then piled all my furniture and crockery on the bed and pinned on the wall a sign carrying the words "To a dear friend, thick smoke and salutation."

By the time poor Solovine got the foul tobacco smoke out of his room and his bed in order, it was morning. The next day, he was threatened with expulsion from the academy if he missed another philosophy session.

My own contact with the philosophy of science and, indeed, with Einstein's philosophy of science, began even before I had learned much in the way of real science—a route that I do not recommend. In 1946 when I was eighteen and a Harvard freshman, I had no idea what I wanted to do with my life. But I had acquired, somehow, a rather romantic idea about the theory of relativity. In particular, I was impressed by the proposition (which I then believed) that there were only five people in the world—or perhaps it was ten—who understood it. (Twenty years earlier Sir Arthur Eddington, when asked if it were true that only three people in the world understood the theory, replied "Who is the third?") I determined to become the sixth, or the eleventh, as the case may have been. I went to the Widner Library to look for a book under the general rubric "relativity," and as luck would have it, hit upon Einstein's *The Meaning of Relativity*—his most difficult book, of which I found I understood very little. At about this time, I heard that the philosopher-physicist Philipp Frank was to give an introductory course in semipopular modern physics and that the theory of relativity would be covered. I enrolled at once, and this course and my subsequent friendship with Philipp Frank, which lasted until his death in 1966, changed the direction of my life. I can imagine no better introduction to Einstein and his life and times, and the philosophy of science than Professor Frank's course. As he wrote, sometime after receiving his doctorate:

> The domain of my most intensive interest was the philosophy of science. I used to associate with a group of students who assembled every Thursday night in one of the old Viennese coffeehouses. We stayed until midnight and even later, discussing problems of science and philosophy....

When I got to know him at Harvard, the Hayes-Bickford Cafeteria in Cambridge had replaced the Viennese coffeehouses, and we often went there for our discussions. He had just published his wonderful biography of Einstein, the product of research collected over a period of forty years.

Between 1908 and 1911, Professor Frank had published several papers on Einstein's then new theory of relativity. He was one of the rare physicists—at the time he was himself still a student, having just taken his Ph.D. in physics from the University of Vienna—who realized immediately the importance of the theory. His personal acquaintance with Einstein dated from 1907, when Einstein was still working in the Patent Office. A paper by Professor Frank on the law of causality had been included in the German chemist Wilhelm Ostwald's *Annalen der Naturphilosophie.* This was not long after the great French polymath Henri Poincaré's *Science and Hypothesis* had been published. In his book and in its successor, *The Value of Science,* Poincaré argued that most of the general principles of physics, such as the conservation of energy, are tautological definitions and as such can never be tested empirically. For example, any apparent violation of energy conservation can always be "explained" by defining a new type of energy: the rest energy associated with any massive object, for instance. These new energies can be assigned the values needed to restore the validity of the law. Professor Frank extended Poincaré's line of reasoning to the law of causality, for which he provided Hume's definition, the proposition that "if, in the course of time, a state *A* of the universe is followed by a state *B* then whenever *A* occurs *B* will follow." He pointed out that this formulation appeared to be empty of content, since no a priori definition of the state *A* is given except that it must be followed by *B*. He received two remarkable responses to his paper: from Lenin, who, in his book *Materialism & Empirio-criticism,* attacked Frank's ideas as antimaterialistic and reactionary; and from Einstein, who wrote to Frank. Many years after having received the letter, Professor Frank wrote about Einstein's reaction.

Einstein's letter was my first personal contact with him. He approved the logic of my argument, but he objected that it demonstrates only that there is a conventional element in the law of causality and not that it is merely a convention or a definition. He agreed with me that, whatever may happen in nature, one can never prove that a violation of the law of causality has taken place. One can always introduce by convention a terminology by which this law is saved. But it could happen that in this way our language and terminology might become highly complicated and cumbersome. What is *not* conventional in the law of causality is the fact that we can save this law by using a relatively *simple* terminology. We are sure that a state A has recurred when a small number of state variables have the same value they had at the start. This "simplicity of nature" is the observable fact which cannot be reduced to a convention on how to use some words.

The same remarks, incidentally, apply to Poincaré's analysis of the conservation of energy. It is not a convention but an observable fact that the physicist needs to introduce rather few types of energy for the law of the conservation of energy to remain valid. In his description of Einstein's reaction to his paper, Professor Frank went on to say: "I realized that Poincaré's conventionalism needs qualifications. One has to distinguish between what is logically possible and what is helpful in empirical science. In other words, logic needs a drop of pragmatic oil."

If I or any of my colleagues had been around in 1907 to discuss the philosophy of science with the twenty-eight-year-old Einstein, we would very likely have concluded that Einstein was a classical, or nearly classical, Machist (after the Austrian physicist Ernst Mach). In reading the running commentary he kept up with himself over the years, it is interesting to note that his philosophy of science constitutes a kind of dialogue with Mach, with Einstein alternately acknowledging Mach's inevitable influence and denying the validity of his ideas. It is said by people who knew Niels Bohr that Bohr had a running dialogue with both the real and, when he was not present, the imaginary Einstein, in which he tried to convince Einstein of the soundness and the finality of the quantum theory. Einstein was a sort of specter that haunted Bohr's philosophical tranquility. In reading Einstein's evolving philosophy of science, I find him having the same kind of dialogue with Mach, even long after Einstein had repudiated Mach's philosophy of science in its most literal form and long after Mach's death in 1916.

In his obituary of Mach, Einstein acknowledged Mach's influence: "Even those who think of themselves as Mach's opponents hardly know how much of Mach's views they have, as it were, imbibed with their mother's milk." By this time, and certainly a few years later, Einstein could be counted as one of Mach's opponents; indeed, in a 1917 letter to his lifelong friend Michelangelo Besso—the only person, incidentally, to be acknowledged in Einstein's great 1905 paper on the special theory of relativity, *"Zur Elektrodynamik bewegter Körpen"* ("On the Electrodynamics of Moving Bodies")—Einstein wrote of Mach's philosophy, "It cannot give birth to anything living, it can only exterminate harmful vermin." At age sixty-seven, however, in his wonderful *Autobiographical Notes,* Einstein wrote, "My attention was drawn to Ernst Mach's *History of Mechanics* around the year 1897. The book exerted a deep and persisting influence on me."

Ernst Mach was born on February 18, 1838, in Chirlitz near Brünn, then the capital of Moravia, which was part of the Austro-Hungarian empire. He shared with Einstein an undistinguished childhood school career. In fact, the Benedictine fathers who ran the gymnasium that Mach attended near Vienna characterized him as *sehr talentlos*—more or less hopeless—and dismissed him. His father, a tutor, intervened to help his son catch up, and in 1853 Mach was able to enroll in another gymnasium and, two years later, in the University of Vienna, where he studied mathematics and physics.

The first decisive philosophical influence on Mach, he later recalled, occurred when he was fifteen. He writes, "I lighted, in the library of my father, on a copy of Kant's *Prolegomena to any Future Metaphysics.* The book made at the time a powerful and ineffaceable impression upon me, the like of which I never afterward experienced in any of my philosophical reading." One is reminded in this passage of the way Einstein described the influence Mach had on *him.* Several years later, Mach had a second decisive revelation: namely, that Kant's celebrated *Ding an Sich,* the 'thing in itself,' which lay behind all appearances and was inaccessible to experiment, was a metaphysical irrelevance. He noted,

The superfluity of the role played by the 'thing in itself' abruptly dawned upon me. On a bright summer day in the open air, the world with my ego suddenly appeared to me as *one* coherent mass of sensations, only more strongly coherent in the ego. Although the actual working out of this thought did not occur until a later period, yet this moment was decisive for my whole view.

This is not the occasion to review Mach's career and to attempt to account for the extraordinary influence he had on scientists, many of whom, such as Einstein, Max Planck, and Ludwig Boltzmann made much more significant contributions to pure science than he was able to do. It is important to note, though, what a strong influence Mach exerted on the young Einstein, and how their views came to diverge. As Mach came to feel that the 'thing in itself' in Kant's metaphysics was superfluous and could be replaced by concepts more intimately related to direct sensory experience, he also came to realize that much of classical physics and, above all, classical mechanics was built on metaphysical constructs. This analysis culminated in Mach's *Science of Mechanics,* published in 1883, when he was forty-five. One of the great polemic works in the history of science, it is dedicated, in Einstein's phrase, to the extermination of "harmful vermin." Mach's argument was directed against the underlying theological and metaphysical assumptions of Newtonian mechanics (primarily Newton's concepts of absolute space, time, and acceleration) and Newton's faulty and circular definition of mass. Newton recognized that his laws took the same form in systems at rest as in uniform motion—Galilean relativity—but he claimed that the two states could be differentiated in the sensorium of God. "He," Newton wrote, "endures for ever and ever, and is everywhere present; and by existing always and everywhere, He constitutes duration and space." On the other hand, *accelerations,* he argued, could be determined absolutely; for this purpose he devised the celebrated rotating bucket experiment in his *Philosophiae Naturalis Principia Mathematica (The Mathematical Principles of Natural Philosophy)*:

If a vessel, hung by a long cord, is so often turned about that the cord is strongly twisted, then filled with water...the vessel by gradually communicating its motion to the water will make it begin sensibly to revolve, and recede by little and little from the middle and ascend to the sides of the vessel forming itself into a concave figure (as I have experienced).

This concern of Newton to define absolute acceleration was hardly academic, because without such a definition his laws of motion are not a complete system. It is essential, for example, to know that the earth is rotating in order to give a complete description of the forces that act on a particle on its surface. For most purposes, the "fixed stars" are good enough as a reference frame, since their proper motions are relatively slow. But Newton was interested in constructing a *complete* system—an absolute system. It is interesting that some of Newton's contemporaries felt that there was something wrong with his distinction between uniform and accelerated motion—to use the modern terminology—that the relativity principle should apply to both. The Irish bishop and philosopher George Berkeley offered a criticism very much like Mach's principle. The Dutch physicist, mathematician, and astronomer Christian Huygens corresponded on the matter with Gottfried Wilhelm von Leibniz in Germany and produced a not very convincing argument, from which he concluded: "It is therefore impossible to state that a body is at rest in infinite space, or that it moves therein; rest and motion are therefore only relative." Huygens's objections soon were overshadowed by the incredible success of Newtonian mechanics, and the theological underpinnings of Newton's theories were more or less forgotten.

The matter of the philosophical premise underlying Newton's mechanics was reopened by Mach. What is fascinating to me is that Mach's discontent does not seem to have been inspired by any new discoveries in physics. The first version of *Science of Mechanics* appeared in 1883, the next in 1888, and the last, revised version in 1912. Nowhere is there a word about the Michelson-Morley experiment, first carried out in 1887, and neither is the name of Einstein mentioned once. What seems to trouble Mach is that Newton's formulations are built on unsound philosophical principles. Mach felt that the distinction Newton made between time as measured by clocks, and space as measured by rulers, and some other sort of absolute time and space beyond these operational procedures, was metaphysical nonsense; and he said so in no uncertain terms. "No one," he wrote, "is competent to predicate things about absolute space and absolute motion; they are pure things of thought, pure mental constructs, that cannot be produced in experience...." Then, he enunciates what is now known as Mach's principle, a resurrection of the early criticism of Newton's criterion for absolute acceleration. Mach says Newton's experiment tells us nothing about how his bucket would behave in empty space because the experiment is not done in empty space. It is done in the real space of the world, which is full of things like the stars. I quote his celebrated remark in full, because it is concise and because it is one of the cornerstones of Einstein's general theory of relativity and gravitation:

Newton's experiment with the rotating vessel of water simply informs us that the relative rotation of the water with respect to the sides of the vessel produces *no* noticeable centrifugal forces, but that such forces *are* produced by its relative rotation with respect to the mass of the earth and the other celestial bodies. No one is competent to say how the experiment would turn out if the sides of the vessel increased in thickness and mass till they were ultimately several leagues thick. The one experiment only lies before us, and our business is, to bring it into accord with the other facts known to us, and not with the arbitrary fictions of our imagination.

Specifically, "Mach's principle" refers to the possibility that the same effect on the water in the bucket could be produced if the bucket were put at rest and we rotated the stars.

The development of Einstein's philosophy of science from the positivism of Hume and Mach to what it finally became is well documented in his own writings. In one of Einstein's letters to Besso, Einstein complained that someone "rides Mach's poor horse to exhaustion. . . ." Besso reminded him: "As to Mach's little horse, we should not insult it; did it not make possible the infernal journey through the relativities? And who knows—in the case of the nasty quanta, it may also carry Don Quixote de la Einstina through it all!" Indeed, one might naïvely interpret the analysis of space and time in terms of clocks and rulers that Einstein gives in his 1905 paper as the purest exercise of Machian positivism imaginable: Time is what we measure with clocks; space is what we measure with rulers, and the physics of these operations is all-important. Within a decade, however, Einstein came to disbelieve (maybe he never believed) that this is what he had intended. It is especially interesting, though, to hear expert testimonial from Werner Heisenberg. In 1926, shortly after he had invented matrix mechanics, Heisenberg was invited to Berlin to give a lecture. After the lecture, Einstein invited Heisenberg to walk home with him, and during the walk asked him, in connection with the new mechanics, "You don't seriously believe that none but observable magnitudes must go into a physical theory?" The question startled Heisenberg, who answered, "Isn't that precisely what you have done with relativity? After all, you did stress the fact that it is impermissible to speak of absolute time, simply because absolute time cannot be observed: that only clock readings, be it in the moving reference system or the system at rest, are relevant to the determination of time." "Possibly I did use this kind of reasoning," Einstein admitted, "but it is nonsense all the same. Perhaps I could put it more diplomatically by saying that it may be heuristically useful to keep in mind what one has actually observed. But on principle, it is quite wrong to try founding a theory on observable magnitudes alone. In reality the very opposite happens. It is the theory which describes what we can observe." By contrast, Mach once wrote, "The object of natural science is the connexion of phenomena, but theories are like dry leaves which fall away when they have ceased to be the lungs of the tree of science."

Indeed, all of Einstein's three great papers of 1905 are non-Machian, something Mach himself must have well understood. The relativity paper has at its base the principle that the speed of light is independent of the uniform motion of its source, a principle for which there was no direct evidence at the time. (The subsequent famous double-star experiments of Wilhelm de Sitter, done in 1913, usually were considered corroborative, but it is not entirely clear what they proved.) When asked in the 1950s by the physicist R. S. Shankland how he had come to the principle of constancy, Einstein replied that it was "because he could think of no form of differential equation which could have solutions representing waves whose velocity depended on the motion of the source...." The Brownian motion paper is generally cited as the convincing argument for the existence of atoms. As is well known, Mach spent the last fifty years of his life denying the existence of atoms. In the opening paragraphs of Einstein's paper on photoelectricity, we find Einstein inventing the light quantum:

The wave theory, operating with continuous spatial functions, has proved correct in representing purely optical phenomena and will probably not be replaced by any other theory. One must, however, keep in mind...in spite of the complete experimental verification of the theory of diffraction, reflection, refraction, dispersion, and so on, that the theory of light that operates with continuous spatial functions may lead to contradictions with observations if we apply it to the phenomena of the generation and transformation of light.

In each of the 1905 papers, Einstein has totally transcended the Machian view that scientific theory is simply the "economical description of observed facts." None of these theories, strictly speaking, begins with "observed facts." Rather, the theory tells us what we should expect to observe.

So far as the general theory of relativity was concerned, Einstein felt that he was carrying out the detailed implementation of Mach's criticism of Newton's bucket experiment, and he said so in one of his letters to Mach. The two men met once in Vienna where Mach had been a Professor of Philosophy since 1895. Professor Frank, who had succeeded Einstein in Prague when in 1912 Einstein left Prague for Zurich, attended the meeting and afterward talked about it often. He recalls it as having taken place in 1913, but Gerald Holton, also one of Frank's disciples, believes that a more likely date is 1911. (It was also in Vienna that Mach had his celebrated confrontation with Ludwig Boltzmann over the existence of atoms. "Have you seen one?'' was Mach's favorite question. In 1898, Mach suffered a stroke, and in 1900 he retired but continued to work. Professor Frank remembers Mach asking him in 1910 to explain Hermann Minkowski's then new four-dimensional formulation of relativity to him. Mach, Professor Frank told me, did not approve.) Describing the meeting, Professor Frank wrote, ''On entering the room one saw a man [Mach] with a grey unkempt beard and a partly good natured, partly cunning expression on his face, who looked like a Slavic peasant and said, 'Please speak loudly to me. In addition to my other unpleasant characteristics I am also almost stone-deaf.' '' Einstein and Mach proceeded to discuss atoms.

EINSTEIN: Let us suppose that by assuming the existence of atoms in a gas we were able to predict an observable property of this gas that could not be predicted on the basis of a non-atomistic theory. Would you accept such a hypothesis even if the calculations of its consequences required very complicated computations, comprehensible only with great difficulty?

MACH: If with the help of the atomic hypothesis one could actually establish a connection between several observable properties which without it would remain isolated, then I should say that this hypothesis was an ''economical'' one; because with its aid relations between various observations could be derived from a single assumption. Nor should I have any objection even if the requisite computations were complicated and difficult.

Professor Frank writes:

Einstein was exceedingly satisfied with this statement and replied ''By 'simple' and 'economical' you mean then, not a 'psychological economy' but rather a 'logical economy.' ''

With *economy* interpreted in this *logical* sense, there was no longer any conflict between Mach's standpoint and Einstein's as to the criteria to be filled by a physical theory. Although Mach made the concession in conversations, yet Einstein saw in his writing only a demand for "psychological economy." Thus for the moment Einstein was satisfied, but he retained a certain aversion to the "Machist philosophy."

In truth, feelings ran deeper than this. Professor Frank was always very diplomatic, and I am not sure if he ever acknowledged the true rift between Einstein and the positivists. In 1921, Mach's *The Principles of Physical Optics* was published posthumously. His preface, dated 1913, reads:

> I am compelled, in what may be my last opportunity, to cancel my views of the relativity theory.
>
> I gather from publications which have reached me, and especially from my correspondence, that I am gradually becoming regarded as the forerunner of relativity. I am able even now to picture approximately what new expositions and interpretations many of the ideas expressed in my book on Mechanics will receive in the future from this point of view. It was to be expected that philosophers and physicists should carry on a crusade against me, for, as I have repeatedly observed, I was merely an unprejudiced rambler endowed with original ideas in various fields of knowledge. I must, however, as assuredly disclaim to be a forerunner of the relativists as I personally reject the atomistic doctrine of the present-day school or church. The reason why and the extent to which I reject the present-day relativity theory, which I find to be growing more and more dogmatical, together with the particular reasons which have led me to such a view—considerations based on the physiology of the senses, epistemological doubts, and above all the insight resulting from my experiments—must remain to be treated in the sequel....

This sequel was never published, and Mach's last words on relativity and the atomic theory deeply offended Einstein, as his letter to Besso, quoted earlier in this chapter, indicates. In a lecture he gave in Paris shortly after having read Mach's preface, Einstein noted that Mach had been a good mechanician but a deplorable philosopher.

In my view, no theoretical physicist, and least of all Einstein, has ever created a deep theory by following Mach's program of beginning with sensory experiences and then simply describing them economically. As Einstein himself often pointed out, even the clocks and measuring rods of the special theory of relativity are not "real" clocks and measuring rods. They are the abstract clocks and rods of thought. As he states in his autobiographical notes: "...strictly speaking, measuring rods and clocks would have to be represented as solutions of the basic equations (objects consisting of moving atomic configurations) not, as it were, as theoretically self-sufficient entities...." He referred to the introduction of these idealized objects as a "sin" that one has the obligation to expiate at some later stage of theoretical development.

By 1908 Einstein realized that not even the idealized clocks and rigid rods of the special theory could be maintained if one included gravitation. Gravitation intertwines space and time. The fact that a simple interpretation of the coordinates in general relativity can only be given locally helps explain why it took Einstein nearly a decade to find the theory. He later wrote, "It is not so easy to free oneself from the idea that coordinates must have an immediate metrical meaning." We know the dates involved in his considerations of ten years because, unlike the case of the special theory, where few existing documents preceded the 1905 paper, Einstein did leave a trail of false starts and partial successes toward the general theory. In the first, his 1907 paper in the *Jahrbuch der Radioaktivität,* he first considers the principle of equivalence between gravitational and inertial mass.

Einstein's prediction on the bending of light rays by the sun's gravitational field was fully worked out in his 1916 paper, "Die Grundlage der allgemeinen Relativitätstheorie'' (The Foundation of the General Theory of Relativity). Once it had been confirmed by the solar eclipse expeditions of 1919, he was flooded with requests to explain the theory and its origins. He responded by writing a number of popular and semipopular papers that also form a continuing philosophical monologue refuting Mach and positivism. Again and again Einstein tells us that in his view physical theories like general relativity cannot be *deduced* from experimental observations. They have an axiomatic basis, the axioms being free creations of the human mind.

Two specific expressions of this view are a lecture Einstein gave on the occasion of Max Planck's sixtieth birthday in 1918, and Einstein's beautiful paper "Physics and Reality," which was published in its English translation by the Franklin Institute in 1936. The paper has a special significance for me, because the well-thumbed reprint I have was sent to me by Einstein himself in 1949, when I was a sophomore. By this time, I had been a student of Professor Frank for about one and one-half years. I possessed that audacity for which sophomores are famous. With some encouragement from Professor Frank, I had written to Einstein to request an interview, since some of the fine points of his theory still eluded me. (At that time I did not even understand what a partial differential equation was.) I received a reply that included a paper expressing his opinions from an epistemological point of view. He mentioned that he did not give oral interviews in order to avoid misinterpretations. (Einstein *had* begun to give oral interviews to various historians of science, from which all who study his life and work have benefited immensely.)

In the course of his birthday lecture for Planck, Einstein said:

The supreme task of the physicist is to arrive at those universal elementary laws from which the cosmos can be built up by pure deduction. There is no logical path to these laws; only intuition, resting on sympathetic understanding of experience, can reach them. In this methodological uncertainty, one might suppose that there were any number of possible systems of theoretical physics, all with an equal amount to be said for them; and this opinion is no doubt correct theoretically. But evolution has shown that at any given moment out of all conceivable constructions, a single one has always proved itself to be absolutely superior to the rest. Nobody who has really gone deeply into the matter will deny that in practice the world of phenomena uniquely determines the theoretical system, in spite of the fact that there is no logical bridge between phenomena and their theoretical principles; this is what Leibniz described as a "pre-established harmony." Physicists often accuse epistemologists of not paying sufficient attention to this fact. Here, it seems to me, lie the roots of the controversy carried on some years ago between Mach and Planck.

In "Physics and Reality," Einstein distinguished between "phenomenological physics"—whose aim was the direct connection of phenomena, and which was obtained "purely inductively from experience"; physics, as he put it, done from the point of view of the theories of knowledge of John Stuart Mill and Ernst Mach—and the theoretical physics that Einstein, above all, practiced—in which the axioms were not a catalogue, but rather free creations of the mind based on a selective view of experience.

The liberty of choice [of the axioms] however, is of a special kind; it is not in any way similar to the liberty of a writer of fiction. Rather, it is similar to that of a man engaged in solving a well-designed word puzzle. He may, it is true, propose any word as the solution; but there is only *one* word which really solves the puzzle in all its forms. It is an outcome of faith that nature—as she is perceptible to our five senses—takes the character of such a well-formulated puzzle...

That this is true, Einstein said, is a fact "which leaves us in awe, but which we shall never understand." One may say, "the eternal mystery of the world is its comprehensibility."

7

Robert Oppenheimer

ROBERT OPPENHEIMER died on February 18, 1967. As far as I know, he left no autobiography, and no satisfactory biography has yet been written of him. Indeed, given the complexity of the man and of his life, I doubt whether a satisfactory biography ever will be written. Oppenheimer and Einstein, for example, pose totally different problems for a biographer. Einstein found in the pursuit of his science an escape from what he referred to as the "merely personal." His life and his science were so intimately joined that even his autobiography reads like a text—a superb one—in modern physics. Einstein seems to have done everything within his power to simplify his personal life so as to free himself to pursue his work. In his early teens, he became a research physicist, and he remained one all his life. There was never a time when he became something else—an administrator, for instance. But Oppenheimer's personal and interior life appear to have been so complex that one wonders how he was able to focus on his science at all. Part of the explanation is found, of course, in his genius—in the facility with which he grasped complex ideas—and part, one would imagine, in his will power, which must have enabled him at times to mute or blot out what was happening inside him.

I was led to think again about these two men while reading *Robert Oppenheimer: Letters and Recollections,* edited by Alice Kimball Smith and Charles Weiner. Smith and

171

Weiner have selected letters written by Oppenheimer between 1922 and 1945, and have provided a superb running commentary, with quotations from some of his correspondents. While it would be interesting to be able at some point to read his later letters as well, the decision to cut off this collection at 1945 is wise, I think, for after that year Oppenheimer became, in Yeats's phrase, "a smiling public man." The penultimate entry here is not a letter at all but a transcript of a talk that Oppenheimer gave on the evening of November 2, 1945, to the members of the Association of Los Alamos Scientists—his farewell speech. The speech is Oppenheimer at his very best. It is eloquent, clairvoyant, lucid; it has no trace of the baroque and often impossible-to-follow turns of phrase that he was sometimes partial to. It ends,

> We are not only scientists; we are men. We cannot forget our dependence on our fellow-men. I mean not only our material dependence, without which no science would be possible, and without which we could not work: I mean also our deep moral dependence, in that the value of science must lie in the world of men, that all our roots lie there. These are the strongest bonds in the world, stronger than those even that bind us to one another, these are the deepest bonds—that bind us to our fellow-men.

Robert Oppenheimer was born on April 22, 1904, in New York City. If, as I. I. Rabi, who had been close to Oppenheimer for nearly fifty years, surmised, Oppenheimer's "problem" was identity—as Rabi put it, "he reminded me very much of a boyhood friend about whom someone said that he couldn't make up his mind whether to be president of B'nai Brith or the Knights of Columbus"—this manifested itself very early, in the matter of Oppenheimer's first name. For whatever reason, on the few occasions that I spoke with Oppenheimer and,

later, with his widow about his early life, they told me un-
equivocally that the "J" in "J. Robert" stood for nothing.
Indeed, as Smith and Weiner point out, by the time
Oppenheimer entered Harvard, in 1922, his transcript read
"J. (initial only) Robert Oppenheimer." Nonetheless there
is a New York City birth certificate for April 22, 1904, that
reads "Julius R. Oppenheim [*sic*]." Julius was the name of
Oppenheimer's father. As was the case with so many
things in Oppenheimer's life, his attitude toward his
parents and their Jewishness was ambiguous. Julius
Oppenheimer immigrated to the United States from
Hanau, Germany, in 1871, and in 1903 he married a young
artist named Ella Friedmann. It was perhaps through her
influence that he developed a small but superb collection
of what was then modern art. The collection included a
van Gogh. (I have an indelible memory of my first conversation with Oppenheimer, which took place in his office at
the Institute for Advanced Study in the fall of 1957. I had
just driven across the country from Los Alamos and was
both exhausted and disheveled. I went to the administrative office at the Institute to get the key to my apartment,
and to my surprise the secretary said that Oppenheimer
wanted to see me. My general ill ease was enhanced by our
contrasting attire—I was wearing a pair of filthy bluejeans
with a matching shirt and Oppenheimer one of the impec-
cable tailored suits of which he was fond—and by his first
question. It was, "What is new and *firm* in physics?" The
word "firm" paralyzed me into what I recall to have been
more or less total silence. Seeing my discomfort, he
pointed in the general direction of the director's mansion
and said kindly, "You must come and visit us at home. We
have a few paintings that you might enjoy." Many weeks
later, at a party there, I saw the paintings, including the
van Gogh. Sometime later, I was told that this was the

collection he had inherited from his father, and that he had never added to it.) The Oppenheimers belonged to the Ethical Culture Society, whose school Robert entered in 1911. His closest friends at the time appear to have been Francis Fergusson, who later became a professor of comparative literature at Rutgers, and Paul Horgan, the novelist, whom Oppenheimer met on a trip to New Mexico, where he had gone to recover from an illness. (I had not known before of the apparent fragility of Oppenheimer's health, both physical and mental, when he was a young man.) In the summer of 1923, Horgan visited Oppenheimer at his parents' summer home in Bayshore, New York. At the end of the visit, the Oppenheimers drove Horgan to Buffalo—a trip that, if Oppenheimer's description of it in a letter to Fergusson is taken literally, seems to have been a nightmare of embarrassment. He writes:

> I think I told you that we were to motor Paul to Buffalo on our way to Quebec. We did. And towards the end there developed such an intricate panorama of complications that I was regaled with a daily scene. Toward the end, you see, mother and father grew a little jealous of Paul, and a little irritated at the ease with which he disregarded obstacles whose conquests formed the central jewels in the Oppenheimer crown. The matter was further embellished by two luscious complexes, oozing itch: mother's and father's which tried to apologize for being Jews; the Horgan's, which whinnied and shied clumsily about richesse and poverty.

But from the comments of Horgan, many years later, one gets the impression that this psychodrama was going on largely in Oppenheimer's head. When Horgan was interviewed by Smith in 1976, he remarked, "The parents were extremely kind to me and very gentle and solicitous about me as a youngster...and apparently very happy in our friendship."

This is not to say that in the atmosphere of the time—and in particular at a university like Harvard—one could not *develop* a complex about being Jewish. Casual anti-Semitism was simply a given—the gentle people of prejudice, as someone put it. (To have some idea of what this was like in British universities, one has only to read, for example, Dorothy Sayer's *Gaudy Night.*) Oppenheimer took his degree in chemistry in 1925 *summa cum laude,* and in three years; he decided to try to do his graduate work, in physics, at Cambridge University. Percy W. Bridgman, the distinguished Harvard physicist, who later won a Nobel Prize, had taught Oppenheimer in an advanced thermodynamics course. It was, Oppenheimer said later, the best science course he took at Harvard. So it was natural for Bridgman to write a letter of recommendation on Oppenheimer's behalf to Sir Ernest Rutherford at Cambridge. The letter was favorable, if cautious. Bridgman wrote, "It appears to me that it is a bit of a gamble as to whether Oppenheimer will ever make any real contributions of an important character, but if he does make good at all, I believe he will be a very unusual success." He added a final paragraph: "As appears from his name, Oppenheimer is a Jew, but entirely without the usual qualifications of his race. He is a tall, well set-up man, with a rather engaging diffidence of manner, and I think you need have no hesitation whatever for any reason of this sort in considering his application." I have no reason to believe that Bridgman, whom I got to know somewhat at the end of his life, was anti-Semitic. It appears to have been customary at the time to append observations of this sort to letters of recommendation. But whatever the causes—a sense of isolation, frustration at not being at the forefront of physics, or, as Francis Fergusson thought, sexual problems—there is no doubt that Oppenheimer had some sort of a nervous breakdown during the year 1925-26 when he was at Cambridge. At one point, he attacked Fergusson, apparently with the intent to strangle him. Oppenheimer sought psychiatric help, and this kind of incident was, as far as I know, never repeated.

The letters in this collection fall into chronological groups. There are the letters from Oppenheimer's student days, which lasted until 1929. In that year, he received a remarkable joint appointment at the University of California at Berkeley and the California Institute of Technology, in Pasadena. He migrated seasonally from one institution to the other, bringing his students with him. The letters from this period, which lasted until he moved to Los Alamos as its director in 1943, reflect both his growing stature in the field of physics and his growing political feelings. Members of his father's family began to arrive as refugees from Germany, and Oppenheimer himself took an interest in various radical causes. He was never a Communist, and when the war in Europe began he seems to have left all of these associations behind. But that he had once maintained them became a source of vulnerability during the McCarthy period. Finally, there are the letters from his Los Alamos days.

Among the early letters are sixteen extraordinary ones to his brother Frank, who was eight years younger. Here it seems that one is coming close to Oppenheimer's real and deep feelings about things. The letters are full of wise and affectionate advice. For example, when Frank Oppenheimer was a teen-ager he wrote to Robert to ask for advice about learning the theory of relativity. His brother answered:

I don't think you would enjoy reading about relativity very much until you have studied a little geometry, a little mechanics, and a little electrodynamics. But if you want to try, Eddington's book is the best to start on. I remember five years ago you were dressed up to act like Albert Einstein; in a few years, it seems, they won't need to disguise you. And you'll be able to write your own speech. And now a final word of advice: try to understand really, to your own satisfaction, thoroughly and honestly, the few things in which you are most interested; because it is only when you have learnt to do that, when you realize how very hard and how very satisfying it is, that you will appreciate fully the more spectacular things like relativity and mechanistic biology.

I cannot think of better advice to offer a young scientist.

Frank Oppenheimer also asked his brother for help in his emotional life. In answering such a letter, Robert wrote, "Don't worry about girls, and don't make love to girls, unless you have to: DON'T DO IT AS A DUTY. Try to find out by watching yourself, what you really want; if you approve of it, try to get it; if you disapprove of it, try to get over it." Whatever one may think of this advice, the puzzling thing to me is: By what experience did Oppenheimer acquire the authority to give it? None of the letters in the book appears to be addressed to women with whom he might have had a romantic attachment. In his letters to friends, there are all sorts of references to women, but these are so detached and dandyesque that the women seem more like stage props than people. And it is just this dandyesque quality that makes the other letters from this period seem bizarre. Here is a young man—one of the most brilliant young men of his generation—writing letter after letter to friends and teachers, and in none of the letters do I, at least, find the smattering of a significant idea. I recall Oppenheimer's telling me once that he enjoyed visiting the Harvard campus because nearly every conversation that he overheard among the students was interesting; the air seemed to be filled with ideas being exchanged.

177

I wonder what he would have felt if he had had to listen to conversations that sounded like his own letters.

To Fergusson he writes:

I am terribly—yes, terribly, eager to see your things, and would even burn my new Jeans Electromagnetics for a glimpse of the Pecos one. I can't tell you how I admire the calm intensity with which you say, "I shall do a big story about that—later on." Quelle patience inattendue et inhumaine! voir Herrick.

To his friend and teacher Herbert Smith he writes:

Aside from the activities exposed in last week's disgusting note, I labor, and write innumerable theses, notes, poems, stories and junk; I go to the math lab and read and to the Phil lib and divide my time between Meinherr Russell and the contemplation of a most beautiful and lovely lady who is writing a thesis on Spinoza—charmingly ironic, at that, don't you think?; I make stenches in three different labs, listen to Allard [Louis Allard, a professor of French] gossip about Racine, serve tea and talk learnedly to a few lost souls, go off for the weekend to distill low grade energy into laughter and exhaustion, read Greek, commit faux pas, search my desk for letters and wish I were dead. Voila.

In none of these letters does Oppenheimer give us a real idea of what he was thinking—what he was understanding (as he advised his brother) "thoroughly and honestly." Take the reference to Meinherr Russell in this last letter. In 1924, Oppenheimer took a course with the philosopher Alfred North Whitehead on the philosophy of science, and the following year he and a classmate persuaded Whitehead to give them a reading course in which the three of them read the *Principia Mathematica,* which Whitehead had written with Bertrand Russell a decade or so previously. Oppenheimer took great pride and pleasure in having taken this course, and in 1962, on the occasion of Russell's ninetieth birthday, he wrote Russell a note, which is included in the present collection:

> It is almost forty years ago that we worked through the *Principia Mathematica* with Whitehead at Harvard. He had largely forgotten, so that he was the perfect teacher, both master and student. I remember how often he would pause before a sequence of theorems and say to us "That was a point that Bertie always liked." I have always thought of this phrase whenever some high example of intelligence, some humanity or some rare courage and nobility has come our way.

But in all these letters there is never the slightest mention of what he learned from working through that extraordinarily difficult book, of why he bothered to do so, or of the controversy that had by then developed over the adequacy of the mathematical foundations that it proposed. Oppenheimer was only twenty-one when he took this course, it is true; but when Kurt Gödel began to *publish* the work that shattered those foundations beyond repair, a few years later, he was only twenty-four.

If one takes these letters at face value, one has the impression of a young man who was an extraordinarily gifted and energetic social and intellectual dandy. But if one reads the comments that Smith and Weiner have collected from Oppenheimer's contemporaries a very different picture emerges. The character created in the letters seems almost to have been a fiction. Take the comment of his college roommate Fred Bernheim:

> He wasn't a comfortable person to be around, in a way, because he always gave the impression that he was thinking very deeply about things. When we roomed together he would spend evenings locked in his room, trying to do something with Planck's constant or something like that. I had visions of him suddenly bursting forth as a great physicist, and here I was just trying to get through Harvard.

The Oppenheimer that emerges from these comments is a rather lonely and isolated young man, deeply dedicated to his science, but unable to make simple and straightforward contact with the people around him.

The year that Oppenheimer spent at Cambridge University appears to have been a personal and professional disaster. But it did have the result that, come what might, he decided to become a theoretical physicist. He later said in an interview, "I had very great misgivings about myself on all fronts, but I clearly was going to do theoretical physics if I could." He applied for permission from the Board of Research at Cambridge to move to Göttingen, in Germany. Göttingen was one of the great centers of theoretical physics—and, above all, of the then new quantum mechanics—in the world. For the first time, he found himself with a group of young theoretical physicists—Pauli, Heisenberg, Paul Dirac—who were his intellectual equals and were doing creative physics of the highest possible order. He later recalled:

In the sense that had not been true in Cambridge and certainly not at Harvard, I was part of a little community of people who had some common interests and tastes and many common interests in physics...something which for me more than for most people is important began to take place; namely I began to have some conversations. Gradually, I guess, they gave me some sense and perhaps more gradually, some taste in physics, something that I probably would not have ever got...if I'd been locked up in a room.

Oppenheimer took his doctorate with the great German-Jewish theoretical physicist Max Born. I have added "Jewish" here because, to judge from the recently published posthumous autobiography *My Life,* Born had a history of identity problems and psychological fragility not dissimilar to Oppenheimer's. The relationship between the two men appears to have been uneasy. A great novel—perhaps several great novels—could be written about the relationship between teachers and their gifted students in science. If there is a common theme, it might be the difficulty of an older person's accepting the fact that a pupil or protégé has produced or is about to produce work that supersedes his own: the mingled feelings of pride, jealousy, and regret. It takes a scientist with the character and assurance of an Einstein to be fully immune to such feelings; while Born was a great physicist, he was not an Einstein. In the Smith-Weiner collection, Oppenheimer is quoted as saying in an interview, "I think it is quite probable that I attended some of Born's lectures, but I don't remember." A very favorable letter of recommendation, written by Born in 1927 to S. W. Stratton, who was president of M.I.T., is included: "We here have a number of Americans, five of them working with me. One man is quite excellent, Mr. Oppenheimer, who studied in Harvard and in Cambridge." But in his autobiography Born writes:

Oppenheimer caused me greater difficulty. He was a man of great talent, and he was conscious of his superiority in a way that was embarrassing and led to trouble. In my ordinary seminar on quantum mechanics, he used to interrupt the speaker, whoever it was, not excluding myself, and to step to the blackboard, taking the chalk and declaring: "This can be done much better in the following manner..." I felt that the other members did not like these perpetual interruptions and corrections. After awhile they complained, but I was a little afraid of Oppenheimer, and my halfhearted attempts to stop him were unsuccessful. At last I received a written appeal, I think that Maria Göppert, then a very young student [she won the Nobel Prize in physics in 1963] was the driving force. They gave me a sheet of paper looking like parchment, in the style of a medieval document, containing the threat that they would boycott the seminar unless the interruptions were stopped. I did not know what to do. At last I decided to put the document on my desk in such a way that Oppenheimer could not help seeing it when he came to discuss his thesis with me. To make this more certain, I arranged to be called out of the room for a few minutes. This plot worked. When I returned I found him rather pale and not so voluble as usual. And the interruptions in the seminar ceased altogether.

Freeman Dyson in his book *Disturbing the Universe* has described his harrowing experience, in the late forties, of giving seminars in the presence of Oppenheimer. By the late fifties, when I attended the same seminars at Princeton, Oppenheimer, who had, by all reports, greatly mellowed, was certainly the dominant and electric personality. As a somewhat superannuated student, I was able to watch the various dramatic encounters among my elders and betters from a fairly safe vantage point. I do recall one notable occasion when a distinguished Swiss theoretical physicist, and an old and very close friend of Oppenheimer's, was giving a seminar. There was an exchange between the two men that went as follows:

Oppenheimer to speaker: "Can you explain so and so?"
Speaker: "Yes."
The speaker then went right on with the lecture, and after a minute or so Oppenheimer said, *"Would* you explain so and so?"
Speaker: "No."
Oppenheimer: "Why not?"
Speaker: "Because then you would ask me another question, and I would have to explain that, and this way my whole seminar time would be used up."
For all of this, the seminars that Oppenheimer presided over were the best and most exciting I have ever attended. They were not comfortable, but they were unforgettable.

Oppenheimer, Rabi, and a few others brought modern physics—and above all, the quantum theory—back to the United States when they returned in the early thirties. But, as Smith and Weiner illustrate, it took Oppenheimer some time to adjust himself to even the best students' relatively limited ability to assimilate information. They give two charming examples. A physicist named Leo Nedelsky began working with Oppenheimer at Berkeley in 1930. Once, when Oppenheimer was leaving Berkeley, he asked Nedelsky to teach his course, remarking that there would be no problem, since the material was all contained in a certain book. When Nedelsky found the book, he saw to his dismay that it was in Dutch. He pointed this out to Oppenheimer, who said, "But it's such easy Dutch." On another occasion, when a student asked about an equation, Oppenheimer told him to consider an equation "underneath" the one he had referred to. "But there isn't one underneath," the student said. "Not below," Oppenheimer replied. "Underneath. I have written over it."

The letters from this period make it clear that teaching and research were the center of Oppenheimer's life. Many of these letters are about physics and may not mean a great deal to the general reader. They indicate that Oppenheimer had a broad range of interests, from the most fundamental problems to the details of experiments. He did not perform experiments, but he could advise experimenters in detail. There is only one casual mention in the letters of what may, in retrospect, turn out to have been Oppenheimer's most notable contribution to physics. In 1939, first with his student George Volkoff and then with a second student, Hartland Snyder, Oppenheimer wrote two papers on the collapse of large stars. In the second paper, the conditions for creating what is now called a black hole were first stated. Under these conditions, Oppenheimer noted, "the star thus tends to close itself off from any communication with a distant observer; only its gravitational field persists.'' The idea was so speculative that it was not taken very seriously until decades later. Black-hole physics is now a respectable and highly active branch of research.

What seems to have been a wonderfully fruitful, almost idyllic, academic life came to an end for Oppenheimer in 1941. In 1939, nuclear fission was discovered. The uranium nucleus was split by Otto Hahn and Fritz Strassman in Germany. The impression that this made on physicists can be judged from the opening phrase in a letter that Oppenheimer wrote to his colleague from Pasadena, William Fowler. ''Dear Willie,'' he writes, ''The U business is unbelievable.'' By 1941, Oppenheimer was deeply engaged in ''the U business,'' and by 1942 it had become nearly a full-time job. In March 1943, Oppenheimer moved with his family—he had married Katherine Puening Harrison in 1940, and a son, Peter, was born in 1941—to Los Alamos. The letters from the early forties show that Oppenheimer had developed into a first-rate administrator—the ideal administrator of an incredibly complex technological project. His new role was probably not what he had in mind when he wrote in 1934 to his brother, who was then studying physics in Cambridge, about ''physics and the obvious excellences of the life it brings,'' but it may have been foreseen. In 1931, Oppenheimer had written to his brother, ''I think that the world in which we shall live these next 30 years will be a pretty restless and tormented place; I do not think that there will be much of a compromise possible between being of it, and being not of it.'' This fascinating collection of letters and commentaries tells us more than has been revealed before about one of the people who defined an age.

8

Nuclear Research:
Shooting the Pussycat

I SPENT the summer months of 1958 and 1959 in La Jolla, California, as a consultant for the then newly founded General Atomic Company. La Jolla was, and I suppose still is, a pleasantly sybaritic beach community with excellent surfing, done mostly on the Wind'n'sea Beach celebrated in Tom Wolfe's *The Pump House Gang*. My connection with General Atomic came about because of my friendship with Freeman Dyson, who was, and still is, a professor at the Institute for Advanced Study in Princeton, where I spent two years from 1957 to 1959. Dyson was invited in 1956 to be a consultant for General Atomic by its then president, Frederic de Hoffmann; sometime later, Dyson asked me to join him. (He has written about these years in his fascinating autobiography, *Disturbing the Universe*.) He arrived that summer, along with the rest of the consultants, at what he describes in his book as a "little red schoolhouse." De Hoffmann had, in fact, rented a schoolhouse that had been abandoned by the San Diego Public School system—since General Atomic then had no buildings of its own. By the time of my appearance the company had acquired its own buildings. But, buildings or not, in 1956 de Hoffmann, who was a tremendous entrepreneur, had managed to attract to La Jolla a stellar group of physicists, including Dyson, with the idea of the company's entering the field of reactor design and construction. Dyson notes in his book that three groups of consultants were formed under the rubrics Safe Reactor, Test Reactor, and Ship Reactor. The latter two were, respectively, a design for a reactor with a very high neutron flux, to be used for materials testing, and a design for a reactor to be used to power merchant ships. Neither of these was ever built by the company.

I recall that Dyson told me he got into the business of designing a safe reactor because no one else (except Edward Teller) in the group wanted to do it. To most of them it did not seem like a very glamorous problem, but Dyson, who is acknowledged to be one of the best problem solvers in physics, took it on as a challenge. In due course—a few weeks' time—he invented the general concept of the TRIGA, an acronym invented by de Hoffmann to stand for "Training, Research, and Isotopes, General Atomic." This reactor was designed for use, primarily at universities and large medical centers, in training students and for the production of short-lived, medically useful isotopes. It sold, according to Dyson, for $144,000 and, at last count, about sixty had been sold. In fact, he notes in his book, "It is one of the very few reactors that made money for the company which built it."

Before getting on to why I am bringing all of this up at the present time I should like to describe briefly in what way the TRIGA is a safe reactor. To explain this in a schematic way, let me first review how a reactor works. Reactors are powered by nuclear fission. In particular the so-called fuel elements of the common reactors consist of long, thin rods containing pellets of uranium that have been "enriched" so as to contain more of the fissionable isotope U^{235} than is normally found in nature. In nature more than 99 percent of the uranium is found in the U^{238} isotope, which is not readily fissionable. In a TRIGA, for example, the fuel elements contain an enrichment of 20 percent of the U^{235} isotope. When a slow neutron encounters a U^{235} nucleus, it has a good chance of splitting it and releasing energy and additional neutrons which can then carry on the chain reaction that produces energy.

This brings me to the second point. If the neutrons are to be made effective, they must be slowed down. This is accomplished by putting the fuel rods in a so-called moderator. In the TRIGA, as in most of the common reactors, the moderator is ordinary water. The fuel elements are in a small swimming pool which glows a pleasant incandescent blue when the reactor is operating. The power generated by the TRIGA is so low that one can stand safely above the pool while the reactor is working. Reactors used by the power industry are at least ten thousand times more powerful, and one cannot approach them when they are in operation. The water in the pool serves the double function of slowing down the neutrons and cooling the fuel elements so they won't melt—the "melt-down." The fissions generate heat, and in a power reactor this heat produces steam, which drives electric turbines. In the power reactors the essential thing, from a safety point of view, is to make sure that under no circumstance does one lose cooling water and thus expose the heated fuel elements. We all know now, from what happened at Three Mile Island, how crucial this is. In power reactors the safety is "engineered." It consists of having many back-up cooling systems which the reactor engineers can bring to bear in an emergency. But, as we saw in the Three Mile Island incident, these safety measures are vulnerable to human error. There the reactor operators shut off the emergency cooling system at a crucial moment. The accident would have been prevented if they had done nothing and let the emergency system operate automatically.

What Teller's group—that is, Dyson—was up to was to create a reactor that was "intrinsically" safe: it would shut itself off no matter what anyone did during an emergency—simply as a law of nature. Dyson's brilliant idea was to design a reactor in such a way that half the moderator was in the water and half was in the fuel elements themselves. The element that slows the neutrons in the water moderator is the hydrogen. Hence Dyson, working with an Iranian metallurgist Massoud Simnad, and others found out how to bond uranium-hydride—a compound of uranium and hydrogen—to a metal compound of zirconium and hydrogen. In this way the fuel elements themselves contain hydrogen; when something goes wrong the hydrogen gets heated up and then, it turns out, it will no longer moderate the neutrons and the whole chain reaction will come to an abrupt stop. In fact, in a TRIGA the reactor shuts itself off in a *few thousandths of a second.* I have watched it do this myself in tests in which the control rods that usually keep the number of neutrons at a safe level were blown out of the reactor by compressed air. What one saw was a brief flash in the swimming pool and then nothing. (By the way, among the people who helped produce the final TRIGA design was Theodore B. Taylor, whose concern for nuclear safety was underscored in John McPhee's book *The Curve of Binding Energy.* Ted Taylor was our group leader at General Atomic when I joined Dyson there in 1958 to try to build an atom-bomb powered spaceship, the *Orion*—a project that was abandoned a few years later. But that is another story.)

Before I come to the point of *this* story I must make a few additional remarks about the safety of nuclear reactors. Prompt shutdown of the chain reaction that keeps a reactor going is unfortunately not the whole safety story. If it were, there would have been no serious incident at Three Mile Island since the operators there managed to shut the chain reaction off in about thirty seconds. Unlike other power sources a reactor continues to generate substantial heat even after the fuel stops "burning." The reason for this is that when the uranium nucleus splits in the fission process it splits into a variety of medium-weight nuclei that are radioactive. These radioactive fission products continue to decay and the motion of the decay products represents energy that manifests itself as heat. The amount of heat that is generated depends on the prior history of how the reactor has been used, but a rough formula is that about 10 percent of the power capacity of the reactor remains as heat when the chain reaction is shut down. To have a clearer idea about the numbers, we may recall that the power of a reactor is usually given in watts—a unit of energy per second—an energy rate. How big is a watt? To get a feeling for this, recall that normal household light bulbs are usually about a hundred watts, which, coincidentally, is the energy rate that is dissipated by the human body. A clothes dryer consumes energy at a rate of about four thousand watts. But a big power reactor at full operation generates about a *billion* watts so that 10 percent of this is about a hundred million watts. When the reactor is shut down, as it was at Three Mile Island, this enormous heat energy must be dissipated if the reactor is not to melt down. It is useful to keep the scale of these numbers in mind in what follows.

Now to the point. As early as 1952, physicists and engineers at Columbia University in Manhattan recognized the need for a safe training reactor that could be operated in a university located within a big city. In 1958 the TRIGA became operational, and by 1963 Columbia had received both government funds and a construction permit from the then Atomic Energy Commission to buy and build a facility for a relatively small TRIGA. The design called for a 250,000-watt reactor. It was to have been run, for training purposes, about eight hours a week at *ten* watts. A few hours a week it would have been run at full power to make isotopes. In the most extreme situation any emergency shutdown would have generated about fifteen thousand watts—the power equivalent of four clothes dryers. This heat would not have been difficult to dissipate. From 1963 until the present, however, Columbia's TRIGA has been tied up in an endless round of litigation between the university and various concerned citizen groups. Finally, in June 1974, the Supreme Court upheld the validity of the original construction permit. In fact the reactor has been built, but it has never been fueled. In 1979, William McGill, then the president of Columbia, announced that it would *never* be fueled as long as he was president. He retired in 1980.

It seems to me that McGill's decision and his reason for it—which, according to the *New York Times,* were "not because of doubts about safety but because of community fears" ("I am much more concerned with the psychological explosion than I am about a nuclear explosion," he stated)—are another illustration of the fact that the energy crisis has so far succeeded in bringing out the worst in nearly everybody. Did it not occur to then President McGill that the same reasoning he used to ban the TRIGA could be used to ban any controversial academic subject at Columbia? Did it not also occur to him that without training facilities, nuclear engineers—both here and abroad—will be even less well equipped to deal with emergencies than the Three Mile Island engineers seem to have been? It should also be noted that no one, no anti-nuclear group, has asked that any of the other sixty-odd TRIGAs be shut down. This in itself is some sort of testimonial to their safety. Columbia's administration has adopted a Luddite position that is unique. It can be compared to General MacArthur's decision to smash the Japanese cyclotrons just after the war on the grounds that these machines were somehow weapons of war. No one can be complacent about nuclear safety after Three Mile Island. But to keep a TRIGA from operating is, as a Columbia professor remarked, like being in an Indian village where a man-eating tiger has been discovered and to respond to this genuine and legitimate concern by shooting someone's pet cat.

9

Topless in Hamburg

A FEW years ago I had the pleasure of interviewing Murray Gell-Mann for the *New Yorker's* "Talk of the Town." Our subject was the quark. Gell-Mann and, independently, George Zweig—who, like Gell-Mann, is now a professor at the California Institute of Technology—invented the quark in 1963. I will come to *why* they did it shortly, but, if I may quote myself, I will begin by explaining where the name quark came from. The quote is from the July 18, 1977, issue of the *New Yorker*.

For a while Gell-Mann did not give them a name. Zweig called them "aces" and the particles made out of them "deuces" and "treys" [thank God *that* didn't stick]. But Gell-Mann had a *sound* for them, and it came out something like "quark"— which, by the way, he pronounces to rhyme with "stork," while many of the European physicists pronounce it to rhyme with "ark." The sound was given an orthography and an etymology by a stroke of serendipity. [I have no recollection of actually having written this sentence, but I am certainly happy to take credit for it.] Gell-Mann had been leafing through and studying "Finnegans Wake" ever since 1939, when his brother bought a first edition of it. And in late 1963, while leafing through it once again, he came across the phrase "Three quarks for Muster Mark!" That did it: now the three objects had a name to go with the sound. But where did Joyce get the word? Gell-Mann, one of whose hobbies is historical linguistics, told us what some of the theories are. Certain Teutonic scholars have noted that *Quark* is the German word for "cottage cheese," and that it traces back

192

to the Late Middle High German *Twarc,* which in turn traces back to the Slavic (TBOPOT in Russian)—perhaps cognate with the Greek τυπός and probably a semantic parallel with the Italian word for cheese, *formaggio,* which came from the Vulgar Latin word *formaticum,* or something made in a "form." They speculate that Joyce might have come across a grocery-store sign in Zurich: *"Drei Mark für Muster-Quark"* ("Three marks for model cottage cheese") and transposed *Mark* and *Quark.* A famous reference to "quark" is a phrase from Goethe—*"Getretner Quark wird breit, nicht stark"* ("Cottage cheese that has been stepped on becomes flattened out, rather than strengthened"), which is a comparison, unfavorable, between cottage cheese and steel. In any case, Joyce scholars think that "quark" is the sound made by the four gulls that mock King Mark in the book, and Gell-Mann thinks that Joyce may also have had a pun in mind on "quark" and "quart," since the book is the dream of a publican—a bartender. Whatever its origin, the name has now become part of the language. There is even, in a projected television series, a pilot of a spaceship (an interplanetary garbage scow) who is called Adam Quark.

Well, as the Italians say, *"Se non è vero, è ben trovato,"* and furthermore I don't think that you are going to find a fuller explanation of the name unless Gell-Mann writes it himself.

The reason that I bring this up now is that I have recently received in the mail a preprint of a paper from M.I.T. entitled, in part, "Search for the Production of a New Quark Flavor...." Before I discuss the significance of its contents I want to make a few sociological observations about it. In the first place, it has a total of *fifty-eight* authors—a good many more, I would imagine, than the total number of physics majors at Harvard when I was an undergraduate. The names of the last eight authors are, respectively, Wu, Wu, Xi, Yang, Yu, Yu, Zhang, and Zhu, which might naïvely lead one to believe that the paper originated in China. But before jumping to hasty conclusions, bear in mind that one of the authors, Samuel C. C. Ting, although Chinese, is from M.I.T. He shared the Nobel Prize in 1977 with Burton Richter—who is neither Chinese nor from M.I.T. but works at Stanford—for their part in starting what is sometimes referred to as "the glorious revolution of 1973"—a sequence of events (of which more later) that appears to have confirmed the existence of the so-called charmed quark. All that having been said, I hasten to add that several of the authors of the paper *are* from China, including, quite possibly, Wu, Wu, Xi, Yang, Yu, Yu, Zhang, and Zhu. The work described in the paper was, in fact, done on a large electron accelerator called PETRA, no doubt an acronym for something, which is located in Hamburg, which is neither in China nor at M.I.T., but in West Germany. Five laboratories collaborated, notably the Physikalisches Institut Techniche Hochschule in Aachen, the Deutches Elektronen-Synchrotron in Hamburg, the Laboratory for Nuclear Science at M.I.T., the Nationaal Institut voor Kernfysica en Hoge-Energiefysica in Amsterdam, and the Institute of High Energy Physics in Peking. I do not know if this is the first physics paper in recent times to be co-authored by Western laboratories and a laboratory from the People's Republic, but it is certainly one of the first. The thrust of the paper, which has ten pages of text and five pages of diagrams, is that these gentlemen, and perhaps ladies, have not found any evidence for the existence of the so-called top quark. Gell-Mann, what have you wrought?

In the good old days, before the Second World War, physicists had actually observed a mere six so-called elementary particles. They were the neutron and proton, which are the constituents of the atomic nucleus; the electron, which is the lightest known particle that carries an electric charge; its anti-particle, now known as the positron; and a thing which behaves like a heavy electron but which is known, for historical reasons, as the "mu meson." Finally, there was the photon—the quantum of electromagnetic energy. In addition, two other particles were conjectured to exist: the so-called pi meson and the neutrino. In fact, when the mu meson first turned up in cosmic rays in 1936, it was, for a brief time, thought to be the pi meson, whose existence had been conjectured the year before by Hideki Yukawa as the hypothetical "glue" which was supposed to hold the nucleus together. When it was learned that this was not the pi meson, I. I. Rabi asked, "Who ordered *that?*"—an excellent question to which, as far as I am concerned, there is still no completely convincing answer. In 1947 the pi meson was finally located. It turned out that nature had played a trick. The pi meson is unstable and decays almost instantaneously—in a few billionths of a second—into a mu meson and a neutrino. The neutrino—an incredibly elusive object that can penetrate some 3,500 *light-years* of lead without a single interaction with a lead nucleus—was finally observed in 1953.

Also in the year 1947 a veritable plethora of new particles began showing up in cosmic ray experiments. It would take an entire book to describe the elation, confusion, and dismay among the physics community as the new particles began to appear. Some flavor of the atmosphere is conveyed by a remark that I heard Oppenheimer make at the time. He proposed awarding a Nobel Prize to the first experimental physicist in the field who, in a given year, did *not* discover a new particle. To get some idea of where we are now, let me remark that the *Reviews of Modern Physics* publishes an annual compendium of data on particles. The 1980 version, for example, is 286 pages long, each page dense with charts and tables of the properties of these objects. My own reaction in the early days—and I think it was not entirely atypical—was that physics was rapidly turning into zoology. To ask *why* there was a K meson or a lambda hyperon seemed to me akin to asking why there are giraffes. Just about this time Gell-Mann appeared at Harvard to give a lecture. When I saw him, some bell rang. Upon looking through some ancient high school year-books, which I still have, I realized why: he and I had over-lapped briefly at Columbia Grammar School in New York. Although he is only a few months older than I am, he grad-uated three years earlier and matriculated at Yale at the age of thirteen. We both took mathematics from the same teacher, a Mr. Reynolds, and Gell-Mann was one of the students Reynolds cited when he wanted to make the point that giants used to roam the corridors of Columbia Gram-mar. (When someone would make a particularly bad mis-take in class, Reynolds used to comment, "In Tarrytown we bury our dead.") In any event, Gell-Mann gave the most lucid lecture I had ever heard about the new particles, and he succeeded (the same scheme was invented indepen-dently by a Japanese physicist named Kazuhiko Nishijima) in giving a precise set of rules which governed their interac-tions. Gell-Mann, who has always had a wonderful facility for inventing names, christened the new objects "strange particles," and it was their "strangeness"—a new kind of non-electromagnetic charge—which governed many of their interaction properties. The field had been trans-formed from zoology back to physics.

In 1959 Gell-Mann suggested that I use a National Science Foundation fellowship which I had won to come to Paris to work with him. I remember his saying, "Stick with me, kid, and I will put you on Broadway." For a year we worked together with some French theoretical physicists. Even then, Gell-Mann was groping toward some unifying scheme that would bring the particles together under one roof. His creative energy was incredible. After a session with him I used to hide out for a day or two to think things over. There would be various telephone messages asking me to call him, and when I finally got my head together I would go to see him. He used to say, "Where have you been? I have discovered *millions* of things!" And he had. This work culminated a little later in the discovery of what Gell-Mann called "the eightfold way." (Some of it was done independently in a Ph.D. thesis by the Israeli physicist Yuval Ne'eman.) For some reason, Gell-Mann's original paper on the eightfold way was never published. It was widely circulated in 1961 as a Caltech report and has been reprinted in a book edited by Gell-Mann and Ne'eman called *The Eightfold Way*. It is an extraordinary paper because, to make the scheme work, particles were needed which at that time had not yet been discovered. They all were discovered, and with just the right properties—or, at least, those that one really wanted.

As the term "eightfold way" would suggest, something in this scheme must have to do with the number eight. Well, one of the things that had to do with that number is that some particles were predicted to come in families of eight. (They were also predicted to come in families of ten and twenty-seven—a point to which I shall return.) But what is a "family"? It has been known for many years that one of the ways nature reveals symmetries is by grouping together apparently distinct objects into states with nearly the same energies. In atomic physics, for example, one often finds two or more levels for the atomic electrons with nearly the same energies—something that is revealed by studying the spectra of these atoms. This sort of "energy degeneracy" was also evident in the particles even in the 1930s. For instance, the neutron and proton have nearly the same mass-energy. It has long been believed that if one could somehow turn off electromagnetism, then the neutron and proton would have the same mass and would become essentially identical. Such a pair of objects is called a doublet. After the pi meson was discovered, it was soon found that there were three kinds: one positively charged, one negatively charged, and a neutral one. They have nearly the same mass—the positive and negative ones have exactly the same mass and the neutral one is slightly lighter—and so, naturally, they are known as a triplet. But until Gell-Mann and Ne'eman did their work, this was about the extent of it. The other particles did not seem to connect together into families in any obvious way. The boldness of the eightfold way was to suggest that, despite superficial differences, there really were families. In fact, the neutron and proton are two members of a family of eight, and the pi mesons are three members of another family of eight. Gell-Mann also noted that it looked as if a family of ten was appearing, and this idea was dramatically confirmed in 1964 in a paper (with only thirty-three authors) which announced the discovery of the so-called omega minus particle—the missing member of the "decuplet" family. (Families of eight are called octets; families of ten are called decuplets; and bachelors are called singlets.)

Where, then, is the quark? I do not, needless to say, have any idea when the first inkling came into Gell-Mann's head that underlying the eightfold-way scheme there might be triplets of particles. When I interviewed him, he thought that the first glimmerings were probably in the early spring of 1963 when he was visiting M.I.T. What I *do* remember distinctly is a visit that Gell-Mann paid to Columbia University in March 1963 to give a colloquium. At Columbia on these occasions it has long been a tradition for the whole group, as well as any visitors who may be around, to go out for a Chinese lunch somewhere on Broadway near the university. T. D. Lee, himself a Nobel Prize winner and a member of that distinguished physics department, usually chooses the restaurant and selects the menu. (It is not a "one from group A and one from group B" selection, I can assure you—nothing but the best.) In any event, I remember walking up Broadway in a freezing wind with a small group that included Gell-Mann and Robert Serber (a very soft-spoken and exceedingly profound theoretical physicist who is now professor emeritus at Columbia and spends much of his time floating around the Caribbean in a sailboat). As we were walking along, Serber asked Gell-Mann where in his scheme—the eightfold way—was the "fundamental representation." What I did not realize at the time was that I had just witnessed the birth of the quark.

The fundamental representation of a symmetry group is the family with the smallest number of members—excluding the bachelor family, which is too small to be interesting. Gell-Mann's eightfold-way group is called by mathematicians "SU(3)," which stands for the "special unitary group in three dimensions." But Gell-Mann's smallest family had eight members, whereas the smallest family possible has only three members. I believe, although my recollection may be faulty, that by the end of the lunch Gell-Mann had worked out the properties of the fundamental representation. I even have a vague memory that he mentioned this in his talk that afternoon. His paper, however, was not published for nearly a year. (As far as I know, Zweig's paper was never published.) What held it up? Perhaps it was the fact that the quarks appeared to be crazy. All particles that have ever been observed have electric charges that are simple integer multiples of the charge of the electron. Why this is we are not sure, but it is a fact. The quarks, however, have fractional charges. In Gell-Mann's original scheme, there were just three quarks and three anti-quarks. Now, we would say that the quarks come in three "flavors." The "up" quark has a charge that is two-thirds of the charge of the electron, while the "down" and "strange" quarks both have charges that are minus one-third. No such objects have ever been seen to this day. Many experiments have been done in a search for real quarks in cosmic rays on the moon, in the ocean, and nearly everywhere else, but—with the exception of a few not completely explained, anomalous experiments—they have never been observed directly.

Why, then, do we believe in them? In the first place, all the observed particles can be made naturally out of quarks. The pi mesons are made out of a quark and an anti-quark, while the proton and neutron can be manufactured from three quarks. In fact, one gets just the right families. The reader may recall that the eightfold way predicted a family of twenty-seven. This family has never been seen, but the simple quark model allows for families of one, eight, and ten members and these alone. It is almost too good to be true. In the second place, these particles can be examined microscopically by bouncing very high-energy electrons off them. If one does this, their quark structure becomes "visible" in a very real sense. The evidence for the quark model seems overwhelming. By now the model has undergone a few very important refinements and I will end this brief survey by describing them, since it will lead me back where I started—namely, being "topless in Hamburg."

One refinement was that Gell-Mann was awarded the Nobel Prize in physics for 1969. There has never been a better merited award. But almost from the beginning it was realized that the so-called Pauli exclusion principle—named after the great Austrian physicist Wolfgang Pauli—was a potential headache for the quark model.

The exclusion principle is such an interesting bit of modern physics that it is worth spending a moment on. In real life, when we say that two things are "identical," we don't really mean it. Even identical twins have different names. But in quantum physics when we say that two photons are identical, we *do* mean it, and this has far-reaching implications. All quantum mechanical particles have a wave nature. One of the most important characteristics of waves is that two or more of them can interfere: They can overlap to produce bright spots and dark spots. When two identical particles occupy the same state, their wave functions can interfere. At this point the discussion divides, since there are two generic classes of particles. One class includes the pi meson and the photon, for which this interference is constructive; these identical particles like to get together. Then there is a second class, where the interference is destructive. This is the Pauli exclusion principle. No two particles of this class can occupy exactly the same state. Its members include the electrons, protons, and neutrons, and Pauli used his principle to give an accounting of the periodic table of elements, among other things. But this class of particles also includes the quarks, and here is where the headache came in.

The most graphic illustration of it is the quark constitution of the omega minus particle, which, as I have mentioned, completed the decuplet. In the original quark model, this object was supposed to consist of three identical strange quarks. But how to stick them together without violating Pauli's principle? It could be done, but only at the expense of standing on one's ear. It then dawned on a number of people—especially O. W. "Wally" Greenberg in 1964—that the way out was to make the quarks non-identical. This meant attaching a new property to them which could distinguish the three strange quarks in the omega minus.

I think that Gell-Mann invented the name "color" for this new property. At least I heard him give a number of early lectures on it in which the quarks were called "red, white, and blue," or whatever color suited the occasion. No one is claiming that the quarks *are* red, white, and blue. Color is just a name given to this new property; one might have called it "dog, cat, and rat." By combining these colored quarks in a lucid fashion, one can beat the Pauli principle, but at the expense of triplicating the number of constituent particles. This might seem like a chimera except that there are experiments—I cannot give the details here—which, in effect, count the number of quarks. These experiments appear to show that this triplication is really there. Gell-Mann christened the theory of these objects "quantum chromodynamics," and its practitioners claim to have shown, with varying degrees of mathematical rigor, that the quarks are dynamically confined to their particles and should not be observed as free, independent objects. Should a certifiable free quark show up, then it will be back to the drawing board.

As early as 1964, a number of theoretical physicists suggested that up, down, and strange quarks, even with color, were not enough. I do not think that Gell-Mann had a hand in this one. The name of the next quark "flavor" —namely, "charm"—first appeared, as far as I know, in a paper by J. D. Bjorken and S. L. Glashow in 1964. This proposal was taken with varying degrees of solemnity until the "glorious revolution of 1973." That year, two experimental groups—one led by the aforementioned Ting and the other by the aforementioned Richter—discovered a new particle which Ting called the J particle and Richter called the ψ particle. (It turned out that "J," if written in the correct way in Chinese, stands for "Ting.") In the interests of fraternal harmony it is often referred to as the "J"/ψ meson. After a certain amount of initial confusion, it became clear that the particle was made up of a charmed and an anti-charmed quark. This was called the discovery of "hidden charm," since charm and anti-charm cancel. "Naked charm" was discovered soon afterward, when several particles were found which were made up of charmed and non-charmed quarks. At the time I recall hearing a delightful lecture by the Italian theorist Sergio Fubini. He had attended a conference in New Orleans and reported that, after a tour of the bars in that city, he had observed a great deal of naked charm but that he had found no evidence of hidden charm.

Now we had four quark flavors and three colors, or a total of twelve quarks. But in 1977 yet a new object was discovered, the so-called Υ particle, which could be made up of none of the above. This did not come as a surprise to many theorists who had been saying all along that there had to be at least two more flavors, which, for reasons known best to them, they called "top" and "bottom." The Υ particle is made up of a "bottom" and an "anti bottom" quark. No comment.

Now we had five flavors and three colors, or fifteen quarks. There were high hopes that the Hamburg experiment would turn up the top quark. It did not, but very likely it is there, waiting to be discovered. Where will it all end? No one knows for sure. If some new quarks turn up in the near future, I will let you know. In the meantime we all have a lot to think about.

10

Time

NO concept is more common and more elusive than that of "time." We are all aware of it in the ebb and flow of our lives—in the passing of innumerable sunrises and sunsets. For most practical purposes, time is a concept that we do not have to analyze very deeply. The ancient peoples found the motions of the sun and stars a perfectly adequate measure of the duration of events, and basically, we do, too. It is for this reason that most of us find the analysis of time by modern scientists—and above all by Einstein—almost an imposition. One is led to wonder why these people appear to be making something complicated of something that appears so simple.

As I will attempt to explain in what follows, the modern scientist's view of time, as complicated as it may at first appear, is based not on whim but on recognition of the fact that our common-sense view of time is no longer adequate to what we now know about the world. If we insist on clinging to the old view, we simply deprive ourselves of the possibility of understanding how the world works.

This does not mean that we must now throw away our watches and clocks, since for practical purposes they are still perfectly adequate; we do not need the Einsteinian revolution to tell the time of day. But the new view of time does mean that when we extend our experience to domains in which clocks can time events that last a billionth of a second or less, and in which objects can move close to the speed of light, we must be prepared for surprises. Physicists have not *invented* these surprises. They are there, part of nature, awaiting our discovery; to deny their existence would be to deny one of the significant experiences of the intellectual life of this century.

In 1687, Issac Newton finally published his *Philosophiae Naturalis Principia Mathematica (The Mathematical Principles of Natural Philosophy)*. It had been a reluctant birth. Some of the work's great ideas—the ideas that were to dominate science for the next two centuries—had been invented by Newton during the famous "plague years" of 1665 and 1666, when at the age of twenty-three he had left Cambridge University and returned to his mother's home in order to avoid the bubonic plague. But there had been gaps in the work, and it was not till about twenty years later that Newton was finally persuaded by the astronomer Edmund Halley to complete the entire work for publication. The *Principia* is written in Latin and laid out like a geometry text, with the axioms, definitions, and rules of inference followed by the theorems. In addition, there are commentaries on some of the terms. These commentaries Newton referred to as *Scholium*. The first of them reads: "Absolute, true and mathematical time, of itself, and from its own nature, flows equably [evenly] without relation to anything external, and by another name is called duration."

This "absolute" time Newton distinguished from a second variety, which he called "relative, apparent and common time." (See chapter 6.) It is this common, or relative, time, he said, that we measure with clocks or, more fundamentally, with any system whose behavior repeats itself periodically. One may wonder why Newton went to such pains to distinguish between two varieties of time. There were, I think, two reasons. Newton was a devoutly religious man. In fact, he spent more time on biblical studies and on alchemy than on physics. He took the Bible to be a literal statement about nature and searched it for clues as to, for example, the age of the universe. And he regarded his scientific system not only as a theory of physics but as an expression of God's work; as such, it had necessarily to be complete. However, Newton's basic law of motion—which states that force is proportional to acceleration—is circular and incomplete if acceleration is not defined. Hence, as I have mentioned before, Newton introduced *absolute time*—and also *absolute space*—in order to define *absolute acceleration,* and so to complete his law. Or so he thought. It was enough for him for these concepts to form part of the "Sensorium of God," sensorium meaning, roughly, "the sensing mind." As Newton wrote of God: "He endures for ever and ever, and is everywhere present; and by existing always and everywhere, He constitutes duration and space."

The second reason for Newton's belief in two kinds of time was, I think, probably psychological. We all feel that time is something that flows on quite independently of any attempt we can make to stop its flow or, indeed, independently of any attempt we make to measure it. Our subjective feeling is that our clocks measure something that is objectively given: "time." It takes a considerable mental effort to analyze the hidden assumptions that go into this idea, and it was not until 1905, when Einstein reopened these matters for physics, that the question of what constitutes a measurement of time was fully analyzed.

This is not to say that Newton's contemporaries were in full agreement with his views about time. It was only later that his theories came to be regarded as complete and unassailable. Indeed, he engaged in a bitter correspondence on the nature of space and time with Gottfried Wilhelm von Leibniz, the German polymath who independently of Newton had also invented the differential calculus. (The notation that we use today is that of Leibniz.) There were five letters written between 1715 and 1716, Newton's end of the correspondence being carried on by a proxy, one Samuel Clarke, to whom it is believed Newton all but dictated letters. Leibniz believed that time is simply a relation by which we order our experience—time does not exist, that is, in the absence of things. In an empty universe, Leibniz held, there would be neither space nor time, since these concepts refer to relations among material objects. In his third letter Leibniz wrote: "...they [space and time] consist only in the successive order of things." This view of time, which was contrary to Newton's, would certainly be acceptable to a modern scientist. Leibniz's view was, however, submerged by the enormous practical success of Newtonian "mechanics"—insights into the nature of motion and natural forces that explained everything from the tides to the motion of the moon and the planets.

In succeeding years, as the power of his system of mechanics became clear, Newton's underlying metaphysical and theological assumptions were forgotten or ignored. Indeed, early in the nineteenth century, after the great French mathematical physicist Pierre Simon de Laplace had presented to Napoleon his now famous work *Celestial Mechanics,* Laplace was asked by the emperor where God could be found among the work's assumptions, to which he responded, "Sire, I had no need for that hypothesis," a remark that Newton would have found absurd.

It is interesting and surely no accident that the development of Newtonian mechanics and the other important scientific discoveries made in Britain and on the Continent

in the early seventeenth and early eighteenth centuries co-
incided with the rise of public interest in the practical consequences of scientific theory. Newton became a contemporary legend because the educated public was receptive to
science as a practical instrument. It was also a period when
empires were being formed—and being defended on the
high seas. Navigation was an urgent piece of national
business. Britain's Royal Society of London for Improving
Natural Knowledge, of which Newton was an early
member, was founded in 1662, and in 1675 the Royal Observatory at Greenwich was founded by Charles II, "in
order to the finding out of the longitude of places for per-
fecting Navigation and Astronomy." To that age, the
"finding out of longitude"—one's location on the globe in
terms of east or west of a given point—was a problem that
had all the practical significance that the development of
energy sources has for us. In fact, in 1707 a British fleet
returning from Gibraltar ran aground and lost 2,000 men
because of an error in navigation. In response to this
disaster, the British Parliament in 1714 offered a quite considerable reward for "such person or persons as shall
discover the longitude at sea."

As I shall explain, to "discover the longitude" meant in
the end the development of an accurate nautical
clock—one that would be unaffected by the pitching and
rolling and abrupt temperature changes undergone by
ships at sea. Longitude is the measurement of the angle
between an arbitrary, internationally accepted, pole-to-
pole line—the line is called the prime meridian and is now
taken to run through Greenwich, England—and the north-
south line that passes through the point where the observer
is located. But these lines of longitude are stationary, and
so they rotate with the motion of the earth. If we remain
stationary some place at sea, the stars above appear to

rotate slowly around a fixed pole—a point in the night sky located somewhere near the so-called North Star, or pole-star. The local "meridian," by definition, is an imaginary "great circle" that passes through us and the north and south celestial poles.

As early as the sixteenth century it had been understood in principle how a navigator could use an accurate clock to determine his position. To begin with, one needed to make a table—an almanac—of the times at which certain given stars passed through the meridian at Greenwich, which was taken as a convenient reference point. This almanac would then be kept in the possession of the ship's navigator. To find the ship's longitude—its east-west position—the navigator would note the time at which a given star passed over his ship. Then, consulting the almanac, the navigator would note the time of the star's passage across the Greenwich meridian. In this way, the navigator could compute the ship's position east or west of Greenwich, England.

Suppose, to take an example, the star crossed overhead one hour later than the corresponding "Greenwich time" indicated in the almanac. The navigator would know that the earth had turned one hour's worth out of twenty-four. Since in twenty-four hours the earth turns a full $360°$, in one hour it would have turned $15°$. Since the apparent rotation of the stars is from east to west—think of the sun—it follows that, in this example, the ship is $15°$ west of Greenwich. All this assumes, of course, that the navigator has a clock that is pinpoint-accurate.

The prize offered by Parliament in 1714 stipulated that £10,000 would be given for a method accurate to within one degree—sixty nautical miles at the equator—while £20,000 (perhaps a million dollars today) would be given for a method accurate to within half a degree. To see what this means in terms of the accuracy of the clock, keep in mind that the earth turns a quarter of a degree per minute. Thus, to win the £20,000 one would have to design a nautical clock accurate to within about two minutes over a six-week voyage. This does not seem like much now, but remember that this marine chronometer would have to keep uniform time on a ship moving in the ocean under often sharply varying conditions of weather, temperature, and wave motion.

The first such timepiece was designed by John Harrison of London in 1759. He had been working on it since the time the prize had been announced, when he was twenty-one. Harrison's clock—the H-4, his fourth model—gained only forty seconds in seven weeks. The K-1, a copy of Harrison's clock, was given to the English round-the-world explorer Captain James Cook, and the K-2, another copy, to Captain William Bligh. Bligh took the K-2 along on his famous voyage on the *Bounty* in 1787.

In a wonderful book called *Man and the Stars,* the British astronomer Hanbury Brown recounts the clock's peregrinations after the voyage came to an abrupt and premature end. When the crew mutinied and cast Bligh adrift in an open boat, the crew "took K-2 with them to Pitcairn [Island], where it stayed until 1808, when it was bought by the captain of a whaler. Again it was stolen and landed in Chile, whence it was returned to England in 1843."

Though Harrison's clocks were a brilliant success, the clockmaker found it was no easy matter to collect the prize he had so clearly won. The Board of Longitude, which was in charge of the contest, insisted that his chronometers be tested again and again, and when it finally conceded that the prize money was his, he was given only half the amount due him. It was not till King George III and Parliament intervened in his behalf that he was finally given the rest of his prize in 1773—when he was eighty years old.

In his book, Hanbury Brown notes that marine chronometers became standard on ships of the nineteenth century and that captains of such ships were expected to provide their own. He quotes Captain Cook, who wrote, "The most expensive article, and what is in some measure necessary in order to come at the utmost accuracy, is a good watch." By 1825, such watches were supplied by the Crown.

None of these advances in technology had any immediate impact on the great philosophical questions that had been left unsettled in the debate between Newton and Leibniz, and, indeed, the next developments came at the hands of the physicists. In 1883, the Austrian physicist-philosopher Ernst Mach published his classic scientific polemic *The Science of Mechanics*. The name Mach is known to most of us only through the "Mach numbers" that measure the velocity of an object relative to that of sound—thus, Mach 3.0 equals three times the speed of sound at sea level, or about 2,280 miles an hour. In his time, however, Mach worked successfully in nearly all of the sciences. Among other things, he was the first man to photograph an object moving faster than the speed of sound, and the first to photograph the shock wave that precedes such a missile.

But it was not this achievement that made Mach the towering influence that he became to his contemporaries. It was, rather, his philosophical skepticism, which he applied to making a withering analysis of Newtonian physics—a physics that by Mach's day had acquired the status of dogma. In his *Autobiographical Notes*, written when he was sixty-seven, Albert Einstein remarked, "It was Ernst Mach who...shook this dogmatic faith; this book [*The Science of Mechanics*] exercised a profound influence upon me in this regard while I was a student. I see Mach's greatness in his incorruptible skepticism and independence.

One of the ideas that Mach devastated in *The Science of Mechanics* was Newton's concept of absolute time. Referring to the *Scholium* mentioned above, Mach wrote,

It would appear as though Newton in the remarks here cited still stood under the influence of the medieval philosophy, as though he had grown unfaithful to his resolves to investigate actual facts...[Newton's] absolute time can be measured by comparison with no motion; it has therefore neither a practical nor a scientific value; and no one is justified in saying that he knows aught about it. It is an idle metaphysical conception."

With all due respect to Isaac Newton!

In his *Autobiographical Notes,* Einstein informs us that the process of liberation from Newton's ideas about time began at the age of sixteen. Since he did not formulate the theory until he was twenty-six, the full process took him about ten years. I will not try to trace here the historical sequence that led to the theory of relativity. What I will attempt to do here is to describe Einstein's analysis of time. This is given in the first few pages of his 1905 paper, which was published under the title *"Zur Elektrodynamik bewegter Körper"* ("On the Electrodynamics of Moving Bodies"). A reader who studies these pages will note that they are almost entirely free of mathematical formulae. It is not ignorance of mathematics that is an obstacle to the understanding of these pages. The obstacle is in part our subjective resistance to the idea that time is somehow "relative," and in part the very compact abstract reasoning presented by Einstein.

The key to understanding Einstein's ideas about time lies in the understanding of how we assign a time to a given event—how we "date" it. As Einstein put it in his paper,

We have to take account that all our judgments in which time plays a part are always judgments of *simultaneous events*. If, for instance, I say, "That train arrives here at 7 o'clock," I mean something like this: "The pointing of the small hand of my watch to 7 and the arrival of the train are simultaneous events.

This does not sound like the stuff of which revolutions are made—but wait! If the event in question is in close proximity to my watch there is nothing very complicated about the procedure. I can look at my watch and record the time of the event. But what do I do if the event is located, say, on the Moon! Clearly, I must resort to some sort of signaling procedure.

In his paper, Einstein restricts himself to signals that are propagated by light. This is because light moving through a vacuum satisfies a very simple physical law: It travels in straight lines with a velocity of about 186,000 miles a second. It was the neglect of the fact that light signals do not propagate instantaneously—do not, that is, travel from their source to your eye with no elapsed time—that misled most of Einstein's predecessors as to the nature of time. Indeed, for most practical purposes we can assume that this light propagation *is* instantaneous; it is only when the speeds of objects become comparable to that of light that the impact of the theory of relativity becomes dramatic. If normal vehicles moved at such enormous speeds, relativity effects would have been discovered long ago.

If a distant event takes place on an object that is stationary with respect to us, there is no problem. We can take into account the time delay, correct for this delay, and assign a time to the distant event without difficulty. But if the distant object is in motion, "simultaneity," as we shall soon see, no longer has a universal meaning. Two events that we judge to be simultaneous will not be judged simultaneous by a moving observer. Once we understand this we will also understand why time is relative.

Einstein was very fond of illustrating this point by examples involving trains. Suppose we are at rest, "standing still," in our system, and we see two lightning bolts strike at two separated points at times that we judge to be simultaneous. We can test this judgment by stationing an observer at the midpoint between these two places. He will note that the light from the two bolts arrives at his eye simultaneously. But suppose there is a moving train whose front end is at the point where one of the bolts strikes down and whose back end is near where the other bolt hits, and suppose that there is an observer watching from a car in the middle of the train. Will this observer also see the light from the two bolts arriving at his eye simultaneously? A moment's thought will convince us that this is not the case. The observer on the train will be moving toward one bolt and away from the other. The light from the bolt toward which he is moving will reach him before the light from the other bolt does. He will conclude then that the two bolts did *not* strike simultaneously—that the bolt ahead struck sooner than the bolt to the rear. This phenomenon is the *relativity of simultaneity*. Since the time of an event is determined by the simultaneity of two events, and since simultaneity is relative, then time itself must be relative.

This is the general, or qualitative, idea about time's relativity. To make it quantitative—to spell it out precisely—one does need some mathematics, although not very much, and this mathematics forms the content of the rest of Einstein's paper. The result is the following: time as measured by any observer at rest with his clock (we can call such a person a "rest observer") will be the same as the time as measured by any other observer at rest with an identical clock. But all observers in motion with respect to these clocks will report a *slowing down* of time.

To be more precise, suppose that a moving observer reports that according to his clock an event has lasted one second. Then to a rest observer this same event will appear to have lasted longer. This is not an optical illusion, nor does it depend on the construction of any given clock. It is a general feature of how time is measured by the two observers, and it can be traced back—given more detail than is possible here—to the relativity of simultaneity. For motions at low speeds this time difference effect, while present, is so small as to be undetectable. To put in some numbers, if an observer moving with half the speed of light finds that an event lasts 1 second, then a rest observer will find that the same event lasts 1.15 seconds; and if the first observer now moves with nine-tenths the speed of light the time dilation factor will be 2.3 seconds, and so on. In the theory of relativity—and in nature itself, so far as we know—the speed of light in a vacuum is the maximum speed that any object can attain.

Many of Einstein's contemporaries found this time-dilation idea absurd. For example, in 1911 W.F. Magie in a presidential address to the American Association for the Advancement of Science stated categorically, "I do not believe that there is any man now living who can assert with truth that he can conceive of time which is a function of velocity." In 1911, Einstein was very much alive and this is precisely what he had been saying. But in 1911 there were neither clocks accurate enough to measure the time dilation for anything like terrestrial speeds, nor were there known objects that moved with speeds approaching that of light. Now we have both. An atomic clock uses as its time calibration the natural frequencies of vibration of atomic electrons. Such a clock, using, for example, cesium atoms, can keep time to an accuracy of one second in 450,000 years. Cesium clocks have been taken aloft in airplanes moving at speeds of a few hundred miles an hour. These airborne clocks measured the time dilation when compared to identical clocks left on the earth. The results checked with the theoretical prediction.

Moreover, since the early 1940s, experiments have been done on subatomic particles that move very close to the speed of light. The first group of these experiments were done on so-called mu mesons, which occur in the cosmic rays that form part of the background radiation that continuously impinges on earth from outer space. For us, the significant property of the mu meson is that it is unstable—it disintegrates radioactively in about a millionth of a second. But this decay, too, is a kind of clock: if the mu meson's lifetime is measured to be a millionth of a second by an observer at rest with respect to the meson, then this brief lifetime will be dilated if it is measured in any other moving system.

This assertion can readily be tested, since cosmic-ray mu mesons move at speeds close to that of light. One can compute how far the mu meson should travel, according to an observer on earth, if its length of travel—its "lifetime"—were not dilated. If one does this, one will find that this travel distance is much shorter than the distance that the mu meson is in fact observed to travel. The discrepancy is accounted for by the time dilation. Such particles can now be produced, more or less at will, in large accelerators, and time dilation is a daily fact of life for people who work on experiments at these machines. A version of one of Einstein's most intriguing predictions about time has also been checked—the so-called traveling twins phenomenon. Einstein noted that the human heart and the other metabolic processes are also clocks. Hence, he said, if there were two identical twins, one of whom stayed at home while the other went on a trip, the traveling twin would return home younger than his sibling; that is, his life span would have been dilated like the lifetime of the mu meson. It is, in fact, possible to create unstable particles in identical pairs in an accelerator, then have one make a trip, and compare its "longer" lifetime with that of the one staying at home, thus confirming, in this sense, the traveling twin prediction.

Remarkable as these developments are, they do not address themselves to the two basic issues about time that I mentioned at the beginning of the discussion. In the first place, they do not resolve the debate between Newton and his opponents as to whether time and space exist in the absence of material objects; and they also do not address the question of the flow of time—of its apparently one-way character. It is to these matters that we now turn. Einstein's 1905 paper on relativity dealt with a particular class of physical systems—those that move uniformly, at constant speeds. The results of the theory, as he then presented it, do not apply to objects that are accelerating. For this reason, his 1905 theory is known as the "special" theory of relativity—"special" since it deals with only a special category of motions.

During the next ten years, however, Einstein worked on the generalization of his 1905 theory, and he published his results in 1916. The "general" theory of relativity that he ultimately created is thought by many scientists to be the most aesthetically beautiful scientific theory that has ever been invented. The key idea that finally led Einstein to the theory lay in a phenomenon that had been well-known ever since the pioneering experiments of Galileo but whose full significance had not been appreciated until Einstein. Galileo observed that, not counting the effects of air resistance, all objects within the gravitational field of the earth fall with the same acceleration. In a vacuum—and this is a common demonstration experiment in freshman physics courses—both a penny and a feather fall with an acceleration that is approximately thirty-two feet per second per second. (On the surface of the moon, because of the moon's lesser mass, this acceleration would be smaller.) Einstein recast this familiar fact in the following language: Suppose that we are in an elevator in space that is being pulled up with some constant acceleration—let's call it g—by means of a cable. To us inside our elevator it will appear as if we are being pressed downward toward the floor of the elevator with a constant force. We may also interpret what is happening to us by saying that our elevator is at rest but that we are in a gravitational field that is acting downwards. Hence we have the equivalence of two apparently unrelated situations: a uniform acceleration *up* or a constant gravitational field *down*.

We may now ask what happens to a clock under these equivalent circumstances. While the special theory of relativity does not, strictly speaking, apply to accelerated motions, we can nonetheless make use of it to get an idea of what will happen. We may think of the acceleration as being composed of small steps, during which the clock is moving uniformly. But a clock in uniform motion runs slow as compared with a "rest clock." Hence this line of reasoning would suggest—and correctly—that an accelerating clock also exhibits time dilation.

But as we have just seen, a uniform acceleration can be equated with—that is, have the same effect as—a gravitational field. Thus, we have reached the important result that a clock in a gravitational field *is also time dilated*. This remarkable prediction of Einstein has now been tested in several ways. The cesium atomic clocks that were flown in airplanes to test the special theory also test the general theory. The gravitational field of the earth is not constant but falls off with increasing distance from the center of the earth. Thus, the higher the plane flies, the less should be the time dilation due to gravity, and, in particular, the effect of gravity should be smaller than the effect on an identical clock on the earth's surface. This was confirmed in 1971 when a cesium clock was flown around the world on a commercial jet at an altitude of about two miles.

In addition to this confirmation of Einstein's ideas, there are the classical experiments first done at Harvard by R. V. Pound and G. A. Rebka in 1960 on what is known as the "gravitational red shift." Atoms emit light of well-defined frequencies—we see them as colors, and this, too, is a kind of clock. And like all clocks, it is retarded when in a gravitational field. In practice, this means that the atomic spectral lines are shifted toward the red end of the spectrum compared to the same lines observed in light emitted from atoms not in a gravitational field. This effect was confirmed by Pound and Rebka and by subsequent investigators.

In relativity theory, time and space are conjoined in a union that is known as space-time. We have seen that time is affected by gravitating matter, and it should perhaps come as no surprise that space is also affected. In empty space, a light ray propagates in a straight line, but if this same light ray is acted on by gravitating matter, it is bent out of that line. Thus, if we were able to construct near gravitating matter a giant triangle made out of light rays, we would discover that this triangle does not obey the celebrated theorem of Euclidean geometry that states that the sum of a triangle's interior angles is exactly 180 degrees. The sum of the angles for this light-ray triangle would not be 180 degrees, and we would conclude that the geometry of space—or, more precisely, space-time—was non-Euclidean. This is summarized by another idea—the notion that space-time is curved, or "warped," by the presence of gravitating matter. In general, relativity theory says that geometry differs from place to place in the universe, depending on the distribution of massive objects. Without such objects, in a certain sense, space and time disappear. As Einstein put it, "There is no such thing as an empty space, i.e., a space without a field. Space-time does not claim existence on its own, but only as a structural quality of the field." Thus, we would say that in his dispute with Newton, Leibniz was right. Space and time in the absence of things is a purely metaphysical concept about which, in Mach's phrase, we know "aught."

I have saved for last the most difficult and intriguing question of all—that is, why time appears to have a direction. Relativity theory by itself does not cast any light on this, and we must look elsewhere. We begin by considering a phenomenon that, at first sight, might seem unrelated to the question of "time's arrow" but in fact will give us important insights. Let us suppose that in one corner of a container of water we deposit a small amount of colored substance such as potassium permanganate. We can guess what will happen. In due time the permanganate, which is deep purple in color, will diffuse throughout the water, which will develop a uniform coloration. We might, if we like, even think of this gradual process as a kind of clock in which "later" corresponds to a greater degree of diffusion. Indeed, children who have been shown picture sequences of processes like the diffusion and asked to order the pictures into "earlier" and "later" have been able to do so quite accurately and with no trouble.

But what is happening on a molecular level to produce

this apparently ordered process of diffusion? The perhaps surprising fact is that what is happening on the molecular level is total chaos. Indeed, if we could follow the molecular interactions, we would find that the permanganate molecules are being bombarded from all sides by the water molecules. In each collision in this idealized situation a permanganate molecule is just as likely to move to one side as to the other. But if we are at a place in the liquid where there are no permanganate molecules, then *some* of the collisions will move permanganates into our area, and subsequent collisions will continue to move them into areas that are free of permanganate, until the permanganate is diffused throughout the water. To use a technical term, on the average, the collisions will increase the disorder, or *entropy,* of the system until in the end there will be an equilibrium in which the entropy will take on its maximum—all the water in the container will be stained an even, purplish color.

I have been careful to use the phrase "on the average" here because in principle there can be improbable collisions in which the entropy *decreases.* There is a celebrated mathematical theorem credited to the great French mathematical physicist Jules Henri Poincaré, who was a contemporary of Einstein and who made significant contributions to relativity theory as well. Poincaré's theorem says that eventually every state in a system like the permanganate and water will repeat itself, and infinitely often. This means that if we could only wait long enough, the permanganate would all collect again at one side of the container. The only difficulty in actually observing such a scenario is that these "Poincaré's cycles" can be longer than the present age of the universe, which is now taken to be some fifteen billion years. This may not be much consolation when we think about aging, which, despite Poincaré's theorem, proceeds inexorably from the cradle to the grave. The entropy-decreasing fluctuations are so rare that they are irrelevant to our destinies.

This constant production of entropy—on the average—is, from a scientific point of view, what is meant by "time's arrow." We can say that "time" flows in the sense of constantly increasing disorder. From this point of view, it is fascinating and poignant to look at the origin and destiny of the universe as a whole—its cosmology. It is well known that the universe is expanding. All the distant galaxies are moving away from us and from each other at speeds that in the case of the most distant galaxies approach that of light. If one traces this expansion backward it appears to have had its origin in a gigantic cosmic explosion—the Big Bang—that took place perhaps fifteen billion years ago. To speak somewhat metaphorically, space and time were created in this explosion. From a scientific point of view, it probably does not make much sense to ask what happened "before"—there *was* no before. At its creation, the universe was at a low ebb in its entropy. Since that time, entropy has been increasing constantly. When a star shines it gives off light energy and this increases the entropy. Entropy increases as the universe expands. Where will it all end? Einstein's theory of gravitation tells us that there are two general possibilities. One is that the expansion will go on forever and the universe will eventually die a slow but inexorable "heat death," in which the temperature of the entire cosmos will approach absolute zero. The other possibility contained in the theory is that the expansion of the universe will slowly decelerate, then stop, and then reverse itself. It may be that in about seventy-five billion years the universe will recontract to its original state—a ball of superdense matter; there will then be a new explosion, and the whole process of expansion and contraction will begin over again. At present, the evidence is not conclusive for either case. However this cosmic process turns out, *we* will not be around to see it.

11

Furth's Reactor and

Fusion

ON A BRIGHT, sunny weekend last May a friend and I drove from New York to Princeton to visit Harold Furth, whom I have known since we were undergraduates at Harvard thirty years ago. He is, I believe, the first physicist to publish in the *New Yorker*. In 1956 he was employed under the general aegis of Edward Teller at the Lawrence Livermore Laboratory near San Francisco. He happened to read an account of a speech given by Teller on antimatter. Furth, whose interests as an undergraduate were about evenly split between physics and creative writing, was inspired to write a poem called "Perils of Modern Living" that was published under his initials H.P.F. The poem began

> Well up beyond the tropostrata
> There is a region stark and stellar
> Where on a streak of anti-matter
> Lived Dr. Edward Anti-Teller...

It goes on to describe the encounter of Teller and Anti-Teller which culminated in a fatal handshake.*

---

*Teller has harbored no hard feelings. He is publishing a major book on controlled fusion research this fall and asked Furth to write one of the chapters.

Furth's Reactor and Fusion

> ...Their right hands
> Clasped, and the rest was gamma rays.

From the time I first knew him, Furth's principal interest in physics was in the phenomenon of magnetism, especially in devices that produced extremely high magnetic fields. At Livermore he was putting this expertise to work in the then nascent controlled nuclear fusion program. The goal of the project was, and still is, to take light elements such as the isotopes of hydrogen—deuterium and tritium—heat them up to temperatures several times that of the interior of the sun, and confine the super hot gas to a small volume so that the hydrogen nuclei have a chance to collide with each other often and violently. In some of these collisions, the nuclei "fuse" with each other, thereby releasing vast quantities of energy according to Einstein's equation $E = mc^2$. Fusion is the basic mechanism which causes the sun and the other stars to shine and it is the basic mechanism that powers a hydrogen bomb. Matter at these incredibly high temperatures—many millions of degrees—is in what physicists call a plasma state. The electrons—electrically charged particles that surround the atomic nucleus—are stripped from the nucleus. This produces a gas of electrons and a companion gas of electrically charged nuclei, which have been stripped of some, or all, of their electrons. These charged particles can be acted on by magnetic fields, and these magnetic fields can be shaped so that they confine the plasma—at least in principle—in a suitable volume. In practice this has turned out to be incredibly difficult. The hot plasma tends to wiggle away, out of the confining magnetic fields. In fact, as Teller once remarked, "It is like trying to confine jelly with rubber bands," the "jelly" being the plasma, and the "rubber bands" being the lines of magnetic force.

In 1967 Furth moved to Princeton where he became a member of the Princeton Plasma Physics Laboratory and a professor in the Department of Astrophysical Sciences. In 1981 he became director of the Plasma Physics Laboratory, which is one of the largest fusion laboratories in the world. It employs over a thousand people and is spread over three sites near the university—over about 600,000 square feet. It now has an annual budget of about 100 million dollars, which is more than a third of the university's total budget. The administration of a complex and often frustrating scientific project like this has its ups and downs. When Furth took over, the director of one of the other large U. S. physics laboratories told him what he thought might be a useful anecdote concerning a newly appointed head of a laboratory who was told that if he got into trouble, he would find two letters in his desk that he should open, one after the other, as needed. After six months he got into trouble and opened the first letter. It read: "Blame the previous director." This worked for awhile, but then he got into even worse trouble, so he opened the remaining letter. It read: "Prepare two letters." So far, Furth has not had to open either letter.

In fact, when we arrived in Princeton last May, Furth told us that just that week the laboratory had achieved a milestone in its program. A large new fusion machine on the site, the PDX (for Poloidal Divertor Experiment), had heated a confined plasma to a temperature of about 70 million degrees centigrade. To appreciate what this kind of temperature means, one should keep in mind that the interior temperature of the sun is about 14 million degrees. Hence, on this quiet Saturday in Princeton, there was within a stone's throw of the campus a device operating that was heating particles to temperatures about five times the temperature of the hottest part of the sun—the place in the sun where solar energy is being manufactured. Furth asked us if we would like to go over and see it; needless to say, we readily accepted his invitation.

A short distance from downtown Princeton is the James Forrestal Campus where the Plasma Physics Laboratory is located. One of the other things under construction (to be operative in 1983) located on the campus is an experimental effort (in part sponsored by the Prudential Life Insurance Company at a cost of a few tens of thousands of dollars) by a group of Princeton physicists—among whom is Theodore B. Taylor, who was a member of President Carter's commission to investigate the accident at Three Mile Island—to produce air conditioning, and possibly heating, at very low cost by filling a hole with a small mountain of ice during the winter, and covering the hole with a plastic insulator. The ice melts in the summer and thus produces the air conditioning. Also on the James Forrestal Campus, also under construction, is the next generation of an experimental fusion reactor—the TFTR (for Tokamak Fusion Test Reactor), which is scheduled to go into operation in late 1982. It will be the largest in our fusion program and will cost about 300 million dollars. These two enterprises represent, perhaps, the extreme opposite ends of the technological spectrum in the attempts to solve our energy problems. Both would use essentially inexhaustible sources of energy.

The fusion laboratory consists of several relatively unprepossessing buildings, among which is a hangarlike structure that will house the TFTR. When we entered the main building, Furth signed us in and got us some radiation badges, because a working fusion reactor is, like the sun, an intense source of radiation. We walked along some labyrinthine corridors and passed a computer center, on the door of which was fastened a notice that read: "To err is human, But to really foul up requires a computer."

We then entered the control room of the PDX. How one reacts to such a display of modern technology depends on one's experience with it. The most complex control rooms of this type that I have seen are those that operate the large particle accelerators, such as the ones at the Fermi Laboratory near Chicago or the ones at CERN near Geneva. The PDX control room is certainly less complicated than these, but it is several times more complicated than the cockpit of a modern airplane. There are about seventy-five scientists associated with the PDX, and, even though it was a Saturday, a large percentage of them were there. Every couple of minutes, there was a banging sound audible in the control room—almost like a tiny explosion. I asked Furth what the noise was. He explained that every few minutes a cold gas of deuterium and hydrogen was injected into the vacuum vessel, where it was to be heated and confined. The pop we heard was the beginning of this cycle. The magnets used to confine the gas were being pulsed. I cannot report that people were running around the control room shouting "Eureka!". On the contrary, everyone was silently glued to various pieces of electronic equipment. Furth asked a few technical questions, then he asked when they were going to shut down the machine for the day. We learned that shutdown was only an hour or so away, so we decided to wander around the laboratory until we could come back and actually go inside the machine area.

The PDX is a highly evolved example of a type of fusion reactor known generically as a tokamak, a Russian acronym for toroidal magnetic chamber. Up until 1958 both our fusion program and that in the Soviet Union were classified. Even workers in these programs had no concrete idea of what their counterparts were doing. In 1958 during the Eisenhower administration, the second of two conferences on Atoms for Peace was held in Geneva; and both the U. S. and the Russians agreed to declassify the entire controlled fusion program. Among the documents that became available was a prescient and extraordinarily far-reaching paper written jointly in 1950 by Andrei D. Sakharov and Igor E. Tamm, both future Nobel Prize winners. (Sakharov is now under house arrest in Gorki because of his activities in the cause of peace and human rights for which he was awarded the Nobel Prize in 1975. If there is a more absurd abuse of a great human being, it is hard to imagine what it would be.) One of the subjects of the 1950 paper was the basic concept of what is now known as the tokamak.

The essential point in a tokamak is the design of magnetic fields in order to confine a heated plasma in a torus. A primary source of the magnetic fields are the coils that are wrapped around the torus. This produces what is known as a "toroidal field." It guides the particles in circles the long way around the torus. But these toroidal magnets alone would not confine the particles in the torus. Inevitably the particles begin to drift across the field lines toward the outer edge of the doughnut, may hit the outer vessel wall, and cool off. There is no fusion. There must be a second magnetic field designed to keep the particles from doing this, and one way of achieving this is to wrap current-carrying windings in a helix outside the torus. This was the invention in 1951 of the Princeton astrophysicist Lyman Spitzer (who, being an enthusiastic mountain climber and skier thought of it while riding up a ski-lift in Aspen). In 1952 the Model A Stellerator was built in Princeton following Spitzer's design. An alternative approach is indicated in a part of the 1950 paper written by

Sakharov alone; he proposed a second method—the toka-mak. In this method, one takes advantage of the fact that a heated plasma is an excellent conductor of electricity. A reactor plasma's conductivity is about thirty times that of copper. Thus the same electric field that heats up the electrons causes them to flow around the torus like the charges in a wire. This current produces a magnetic field that is perpendicular to the toroidal field. The combination of the two fields is enough to persuade the plasma particle to follow the helical orbits inside the doughnut and thus, in principle, to solve the problem. In 1962 the late Lev A. Artsimovich of the Kurchatov Institute in Moscow headed a team that completed the T-3 Tokamak. In 1968 this machine heated electrons to over ten million degrees, and the nuclei to about half that. These temperatures were maintained for a few hundredths of a second. For the first time the dream of controlled fusion seemed realizable, and a kind of shock wave went through the international fusion community. (Furth said it was known as tokamania.) From that time on, every major industrial-scientific country in the world has been in the business of making tokamaks.

Experimental tokamaks come in various sizes. The TFTR will have a major radius of about eight feet and a minor radius of three feet—a very fat doughnut. A working fusion tokamak power reactor, when eventually built, will have dimensions that are at least twice this—a large but not gargantuan machine. High energy particle accelerators can have dimensions of several miles. There is one at CERN, for example, in which particles are accelerated in a ring that runs through two countries, Switzerland and France. The Stanford Linear accelerator is two miles long, and the next generation of the accelerator at CERN will have a circumference of about eighteen miles!

On purely theoretical grounds, it can be shown that the minimum size of a tokamak, which would produce more power than it consumes, can have a major radius greater than about sixteen feet and a minor radius greater than about four feet. There are small experimental tokamaks which have radii substantially less than this.

As one might imagine from the name, the shape of Furth's reactor is a torus. (The PDX itself has a somewhat modified torodial shape, so that in cross section its vacuum vessel looks more like a race track than a circle.) A proper torus—a doughnut—has two significant dimensions that characterize its size: the major and minor radii. The major radius measures the distance from the axis of symmetry to the middle of the doughnut. The minor radius is simply the radius of the doughnut, a measure of its thickness. The PDX has a vacuum vessel about five feet thick and about twenty feet around. I give these numbers to show that our walk around the reactor was not exactly an all-day hike.

The first thing that struck me about being able to go inside the machine area just after it shut off was that we were able to do it at all. Here was a machine that a few minutes earlier had been heating matter to temperatures much hotter than the sun and that had been emitting radiation but nonetheless was now cool enough so that we could wander around it a few minutes later. For reasons I will explain later, a real fusion power reactor will have significant problems of radioactivity associated with it. But, nevertheless, there is an important difference, a fundamental difference, in the environmental problems it poses, as compared to a fission reactor. A working fusion reactor—not to be confused with the much smaller PDX—will have an inventory of radioactive material at least a hundred times less active than, for example, a fission breeder reactor. Furthermore, one can choose the type of radioactive material it produces, so that it decays to biologically safe levels in *hundreds* of years, as opposed to tens of thousands.

An additional reason for a low level of hazard is that a fusing plasma contains very little material. Its density is about a million times less than the density of the earth's atmosphere. To make things more quantitative, in a gas under standard conditions there are about 10^{21} molecules in each cubic inch. (10^{21} means 1 followed by twenty-one zeros; a million, for example, is 10^6.) On the other hand, in the plasma in the PDX, when it was operating, there were less than 10^{15} particles per cubic inch, a million times less than in a normal gas. Therefore there is very little matter in such a plasma. Although the temperature in the working machine is much hotter than the interior of the sun, the material is so diffuse its heat content is about comparable to that in the steam from a tea kettle. But, as Furth pointed out, this does not mean that one would want to put one's hand into the machine while it is operating. The whole plasma will cool off on any intruding object, and its total heat content is enough to boil a quarter-pound ice cube.

As we entered the machine area, the first things I noticed were the regularly spaced magnet coils that wrap around the torus. One may imagine a doughnut which has been threaded through a series of circular rings. My immediate thought was about my watch. I remembered the days in the early 1950s when Furth and I were working at the Harvard cyclotron. In this ancient machine, the particles were guided by magnetic fields produced by an iron magnet which had a great deal of residual magnetism, even when the machine was turned off. In fact, there was so much magnetism that, it would not only magnetise one's watch, but it would actually grab iron tools out of one's hand and fling them up against the magnet. Furth assured me that the copper-wound electromagnets used at the PDX had negligible residual magnetism, so that one's watch was safe.

These are not the kind of magnets that will be used in a working commercial fusion power reactor. The reason is that these magnets consume too much power. The TFTR magnets, when pulsed, will use several times more power than the whole community of Princeton. Future fusion reactors will use superconducting magnets. A superconductor is a material, like niobium-tin, that loses all of its resistance to the conduction of electricity when it is cooled to a few degrees above absolute zero—the lowest possible temperature, which is −273.15 degrees centigrade. The use of these magnets will add to the cost and technical complexity of the machine, but they seem to be an absolute necessity. They will be used in the next-generation particle accelerator as well. At the present time, under the auspices of the "large coil program" at the Oak Ridge National Laboratory in Tennessee, six large superconducting magnets are being built—three here and three abroad—for the fusion program. When such coils are operated in a reactor, they must be kept shielded from radiation, which would heat up the superconductor and cause it to lose its superconducting properties.

The next things I noticed on our tour were some fuming containers holding liquid helium, which is used to trap and pump away excess gas from inside the torus when the machine is running. Then Furth, who likes to live dangerously (he used to be a rock climber), led us through a laser beam with no apparent ill effects. The laser is one of the diagnostic tools used to measure the characteristics of the heated plasma. Clearly, one cannot stick a conventional thermometer into the plasma to measure its temperature. The thermometer would be vaporized instantly. Instead, both laser light and microwaves are scattered off the charged particles in the plasma. In this way the temperature and density of the plasma can be measured continuously during the working cycle throughout the machine. The peak temperatures occur in the center of the plasma which is, relatively speaking, very cool at its outer edges.

This raises the fundamental question of how the plasma in a tokamak is heated up in the first place. To begin with, a cold gas of, for instance, ordinary hydrogen and heavy hydrogen is injected into the machine. This gas is acted upon by a short, strong electric field pulse, which knocks some of the electrons off the neutral gas atoms. This is what happens when a bolt of lightning goes through the atmosphere. Now one has a "cold plasma," only a few hundred thousand degrees or so. The electrons in it, which are relatively light particles, can now be accelerated by acting on them with a weaker electric field pulse, lasting a fraction of a second. The now "heated" electrons bump into the heavy ions in the plasma and can heat them up to about 10 million degrees. This kind of heating is called "ohmic" or resistive heating, and it is what warms up an ordinary toaster. Some of the smaller experimental tokamaks, such as the Alcator machines, which have been built under the direction of Bruno Coppi at M.I.T., have achieved very dense and well-confined plasmas with purely ohmic heating, but it remains to be seen if such small machines can really reach the fusion reactor regime.

The large tokamaks, such as the PDX, make use of a second heating method to complement the ohmic heating. Hydrogen atoms are stripped of their electrons, then are accelerated to a high velocity. These high velocity hydrogen nuclei, protons, then enter an area where they pick up electrons again. The neutralized atoms are shot into the plasma, and collide with the particles in it and heat them up. This combination of techniques is what has heated the plasma in the PDX to its supersolar temperature.

As we were wandering around the PDX, I noticed a high shielding wall to protect the experimenters from the radiation produced by the operating machine. One of the most important forms of radiation is that produced by the fusion products themselves. In fact, it is just the energy of this radiation that is the object of the entire exercise—the desired fusion power. The working "fuel" used in the PDX and the other large experimental tokamaks is the heavy hydrogen nucleus, the deuteron. The nucleus of ordinary hydrogen is the proton, a positively charged particle that has about two thousand times as much mass as an electron. In a neutral atomic hydrogen atom, an electron and a proton are bound together with the electron being a great distance away. In fact if the proton had the diameter of a foot, the electron would be on average about two miles away in a hydrogen atom. The next most complex nucleus is obtained by attaching a neutral particle of comparable mass—the neutron—to the proton. This marriage of neutron and proton is the deuteron, the nucleus of *heavy* hydrogen. Heavy hydrogen can combine with oxygen to make heavy water. In fact, each gallon of water we drink contains about one six thousandth of a gallon of heavy water. Considering how much water there is in the oceans the supply of deuterium is essentially inexhaustible.

Of course it takes energy to separate water and heavy water, and this must go into the energy balance when one decides whether fusion is a practical power source. Two deuterons in a reactor can fuse in two distinct ways with about a fifty-fifty chance. On the one hand they can fuse to make a still heavier isotope of hydrogen, the triton, because it consists of three particles: two neutrons and a proton. An extra, free proton is also emitted in this reaction. On the other hand, the final fusion products can be a light isotope of helium, consisting of two protons and a neutron, plus an extra, free neutron. In both cases, the total mass of the final particles produced in the fusion is less than the mass of the two deuterons that entered the fusion reaction. The mass-loss shows up as energy—the energy of motion of the final particles, according to Einstein's equation $E = mc^2$, where m here stands for the loss of mass. How much energy is gained in this enterprise? To put things in practical units, if we could fuse all of the deuterons in one gram of deuterium—less than a thousandth of a pound—the energy produced would be the equivalent of that produced by two tons of oil; or, to put it another way, one gallon of ordinary water containing the natural component of deuterium has an equivalent energy value of nearly four hundred gallons of gasoline. In fact, the energy cost of extracting deuterium from water is essentially negligible compared to the gain in energy if the deuterium is fused.

This raises the question of why the oceans do not simply burn themselves up spontaneously by the fusing of deuterium. The answer to this question will give us a deep insight into the technical challenges presented by controlled fusion. A well-known fact about electric charges is that two like charges—for example, two positive charges—will repel each other. But, atomic nuclei are positively charged so two nuclei tend to repel each other electrically. According to classical physics—the physics of Newton and his nineteenth-century successors—nuclei could never get together to fuse. They would simply fly apart if they approached each other. But the atomic world is not governed by classical physics. The physics of this domain is quantum mechanics. This theory assigns nonvanishing probabilities to nuclear reactions that are forbidden by classical physics.

For cold, slowly moving nuclei, these probabilities are negligibly small, so that for all practical purposes the deuterons in the ocean do not fuse. They can essentially never get beyond the electrical barrier so that the strong, short-ranged, nuclear forces can take over to cause nuclear fusion. To get them to fuse with any decent probability they must be heated up to incredible temperatures as in a tokamak. A very important temperature is what is known as the "ignition temperature." This is the temperature at which the fusions supply enough energy to maintain the temperature in the plasma without supplying any heating from the outside. The plasma "ignites"—as a log does—and burns of its own accord once it has been sufficiently heated. The ignited log produces much more energy than was required to heat it up to ignition, and so will an ignited fusing plasma.

But the ignition temperature depends not only on the materials in the reactor but also on how long they can be confined. The worse the confinement, the hotter the plasma must be before it will ignite, since the rate of the fusion reactions increases with temperature. If perfect confinement could be achieved, a plasma of deuterium and tritium would ignite at about 60 million degrees centigrade while a plasma of pure deuterium would have an "ideal" ignition temperature eight times higher. As it is, the confinement in the present generation of machines is not perfect. Workers in the field have devised a numerical criterion for the confinement that is called the "Lawson number" after the British physicist R. D. Lawson. Without going into details as to how this number is defined, it is worthwhile to point out that the PDX achieves a Lawson number that is about a hundred times too small for ignition at the temperature at which it operates. There are machines, such as the M.I.T. Alcator, which have achieved Lawson numbers close to what is needed but with temperatures that are much too low. It is expected that the next generation of machines will achieve both temperatures and confinement that will bring them close to the conditions needed for the break-even point or possibly for ignition. The PDX that Saturday in May was operating at a temperature of only 70 million degrees—well below ignition. It reached this maximum temperature for less than a tenth of a second. Nonetheless in each cycle something like 10^{13} fusions—ten thousand billion—were taking place. In about half of these fusions, an energetic free neutron was produced. These neutrons, neutral particles, can readily penetrate matter so they must be shielded against—thus the shielding wall.

In view of all the ingenuity that has gone into this enterprise, one may wonder how the sun and the stars have gone about the business of fusion for billions of years, without the benefit of physicists. The center of the sun is essentially a plasma of protons and electrons at a temperature of about fourteen million degrees. These protons become transformed into helium by a series of reactions that physicists have understood only since the late 1930s, because of the pioneering work of the German physicist C. F. von Weizsacker, and then that of H. A. Bethe and C. L. Critchfield. Bethe went on to describe the mechanism, the carbon cycle, which is responsible for the energy production in those stars hotter and more massive than the sun—a work for which he received the Nobel Prize in 1967. The reaction that triggers the production of solar energy is the combination of two protons into a deuteron along with a free, positively charged electron and a bizarre particle called the neutrino that readily escapes from the sun. These neutrinos are so elusive that they can penetrate several light years of lead without a single interaction. Unlike the nuclear forces that cause the fusions in a tokamak, this trigger reaction is what physicists refer to as a weak interaction. It proceeds so slowly that although such weak interactions have been extensively studied in the laboratory, they are essentially useless as the source of a practical fusion power machine. This weak interaction process is successful in the sun because the number of protons available for fusion is immense—about 10^{57}—so that even unlikely reactions become sufficiently frequent to be practical. In the sun the plasma confinement is achieved gravitationally: The huge mass holds itself together long enough for the weak interactions to occur.

There is another instance where the fusion process successfully produces a vast amount of energy—the hydrogen bomb. Here the basic process is the fusion of a deuteron and a triton—the nucleus of super heavy hydrogen—to produce helium and the energetic neutron. For this reaction, the ignition temperature is about 60 million degrees—about one eighth of the pure deuterium ignition temperature. In a hydrogen bomb these temperatures are achieved by first exploding an ordinary nuclear fission bomb. In fact, the reaction rates in a deuterium-tritium plasma are about a hundred times faster than those in a pure deuterium plasma, which raises the question why this plasma is not used in the PDX or, more generally, in terrestrial fusion reactors. This, however, *is* what will be used in the next generation of reactors, although the drawback is that the triton is not a stable nucleus. It decays into an isotope of helium in about twelve years. This means that there is no natural tritium, for instance, in ordinary water. The tritium must be manufactured.

It is not the case, however, that any pair of nuclei can be fused into almost anything. There is a catch—the "curve of binding energy." Nuclei can be fused only if the resulting products are less massive than the nuclei that enter the reaction. Thus, for example, helium nuclei can be fused into carbon. Carbon can fuse into silicon and so on. But the whole process stops at iron. No element heavier than iron can be formed in fusion reactions. This poses the question of where these heavy elements—lead, uranium and so on, come from. The answer is rather surprising. When stars like the sun produce energy they ultimately contract, and there are three possible results. They can fuse all of their material and then quietly fade into oblivion—this is what will happen to our sun in several billion years. Stars substantially more massive than the sun may contract indefinitely and eventually become black holes. And in intermediate cases, stars eventually explode in a stupendous explosion that is known as a supernova. In the course of this explosion energetic neutrons can be absorbed by iron. This is the iron that was produced in the stars by the fusion of lighter elements. It is this neutron absorption manufacturing process that makes the heavy elements. It is not what we call fusion, since fusion releases energy while this process uses up energy. It would appear as if every atom in the universe belonging to an element heavier than iron is born in some supernova explosion. In a very real sense we are all children of the stars.

After having looked at fusion research, we may turn finally to several practical questions. How close are we to having a real fusion power reactor? What will it look like? What will it cost? And do we need it? A comment on the first question is that while the tokamak is, at present, the most advanced fusion game in town, it is not the only game in town. As Furth has remarked, "There are lots of possibilities for magnetic bottles (devices that confine plasmas with magnetic fields). The day of the inventor is not over, by any means." Among the possibilities are the so-called mirror machines. Here the plasma is guided along straight lines rather than around a closed orbit. At the ends of the machine, magnetic fields block the motion of the particles and bounce them backwards. In principle, the particles would oscillate back and forth indefinitely between the magnetic "mirrors." In practice, particles tend to leak out the ends and thus spoil the confinement. One way to deal with this is to put the mirrors in tandem. One interesting idea is to link a few dozen mirror machines in a ring so that they form a broken torus. This concept is known as an "Elmo Bumpy Torus." There is a bumpy torus machine operating now at Oak Ridge in the United States, and work is being done on them in Japan. So far they do not compare in either temperature or confinement with the large conventional tokamaks, but they may play an important role in the future. Apart from these magnetic bottle machines, there has been a substantial effort to make fusion machines by heating and confining cold pellets of material, blasting them with an intense laser beam—what is known as inertial confinement. This effort is also, at present, well behind the tokamaks. In the fall of 1980 the Congress passed the "Magnetic Fusion Energy Engineering Act of 1980," which stated that "The United States must aggressively pursue research and development programs in magnetic fusion designed to foster advanced concepts and advanced technology and to develop efficient, reliable components and subsystems." Following the passage of this bill, President Carter proposed to raise the 394 million-dollar budget for 1981 to a budget of 505 million dollars for magnetic fusion research in 1982. President Reagan has cut this to 460 million dollars—still a sizeable increase over 1981, and a sign of strong support in the present climate of austerity. The next generation of large tokamaks—the Tokamak Fusion Test Reactor at Princeton and the Joint European Torus at Cullam, En-

241

gland, scheduled to become operative in 1983, a year after the Princeton machine—are reactors that have been designed to produce sizeable amounts of fusion power in short periods but no electricity. To have some notion of the power scale, we may recall that a typical modern nuclear fission power plant produces something like a billion watts of power. This new generation of large experimental fusion machines is expected to produce power at a four hundredth of this level. The next step, according to the present Department of Energy plan, would be to set up a Center for Fusion Engineering, an organization that will be managed mainly by construction and manufacturing industry, rather than by the universities or the national laboratories. The first year in which this entity could be approved is 1984. Its task would be to construct the Fusion Engineering Device—a focus for the study of the engineering connected with a burning plasma. The FED is expected to employ the tokamak concept. Preliminary design studies for this have already been carried out, and it is hoped the FED will become operational in the early 1990s. At this time alternate nonmagnetic confinement schemes will get a chance to compete for a fusion demonstration plant. This should be the final prototype of a real fusion power plant, which will make electricity in an economically promising way. If all goes well, it will begin to operate not long after the year 2000. The total cost of all of this has been estimated to be around twenty billion dollars.

What would the final plant be like, and how safe and how environmentally benign would it be? At the heart of it there would be the fusion reactor. If it is a tokamak, it might have a major radius of about twenty feet, and a thickness of about twelve feet—a large, fat doughnut. Stainless steel or an alloy of titanium, zirconium, and molybdenum might be used to make it. The doughnut skin would constitute the first wall of the shielding blanket which, in its entirety, might be about three feet thick. Since a deuterium-tritium plasma would be used in these first-generation machines, this blanket would be subject to an intense flux of energetic neutrons—a flux comparable to that in a fission reactor.

But the safety problems of the two reactors are totally different. In a fusion reactor there is no possibility of a runaway accident. If the plasma confinement fails, the machine simply shuts itself off, since the fusions stop. Even if *all* of the fuel in the fusion machine were to react at once, there is so little of it that the temperature rise at the blanket would be only about a hundred degrees centigrade. This is a completely negligible rise compared to what happens when an accident in a fission reactor allows the fission products to heat up their containment structures. Neutron shielding, however, is not a difficult engineering problem since many common substances, such as boron, absorb neutrons like a sponge. Tritium, while radioactive, has a very low activity, and only relatively small amounts would be used—perhaps twenty pounds per billion watts of electricity produced. (In some of the weapons programs, tritium has been released in accidents. It goes into the atmosphere and disappears without a trace.) The blanket would become radioactive and also radiation damaged. It is estimated that in a billion-watt fusion reactor something like 150 cubic yards of radioactive material would have to be dealt with—disposed or recycled—each year, a moderately substantial but not a gargantuan amount. The advantage here would be that the shielding material could be chosen so that the radioactive material would be as short-lived as possible—years or decades.

In a fission reactor, though, there is no choice. Nature has chosen the fission products and some of these must be safely buried for many centuries.

A shielding blanket in such a reactor contains lithium. The reason for this is when a neutron hits a lithium nucleus, it can break it up into helium and tritium. Hence tritium fuel can be manufactured in the blanket as the reactor works. The machine produces its own fuel as it goes along. The blanket must be kept "cool"—perhaps at a temperature of four to five hundred degrees centigrade. To manage this, a coolant circulates in the blanket. It removes heat from the blanket, and this heat can be used to make steam which in turn can run an electric generator in the conventional way.

Thus the tokamak functions as a large and very expensive steam generator. How expensive? Essentially all of the expense will be in the capital construction of the machine. Less than 10 percent is expected to go into fuel and operations. To compete with conventional methods of electric generation—if, indeed, these are even available in the next century or later—it has been estimated that construction costs must be no greater than 3000 dollars per kilowatt of electricity generated. Thus a billion-watt fusion plant to be competitive should not cost more than three billion dollars. Whether this fusion cost can be realized is somewhat like having asked the Wright brothers what the cost of a Boeing 747 would have been in 1981. Cost estimates have been made, but it seems fair to say that these vary according to the eye of the beholder.

Finally, I would like to deal with the question of whether we *should* spend the vast sums of money needed to turn fusion power from a laboratory study into a practical power source. It is worthwhile to point out that all of the industrial countries have decided, in varying degrees, that fusion power is enough of a realistic and attractive prospect to spend substantial resources on. An interesting instance is that of the Chinese. Work on controlled fusion in China goes back as far as 1955, when Chairman Mao identified it as a potentially profitable area of research. With the endorsement of Chou En-lai work began in China on magnetic mirror machines and, eventually, on tokamaks. The tokamak, like most good scientific ideas, has succeeded in crossing ideological and political barriers. When the Gang of Four took control of China, scientists were sent to the countryside to do physical labor, and essentially all scientific activity came to a halt. With the new regime, science has been reborn in China. Large numbers of Chinese graduate students are now coming to this country to study in our universities—many to study fusion. Many of them are in their late thirties and early forties, having had their education disrupted, and are among the best graduate students my colleagues have ever seen. The fusion program in China, though, is well behind other programs—ours, the Japanese, which is in the process of becoming one of the strongest in the world, the joint Western European, and the Soviet Union's.

Of course the fact that all of these countries are working on fusion does not mean that it is the right thing to do. Indeed, some critics of the fusion program would, and have, claimed that this is yet another example of a collective technological delusion. On the basis of what I have been able to learn about the general energy question, I believe—as someone who has no personal stake in this field nor, indeed, in any area of energy research—that these critics are wrong. If there were a totally environmentally safe, cheap way of making the electricity we need now and in the near future, and if the discovery of such a method meant the abandonment of power reactors—fission and fusion—I would be the first person to endorse it. However, I do not see such a method. To explain why I have come to this conclusion, let me describe in somewhat more detail how I have reached it. About 30 percent of our total energy consumption goes into making electricity. At the present time this percentage appears to be slightly declining. This probably reflects both conservation—increased efficiency—and industrial stagnation. But almost every scenario that I have read for the year 2000 predicts that we will use substantially more electricity than we use now. Some recent figures on how electricity is presently generated—what energy sources are used—show the following:

Coal	45%
Nuclear	13
Hydroelectric	13
Natural gas	13
Oil	16

More than half the coal we mine—the total is about 600 million tons a year—goes to make electricity. The above percentage is increasing throughout the world and will certainly continue to do so in the near future. Coal is a finite resource. There is plenty of it now, but it will not last forever. It may well be that late in the next century coal will be regarded in somewhat the same way that we regard our diminishing supply of oil and natural gas. But apart from this, coal presents problems of pollution that appear to be essentially ineluctable. The sulfur content of coal can very likely be dealt with by the use of expensive "scrubber" technology. The nitrogen, which when combined with water, produces the main content of the acidic rain that threatens our water environments, seems all but immune to present technology. And no technology can cope with the increase in carbon dioxide in the atmosphere that accompanies the burning of any fossil fuel—this is simply part of the burning reaction. Coal is one of the worst sources of this pollution. (Synthetic fuels extracted from coal are even worse.) This carbon dioxide traps the heat which the earth reradiates each day and thus heats the atmosphere—causing what is known as the "greenhouse effect." The amount of carbon dioxide in the atmosphere has been steadily increasing. If it were doubled, which could well happen if we end up by burning all our coal, it is believed that the average global temperature would increase by three degrees centigrade. This would change climates in a serious and unpredictable way. It would probably be enough to melt the west Antarctic ice cap, which, if it melted completely, would raise the ocean levels by fifty feet. All of this has inspired one of the few energy jokes I have heard. The *good* news is that we have a lot of coal—the *bad* news is that we may have to use it.

Despite the present surfeit of oil, no serious observer believes that this is anything but a rapidly diminishing resource. To use it up to make electricity is, as far as I am concerned, like making coat hangers out of platinum. Natural gas is more abundant, but unless the conjectures are correct that deep in the earth there are vast amounts left over from the formation of the planet, this too will run out some time in the next century. Hence in this country our descendants will have to find a replacement for 30 percent of the fuel we now use to make electricity. This is *our* problem. But where will developing countries find the resources they need to make the electricity that will be needed to bring them into the modern world? Few of them have coal or oil resources. There will be some additional use of biomass as a fuel source. This, however, turns out to have about half the energy content of an equivalent amount of coal—which means that twice as much would have to be burned to achieve the same energy total. Furthermore if we grow it for burning, this means we have less available space for growing food which is already in short supply. Hydroelectric power might be expanded somewhat by damming every stream in sight. But is this something that environmentally sensitive people really want to do? Wind power might sound nice—until one looks at the numbers. Assuming an average wind speed of 20 miles an hour—a hefty wind—it would take fifty thousand very large windmills to equal the output of one billion-watt power station—one prospective fusion plant. Hence it would take millions of windmills to make a real dent in our energy requirements. Can this really make any sense as a method for solving our energy problems?

The dangers and difficulties with fission reactors are too well known to merit extensive discussion here. I believe that despite these difficulties, they represent a safer and more environmentally attractive option than using vast amounts of additional coal. But uranium is also a finite resource, and it can be stretched in the future only by using breeder reactors to make new fuel. But these reactors can also be used for making ammunition for atomic bombs; this, coupled with the other safety problems, may be enough to limit their future use—at least in this country. There are no plans here at present to build nuclear power reactors beyond those that the utilities have already ordered. Incidentally, one of the reasons that the nuclear power program may be in such difficulties is that for economic reasons the design of these plants was essentially frozen before enough chance was given for novel ideas to be fully heard. This is a mistake that the fusion program should not repeat.

This leaves us essentially with fusion and the sun. Everyone agrees that solar energy will play a more substantial role by the end of this century. The disagreements are quantitative—how much of a role and in what areas. There is no argument that wherever possible solar heating and architecture designed to use the sun as effectively as possible should be used. This is an environmentally sound and economically attractive alternative that can do us—whenever applicable—nothing but good. Solar electricity is another matter. This is a domain that appears to have become so emotionally charged that rational discussion has become more and more difficult. I can report only what I have come to believe. In the first place the notion that this is a low technology—a cottage industry—enterprise strikes me as sheer nonsense. There are two basic problems still to be resolved:

1. The improvement of the economics and the efficiency of the solar collectors—the solar cells
2. The development of an economical method of storage of electricity when the sun is not shining

There has been substantial progress in the first problem area. The price per watt of installed solar cells came down from $42.00 per peak watt—the watt at high noon on a clear day—in 1975 to $7.00 in 1980. To be competitive with other methods of making electricity, this price would have to come down by at least another factor of ten—something that will require all of the research ingenuity available. It must also be understood that these collectors take space. With the presently available cells, it takes about sixteen square feet of collector, at the latitude of New York, to illuminate one 50-watt bulb averaging over night and day and allowing for clouds. (The same array at high noon on a bright day would illuminate a 170-watt light bulb.) The problem of finding a suitable storage device is, as far as I know, essentially unsolved. I believe the idea of a conspiracy by the oil companies and others to deprive us of solar energy is ridiculous. Anyone who could solve the problem of producing cheap solar electricity would become enormously wealthy—a goal to which large industrial companies are hardly indifferent. Most responsible people believe that in the year 2000 solar electricity might account for just a small percentage of the total.

As Furth has pointed out, there is a parallel between progress from "traditional" solar power toward fusion, and the development of agriculture. At first, mankind was satisfied to collect roots and berries, then he gradually learned to grow them at will. If fusion power can be made practical, we can collect power of the type the sun supplies by growing it at will. We can make limitless amounts of electricity from the water in the oceans.

12

Can TV Really
Teach Science?

AS A WORKING SCIENTIST and science writer, I should be overjoyed by what appears to be a boom in the popularization of science. Apart from the several books that are selling in the hundreds of thousands of copies, there are the new magazines such as *Omni, Science Digest, Science 81,* and *Discover,* as well as the television programs "Cosmos," "Connections," "The Search for Solutions," and "The Body in Question." "Cosmos" was one of the most popular series ever to run on public televison.

I *should* be overjoyed, but I am not. Not quite.

It is now a cliché that scientists are human beings. We scientists have come a long way from the celebrated Thurber drawing in his book *The Thurber Carnival* that shows the capture of three physicists by a Thurber woman. I have no idea where Thurber got the idea that physicists look like *that*—one resembles the Smith brothers on the cough drop box—when, as we all now know, they really look like Carl Sagan.

As human beings, we like to communicate about our work. Give us only a half-attentive audience, and we cannot be stopped. If, then, the seemingly widespread interest in science is real, nearly everybody should be as eager to listen to us as we are to discuss whether neutrinos are massive or whether a "top" quark exists.

There is an important corollary to this potentially happy state of affairs. Science is now incredibly expensive, and you, the taxpayer, are paying for most of it. In my own field of elementary particle physics, annual funding in this country is about $375 million, most of it dispensed by the Department of Energy and some by the National Science Foundation. Much of the money goes to maintain and construct high-energy accelerators and to experiment with them. Some supports students and young postdoctorals and the like.

I have always believed that the only enduring and enlightened reason for public support of this kind of highly abstract fundamental science must be that people, in the long run, see the work for what it really is—the best effort that humans have so far been able to muster to inquire about what we and the rest of the universe are made of.

The public supports this research, but its interest is quixotic; it expects staggering discoveries that will open new worlds. In actuality, research may be slow-moving and findings difficult to understand. Eventually some of this research may have important practical spin-offs, but to boost public support for this reason is to risk causing disillusionment. I cannot imagine anyone's claiming a practical use for the quark, yet, in my view, it is worth every nickel we have spent on its research because it seems to be the basic building block of the universe.

To earn public support in the short term, we scientists must convince the public that humanity is getting a rich reward in discoveries, however indirect it may be. And if all the attention popular science is now getting means that these discoveries are being communicated effectively, then I am all for it.

But is that what it means? And, above all, is television, the most pervasive public medium, communicating science in a meaningful and enduring way?

I would like to ask a random sampling of the millions of viewers of "Cosmos" what they remember of it apart from a lasting image of Carl Sagan's profile. Sagan was never very concerned about what people would remember. In a press release issued before the series was aired last fall, he wrote, "I would be very pleased if viewers left the entire "Cosmos" series without remembering a single fact—provided they found rekindled some of that ancient human joy in understanding the natural world...." If I took such a poll, I might discover that Sagan was wrong, that people can recall a great deal. But a clue to what I would probably find came in a segment of a recent television news program. The anchorman said that he gathered from watching "Cosmos" that we were evolving from a carbon-based into a silicon-based species. Since computers, he continued, are made of silicon, we must be evolving into computers. What a splendid idea, an improvement on a notion held by a friend of mine that since everything we do requires less and less physical effort we are evolving into Bartlett pear-shaped beings, with one tiny stem for a brain and two tiny stems to push buttons. If the millions spent on "Cosmos" have left the impression that we are evolving into IBM machines, then what has been accomplished?

In fact, a close look at many of the new popular-science books and magazines leaves me with a similar feeling of disquiet. In trying to make science "interesting," these publications seem determined to transform it into a kind of entertainment. Quantum mechanics sells if it can be communicated as a psychedelic mishmash of physics and Eastern mysticism. Recombinant DNA sells either if it cures cancer or if it can scare the wits out of us with clones or monster bacteria. Cosmology sells if it becomes a religious experience. In short, science sells if it is no longer presented as science. In fairness to Sagan and leaving aside the inevitable inaccuracies that troubled the scientists and the historians who watched "Cosmos," the obvious intent was to convey the heart and soul of the scientific enterprise. But, somehow, this got lost along the way. Even Adrian Malone, executive producer of "Cosmos," has been quoted as saying, "It [the series] has moments. It's very professional. It's very glossy. But it's not right." What went wrong, and what are the lessons to be drawn from it?

Let me give a concrete example. In the second episode, Sagan wanted to explain artificial selection, the process by which species can be altered if, for some reason, we choose to select varieties that have some trait we are interested in. This is an important point because many people, even in this day and age, do not believe in evolution. Artificial selection demonstrates that evolution is a working fact and not a theory. To explain this, Sagan recounted the destruction of the Heike samurai fleet, in 1185, and the intentional drowning of the seven-year-old emperor by his guardian. According to the legend, the Heike samurai still wander Japan's Inland Sea in the form of crabs that have a design on their carapaces that looks like the face of a warrior. Sagan raised the fascinating question of how these crabs came to bear this design. The answer seems to be that fishermen, in honor of the slain Heike, were reluctant to keep the crabs that bore the samurai-like design. Those crabs, then, had a better chance of surviving and passed the trait on to subsequent generations.

I was unfamiliar with this phenomenon. It seemed to me a fine illustration of artificial selection. In the television program, however, an attempt was made to re-create the legend visually. The samurai warriors had a go at one another at the edge of the sea. After the Heike lost, the little emperor was rowed into deep water and gently put overboard to drown. One was not quite sure whether to laugh or cry. The only certainty was that the viewer was totally distracted from the ostensible business at hand. In the book *Cosmos,* I might add, artificial selection and the samurai legend are discussed unobtrusively, and the scientific lesson is never lost.

Misuse of the visual in "Cosmos," a misuse that I felt was characteristic of the series, led me to formulate the first of Bernstein's three laws: DO NOT TRY TO MAKE THINGS MORE VISUAL THAN THEY REALLY ARE. (I like to believe that in the best of all possible worlds my three laws would govern the presentation of science on television. Arthur Clarke once told me *his* three laws and added: "If three laws were good enough for Newton, they are good enough for me.")

My second law, which, if the truth be told, I stole from the Danish physicist Niels Bohr, has to do with the impossibility of anyone's being a genuine polymath. It is: DO NOT SPEAK MORE CLEARLY THAN YOU THINK. The last person who was said to understand all of modern physics was the late Enrico Fermi and physics is just *one* science. To be sure, some scientists are knowledgeable in a variety of disciplines; I've always felt that Freeman Dyson knows more about everything than I know about anything. But the limitations that most of us suffer from mean that we run the risk of not knowing quite what we are talking about when we try to explain things outside our own fields.

Yet, as scientists trying to popularize our enterprise, we do have some advantages. We do have a specialty in which we are genuinely expert, in which we have written papers, taught students, and the rest. Sagan, for example, is a professional planetary astronomer. A firm background in one scientific area helps us to learn other scientific disciplines with less difficulty. But this does not mean that we should communicate information about these alien fields to lay people as if it were crystal clear. I have written articles, to cite an example, about computer science, a subject in which I am far from being an expert, but in doing so I have tried to learn from the best professionals whom I could find. I have always felt that if I could share, rather than disguise, this sense of a learning experience with my readers, communication between us would be improved. If I were to give grades to the scientific television communicators on the basis of their abilities to resist the temptation of appearing as polymaths, I would give Jonathan Miller an *A,* Jacob Bronowski a *B,* Sagan a *D,* and Nigel Calder an *F.*

My third law, DON'T OVERPLAY YOUR HAND, was inspired by Calder in a remarkable paragraph in his book *The Key to the Universe,* also the title of his 1977 television program on the new discoveries in elementary particle physics. He writes:

After a year and a half, the theorists who favoured charm were far into a second period of worrying and waiting. ["Charm" is the name assigned to one type of quark. At present there are five known types, labeled "up," "down," "strange," "charmed," and "bottom." Most physicists would bet that there is at least one more type, the so-called "top" quark.] I [Calder] worried, too, in those first few months of 1976. This book and the associated television programme were intended to lay before the public the splendid fruits of recent research into the workings of the universe. But were the fruits after all rotten?

When I read this, I was absolutely appalled. Does this mean that scientists should now go about their work so that their discoveries will neatly fit into someone's television or book publication schedule? Is research going to become like "Monday Night Football," whose West Coast games are played at the dinner hour so we in New York can watch them at 9 P.M.? I had visions of someone trying to evaluate an integral in his office at Princeton while, in the corridor outside, the television cameras were all set up to announce a breakthrough. What if there is no breakthrough?

Calder was lucky. He did his documentary at a time when elementary particle physics was in one of its most productive phases. I think that a whole world view began to emerge, one that is now even richer and more certain than it was in 1977. But it is quite possible that elementary particle physics is entering a more reflective period, a period of consolidation. If this is so, we who work in this field would, in my opinion, be making a terrible mistake if we encouraged the general public to believe that something spectacular was about to happen every few months. We must not promise, for the sake of television, that we can deliver great discoveries on schedule.

In this respect, I have often mused on the fate of the space program. The first moon landings were absolutely heart-stopping. But they rapidly became pure media events, and the power of such events, as we all know, evaporates into thin air like water in the desert. The only way to sustain that level of interest is constantly to raise the ante—to land on Mars, and then Saturn. If science is not appreciated for its own sake, I do not think that the present level of public interest can be sustained, and that would be a real tragedy, a lost opportunity.

How, then, can science be televised? A possible clue might be in the most satisfactory intellectual television series I have ever watched, Lord Kenneth Clark's "Civilisation." I am well aware of the criticisms that have been made of this series. For example, the critic Robert Hughes remarked that the programs resembled "an illustrated slide show [in which] Clark was constantly popping up in front of a work of art to talk about it—standing in front of Chartres Cathedral, for instance, like a slide lecturer."

But isn't this just the point? Clark, unlike Sagan, did not feel that he had to resort to models of questionable accuracy. "Cosmos" used paintings that depicted astronomical phenomena in such a way that one did not know where the real thing left off and the art began. Clark was content to show us the genuine articles. I thought it made seeing them even more memorable. Has anyone who watched this series been able to forget it? Do we have the same feeling about "Cosmos?"

The closest I have seen to ideal televised science is a "Nova" program on molecular biology. It was narrated by Isaac Asimov, hardly a shrinking violet. Though molecular biology is close to Asimov's own area of scientific expertise, he apparently felt himself in the presence both of a scientific experience that took him outside of his own learning, and of scientists whose work and insights were much deeper than his own. The program resembled a series of wonderful classroom lectures heard in college and remembered almost word for word.

Suppose we try to re-create on television, for example, the series of lectures (later published as *The Character of Physical Law*) that Richard Feynman, one of the most hypnotic lecturers in science, gave at Cornell University in 1964. Suppose this were done on film in a small classroom setting, with people being able to raise their hands and say, "I don't understand." After all, this is still the most effective way we know of teaching. Would people watch this on television? I am not sure, but it might be worth trying, and it could probably be done for what it cost to make fifteen minutes of a single episode of "Cosmos."

PART III

Out of My Mind:
Entertainments, Serious
and Otherwise

13

How About a Little Game?

Stanley Kubrick

ON PLEASANT AFTERNOONS, I often go into Washington Square Park to watch the Master at work. The Master is a professional chess player—a chess hustler, if you will. He plays for fifty cents a game; if you win, you get the fifty, and if he wins, he gets it. In case of a draw, no money changes hands. The Master plays for at least eight hours a day, usually seven days a week; in the winter he plays indoors in one or another of the Village coffee-houses. It is a hard way to make a living, even if you win all your games; the Master wins most of his, although I have seen him get beaten several games straight. It is impossible to cheat in chess, and the only hustle that the Master perpetrates is to make his opponents think they are better than they are. When I saw him one day recently, he was at work on what in the language of the park is called a "potzer"—a relatively weak player with an inflated ego. A glance at the board showed that the Master was a rook and a pawn up on his adversary—a situation that would cause a rational man to resign the game at once. A potzer is not rational (otherwise, he would have avoided the contest in the first place), and this one was determined to fight it out to the end. He was moving pawns wildly, and his hands were beginning to tremble. Since there is no one to blame but yourself, nothing is more rankling than a defeat in chess, especially if you are under the illusion that you are better than your opponent. The Master, smiling as seraphically as his hawklike angular features would allow, said, "You always were a good pawn player—especially when it comes to pushing them," which his deluded opponent took to be a compliment. At a rook and four pawns down, the potzer gave up, and a new game began.

My acquaintance with the Master goes back several years, but it was only some time later that I learned of a connection between him and another man I know—the brilliant and original filmmaker Stanley Kubrick, who has been responsible for such movies as *Paths of Glory, Lolita, Dr. Strangelove, 2001: A Space Odyssey, Barry Lyndon,* and *The Shining.* The Master is not much of a moviegoer—his professional activities leave little time for it—and, as far as I know, he has never seen one of Kubrick's pictures. But his recollection of Kubrick is nonetheless quite distinct, reaching back to the early 1950s, when Kubrick, then in his early twenties (he was born in New York City on July 26, 1928), was also squeezing out a small living (he estimates about three dollars a day, "which goes a long way if all you are buying with it is food") by playing chess for cash in Washington Square. Kubrick was then living on Sixteenth Street, off Sixth Avenue, and on nice days in the spring and summer he would wander into the park around noon and take up a position at one of the concrete chess tables near MacDougal and West Fourth streets. At nightfall, he would change tables to get one near the street light. "If you made the switch the right way," he recalls, "you could get a table in the shade during the day

and one nearer the fountain, under the lights, at night."
There was a hard core of perhaps ten regulars who came to
play every day and, like Kubrick, put in about twelve hours
at the boards, with interruptions only for food. Kubrick
ranked himself as one of the stronger regulars. When no
potzers or semi-potzers were around, the regulars played
each other for money, offering various odds to make up
for any disparities in ability. The best player, Arthur Feldman, gave Kubrick a pawn—a small advantage—and, as
Kubrick remembers it, "he didn't make his living off me."
The Master was regarded by the regulars as a semi-
potzer—the possessor of a flashy but fundamentally unsound game that was full of pseudotraps designed to en-
mesh even lesser potzers and to insure the quickest possible
win so that he could collect his bet and proceed to a new
customer.

At that time, Kubrick's nominal non-chess playing oc-
cupation (when he could work at it) was what it is
now—making films. Indeed, by the time he was twenty-
seven he had behind him a four-year career as a staff
photographer for *Look,* followed by a five-year career as a
filmmaker, during which he had made two short features
and two full-length films—*Fear and Desire* (1953) and
Killer's Kiss (1955). By all sociological odds, Kubrick
should never have got into the motion picture business in
the first place. He comes from an American Jewish family
of Austro-Hungarian ancestry. His father is a doctor, still
in active practice, and he grew up in comfortable middle-
class surroundings in the Bronx. If all had gone according
to form, Kubrick would have attended college and probably ended up as a doctor or a physicist—physics being the
only subject he showed the slightest aptitude for in school.
After four desultory years at Taft High School, in the
Bronx, he graduated, with a sixty-seven average, in 1945,

the year in which colleges were flooded with returning ser-
vicemen. No college in the United States would even consider his application. Apart from everything else, Kubrick
had failed English outright one year and had had to make
it up in the summer. In his recollection, high-school
English courses consisted of sitting behind a book while
the teacher would say, "Mr. Kubrick, when Silas Marner
walked out of the door, what did he see?" followed by a
prolonged silence caused by the fact that Kubrick hadn't
read *Silas Marner,* or much of anything else.

When Kubrick was twelve, his father taught him to play
chess, and when he was thirteen, his father, who is something of a camera bug, presented him with his first camera.
At the time, Kubrick had hopes of becoming a jazz drum-
mer and was seriously studying the technique, but he soon
decided that he wanted to be a photographer, and instead
of doing his schoolwork he set out to teach himself to become one. By the time he left high school, he had sold
Look two picture stories—one of them, ironically, about
an English teacher at Taft, Aaron Traister, who had succeeded in arousing Kubrick's interest in Shakespeare's
plays by acting out all the parts in class. After high school,
Kubrick registered for night courses at City College, hoping to obtain a *B* average so that he could transfer to
regular undergraduate courses, but before he started going
to classes, he was back at *Look* with some more pictures.
The picture editor there, Helen O'Brian, upon hearing of
his academic troubles, proposed that he come to *Look* as
an apprentice photographer. "So I backed into a fan-
tastically good job at the age of seventeen," Kubrick says.
Released from the bondage of schoolwork, he also began
to read everything that he could lay his hands on. In
retrospect, he feels that not having gone to college and
having had the four years to practice photography at *Look*

and to read on his own was probably the most fortunate thing that ever happened to him.

It was while he was still at *Look* that Kubrick became a filmmaker. An incessant moviegoer, he had seen the entire film collection of the Museum of Modern Art at least twice when he learned from a friend, Alex Singer (now also a movie director), that there was apparently a fortune to be made in producing short documentaries. Singer was working as an office boy at the March of Time and had learned—or thought he had learned—that his employers were spending forty thousand dollars to produce eight or nine minutes of film. Kubrick was extremely impressed by the number of dollars being spent per foot, and even more impressed when he learned, from phone calls to Eastman Kodak and various equipment rental companies, that the cost of buying and developing film and renting camera equipment would allow him to make nine minutes of film, complete with an original music score, for only about a thousand dollars. "We assumed," Kubrick recalls, "that the March of Time must have been selling their films at a profit, so if we could make a film for a thousand dollars, we couldn't lose our investment." Thus bolstered, he used his savings from the *Look* job to make a documentary about the middleweight boxer Walter Cartier, about whom he had previously done a picture story for *Look*. Called *Day of the Fight,* it was filmed with a rented spring-wound thirty-five-millimeter Eyemo camera and featured a musical score by Gerald Fried, a friend of Kubrick's who is now a well-known composer for the movies. Since Kubrick couldn't afford any professional help, he took care of the whole physical side of the production himself; essentially, this consisted of screwing a few ordinary photofloods into existing fixtures. When the picture was done—for thirty-nine hundred dollars—Kubrick set out to sell it for forty thousand. Various distributing companies liked it, but, as Kubrick now says ruefully, "We were offered things like fifteen hundred dollars and twenty-five hundred dollars. We told one distributor that the March of Time was getting forty thousand for *its* documentaries, and he said, 'You must be crazy.' The next thing we knew, the March of Time went out of business." Kubrick was finally able to sell his short to R.K.O. Pathé for about a hundred dollars more than it had cost him to make it.

Kubrick, of course, got great satisfaction out of seeing his documentary at the Paramount Theatre, where it played with a Robert Mitchum-Ava Gardner feature. He felt that it had turned out well, and he figured that he would now instantly get innumerable offers from the movie industry—"of which," he says, "I got none, to do anything." After a while, however, he made a second short for R.K.O. (which put up fifteen hundred dollars for it, barely covering expenses), this one about a flying priest who traveled through the Southwest from one Indian parish to another in a Piper Cub. To work on the film, Kubrick quit his job at *Look,* and when the film was finished, he went back to waiting for offers of employment, spending his time playing chess for quarters in the park. He soon reached the reasonable conclusion that there simply wasn't any money to be made in producing documentaries and that there were no film jobs to be had. After thinking about the millions of dollars that were being spent on making feature films, he decided to make one himself. "I felt that I certainly couldn't make one worse than the ones I was seeing every week," he said. On the assumption that there were actors around who would work for practically nothing, and that he could act as the whole crew, Kubrick estimated that he could make a feature film for something like ten thousand dollars, and he was able to raise this sum from his father and an uncle, Martin Perveler. The script was put together by an acquaintance of Kubrick's in the Village, and, as Kubrick now describes it, it was an exceedingly serious, undramatic, and pretentious allegory. "With the exception of Frank Silvera, the actors were not very experienced," he said, "and I didn't know anything about directing *any* actors. I totally failed to realize what I didn't know." The film *Fear and Desire* was about four soldiers lost behind enemy lines and struggling to regain their identities as well as their home base, and it was full of lines like "We spend our lives looking for our real names, our permanent addresses." Despite everything, the film got an art-house distribution," Kubrick said. "It opened at the Guild Theatre, in New York, and it even got a couple of fairly good reviews, as well as a compliment from Mark Van Doren. There were a few good moments in it. It never returned a penny on its investment."

Not at all discouraged, Kubrick decided that the mere fact that a film of his was showing at a theatre at all might be used as the basis for raising money to make a second one. In any case, it was not otherwise apparent how he was going to earn a living. "There were still no offers from anybody to do anything," he said. "So in about two weeks a friend and I wrote another script. As a contrast to the first one, this one, called *Killer's Kiss,* was nothing but action sequences, strung together on a mechanically constructed gangster plot."

Killer's Kiss was coproduced by Morris Bousel, a relative of Kubrick's who owned a drugstore in the Bronx. Released in September, 1955, it, too, failed to bring in any revenue, so, broke and in debt to Bousel and others, Kubrick returned to Washington Square to play chess for quarters.

The scene now shifts to Alex Singer. While serving in the Signal Corps during the Korean War, Singer met a man named James B. Harris, who was engaged in making Signal Corps training films. The son of the owner of an extremely successful television-film distribution company, Flamingo Films (in which he had a financial interest), Harris wanted to become a film producer when he returned to civilian life. As Harris recalls it, Singer told him about "some guy in the Village who was going around all by himself making movies," and after they got out of the army, introduced him to Kubrick, who had just finished *Killer's Kiss*. Harris and Kubrick were both twenty-six, and they got on at once, soon forming Harris-Kubrick Pictures Corporation. From the beginning, it was an extremely fruitful and very happy association. Together they made *The Killing, Paths of Glory,* and *Lolita.* They were going to do *Dr. Strangelove* jointly, but before work began on it, Harris came to the conclusion that being just a movie producer was not a job with enough artistic fulfillment for him, and he decided to both produce and direct. His first film was *The Bedford Incident,* which Kubrick considers very well directed. For his part, Harris regards Kubrick as a cinematic genius who can do anything.

The first act of the newly formed Harris-Kubrick Pictures Corporation was to purchase the screen rights to *Clean Break,* a paperback thriller by Lionel White. Kubrick and a writer friend named Jim Thompson turned it into a screenplay, and the resulting film, *The Killing,* which starred Sterling Hayden, was produced in association with United Artists, with Harris putting up about a third of the production cost. While *The Killing,* too, was something less than a financial success, it was sufficiently impressive to catch the eye of Dore Schary, then head of production for M-G-M. For the first time, Kubrick received an offer to work for a major studio, and he and Harris were invited to look over all the properties owned by M-G-M and pick out something to do. Kubrick remembers being astounded by the mountains of stories that M-G-M owned. It took the pair of them two weeks simply to go through the alphabetical synopsis cards. Finally, they selected *The Burning Street,* by Stefan Zweig, and Kubrick and Calder Willingham turned it into a screenplay—only to find that Dore Schary had lost his job as a result of a major shuffle at M-G-M. Harris and Kubrick left soon afterward. Sometime during the turmoil, Kubrick suddenly recalled having read *Paths of Glory,* by Humphrey Cobb, while still a high-school student. "It was one of the few books I'd read for pleasure in high school," he says. "I think I found it lying around my father's office and started to read it while waiting for him to get finished with a patient." Harris agreed that it was well worth a try. However, none of the major studios took the slightest interest in it. Finally, Kubrick's and Harris's agent, Ronnie Lubin, managed to interest Kirk Douglas in doing it, and this was enough to persuade United Artists to back the film, provided it was done on a very low budget in Europe. Kubrick, Calder Willingham, and Jim Thompson wrote the screenplay, and in January of 1957 Kubrick went to Munich to make the film.

Seeing *Paths of Glory* is a haunting experience. The utter desolation, cynicism, and futility of war, as embodied in the arbitrary execution of three innocent French soldiers who have been tried and convicted of cowardice during a meaningless attack on a heavily fortified German position, comes through with simplicity and power. Some of the dialogue is imperfect, Kubrick agrees, but its imperfection almost adds to the strength and sincerity of the theme. The finale of the picture involves a young German girl who has been captured by the French and is being forced to sing a song for a group of drunken French soldiers about to be sent back into battle. The girl is frightened, and the soldiers are brutal. She begins to sing, and the humanity of the moment reduces the soldiers to silence, and then to tears. In the film, the girl was played by a young and pretty German actress, Suzanne Christiane Harlan (known in Germany by the stage name Suzanne Christiane), and a year after the film was made, she and Kubrick were married. Christiane comes from a family of opera singers and stage personalities, and most of her life has been spent in the theatre; she was a ballet dancer before she became an actress, and currently she is a serious painter, in addition to managing the sprawling Kubrick household, which includes three daughters.

Paths of Glory was released in November 1957, and although it received excellent critical notices and broke about even financially, it did not lead to any real new opportunities for Kubrick and Harris. Kubrick returned to Hollywood and wrote two new scripts, which were never used, and worked for six months on a Western for Marlon Brando, which he left before it went into production. (Ultimately, Brando directed it himself, and it became *One-Eyed Jacks*.) It was not until 1960 that Kubrick actually began working on a picture again. In that year, Kirk Douglas asked him to take over the direction of *Spartacus,* which Douglas was producing and starring in. Shooting had been underway for a week, but Douglas and Anthony Mann, his director, had had a falling out. On *Spartacus,* in contrast to all his other films, Kubrick had no legal control over the script or the final form of the movie. Although Kubrick did the cutting on *Spartacus,* Kirk Douglas had the final say as to the results, and the consequent confusion of points of view produced a film that Kubrick thinks could have been better.

While *Spartacus* was being edited, Kubrick and Harris bought the rights to Vladimir Nabokov's novel *Lolita*. There was immense pressure from all sorts of public groups not to make *Lolita* into a film, and for a while it looked as if Kubrick and Harris would not be able to raise the money to do it. In the end, though, the money was raised and the film was made, in London. Kubrick feels that the weakness of the film was its lack of eroticism, which was inevitable given the cinematic restraints of the time. "The important thing in the novel is to think at the outset that Humbert is enslaved by his 'perversion,' " Kubrick says. "Not until the end, when Lolita is married and pregnant and no longer a nymphet, do you realize—along with Humbert—that he loves her. In the film, the fact that his sexual obsession could not be portrayed tended to imply from the start that he was in love with her."

It was the building of the Berlin Wall that sharpened Kubrick's interest in nuclear weapons and nuclear strategy, and he began to read everything he could get hold of about the bomb. Eventually, he decided that he had about covered the spectrum, and that he was not learning anything new. "When you start reading the analyses of nuclear strategy, they seem so thoughtful that you're lulled into a temporary sense of reassurance," Kubrick has explained. "But as you go deeper into it, and become more involved, you begin to realize that every one of these lines of thought leads to a paradox." It is this constant element of paradox in all the nuclear strategies and in the conventional attitudes toward them that Kubrick transformed into the principal theme of *Dr. Strangelove*. The picture was a new departure for Kubrick. His other films had involved putting novels on the screen, but *Dr. Strangelove,* though it did have its historical origins in *Red Alert,* a serious nuclear suspense story by Peter George, soon turned into an attempt to use a purely intellectual notion as the basis of a film. In this case, the intellectual notion was the inevitable paradox posed by following any of the nuclear strategies to their extreme limits. "By now, the bomb has almost no reality and has become a complete abstraction, represented by a few newsreel shots of mushroom clouds," Kubrick has said.

People react primarily to direct experience and not to abstractions; it is very rare to find anyone who can become emotionally involved with an abstraction. The longer the bomb is around without anything happening, the better the job that people do in psychologically denying its existence. It has become as abstract as the fact that we are all going to die someday, which we usually do an excellent job of denying. For this reason, most people have very little interest in nuclear war. It has become even less interesting as a problem than, say, city government, and the longer a nuclear event is postponed, the greater becomes the illusion that we are constantly building up security, like interest at the bank. As time goes on, the danger increases, I believe, because the thing becomes more and more remote in people's minds. No one can predict the panic that suddenly arises when all the lights go out—that indefinable something that can make a leader abandon his carefully laid plans. A lot of effort has gone into trying to imagine possible nuclear accidents and to protect against them. But whether the human imagination is really capable of encompassing all the subtle permutations and psychological variants of these possibilities, I doubt. The nuclear strategists who make up all those war scenarios are never as inventive as reality, and political and military leaders are never as sophisticated as they think they are.

Such limited optimism as Kubrick has about the long-range prospects of the human race is based in large measure on his hope that the rapid development of space exploration will change our views of ourselves and our world. Most people who have thought much about space travel have arrived at the somewhat ironic conclusion that there is a very close correlation between the ability of a civilization to make significant space voyages and its ability to learn to live with nuclear energy. Unless there are sources of energy that are totally beyond the ken of modern physics, it is quite clear that the only source at hand for really elaborate space travel is the nucleus. The chemical methods of combustion used in our present rockets are absurdly inefficient compared to nuclear power. A detailed study has been made of the possibilities of using nuclear power to propel large spaceships. Indeed, if we are to transport really large loads to, for example, the planets, it is very likely essential that it be done with nuclear power. Thus, any civilization that operates on the same laws of nature as our own will inevitably reach the point where it learns to explore space and to use nuclear energy about simultaneously. The question is whether there can exist any society with enough maturity to peacefully use the latter to perform the former. In fact, some of the more melancholy thinkers on this subject have even come to the conclusion that the earth has never been visited by beings from outer space because no civilization has been able to survive its own technology. That there *are* extraterrestrial civilizations in some state of development is firmly believed by many astronomers, biologists, philosophers, physicists, and other rational people—a conclusion based partly on the vastness of the cosmos, with its billions of stars. It is presumptuous perhaps to suppose that we are its only living occupants. From a chemical and biological point of view, the processes of forming life do

not appear so extraordinary that they should not have occurred countless times throughout the universe. One may
try to imagine what sort of transformation would take
place in human attitudes if intelligent life should be
discovered elsewhere in our universe. In fact, this is what
Kubrick did in *2001: A Space Odyssey,* which, in the words
of Arthur Clarke, the coauthor of its screenplay, is "about
the first contact"—the first human contact with extraterrestrial life.

It was Arthur Clarke who introduced me to Kubrick. We
met in New York several years back, when he was working
on a book about the future of scientific ideas and wanted
to discuss some of the latest developments in physics. I
always look forward to his occasional visits from Sri
Lanka, and when he called me up one evening some time
ago, I was very happy to hear from him. He lost no time in
explaining what he was up to. "I'm working with Stanley
Kubrick on the successor to *Dr. Strangelove,"* he said.
"Stanley is an amazing man, and I want you to meet him."
It was an invitation not to be resisted, and Clarke arranged
a visit to Kubrick soon afterward.

Kubrick was at that time living on the Upper East Side,
in a large apartment whose decor was a mixture of Christiane's lovely paintings, the effects of three rambunctious
young children, and Kubrick's inevitable collection of
cameras, tape recorders, and hi-fi sets. Christiane once
said that "Stanley would be happy with eight tape
recorders and one pair of pants." Kubrick himself did not
conform at all to my expectations of what a movie mogul
would look like. He is of medium height and has the bohe-
mian look of a riverboat gambler or a Rumanian poet. (He
now has a considerable beard, which gives his broad
features a somewhat Oriental quality.) He had the vaguely
distracted look of a man who is simultaneously thinking

about a hard problem and trying to make everyday conversation. During our meeting, the phone rang incessantly, a messenger arrived at the door with a telegram or an envelope every few minutes, and children of various ages and sexes ran in and out of the living room. After a few attempts at getting the situation under control, Kubrick abandoned the place to the children, taking me into a small breakfast room near the kitchen. I was immediately impressed by Kubrick's immense intellectual curiosity. When he is working on a subject, he becomes completely immersed in it and appears to absorb information from all sides, like a sponge. In addition to writing a novel with Clarke, which was the basis of the script for *2001,* he was reading every popular and semipopular book on science that he could get hold of.

During our conversation, I happened to mention that I had just been in Washington Square Park playing chess. He asked me whom I had been playing with, and I described the Master. Kubrick recognized him immediately. I had been playing a good deal with the Master, and my game had improved to the point where I was almost breaking even with him, so I was a little stunned to learn that Kubrick had played the Master on occasion, and that in his view the Master was a potzer. Kubrick went on to say that he loved playing chess, and added, "How about a little game right now?" By pleading another appointment, I managed to stave off the challenge.

I next saw Kubrick in London, where I had gone to a physicists' meeting and where he was in the process of organizing the actual filming of *2001.* I dropped in at his office in the M-G-M studio in Boreham Wood, outside London, one afternoon, and again was confronted by an incredible disarray—papers, swatches of materials to be used for costumes, photographs of actors who might be used to play astronauts, models of spaceships, drawings by his daughters, and the usual battery of cameras, radios, and tape recorders. Kubrick likes to keep track of things in small notebooks, and he had just ordered a sample sheet of every type of notebook paper made by a prominent paper firm—about a hundred varieties—which were spread out on a large table. We talked for a while amid the usual interruptions of messengers and telephone calls, and then he got back to the subject of chess: "How about a little game right now?" He managed to find a set of chessmen—it was missing some pieces, but we filled in for them with various English coins—and when he couldn't find a board he drew one up on a large sheet of paper. Sensing the outcome, I remarked that I had never been beaten five times in a row—a number that I chose more or less at random, figuring that it was unlikely that we would ever get to play five games.

I succeeded in losing two rapid games before Kubrick had to go back to London, where he and his family were living in a large apartment in the Dorchester Hotel. He asked me to come along and finish out the five games—the figure appeared to fascinate him—and as soon as he could get the girls off to bed and order dinner for Christiane, himself, and me sent up to the apartment, he produced a second chess set, with all the pieces and a genuine wooden board.

Part of the art of the professional chess player is to unsettle one's opponent as much as possible by small but legitimate annoying incidental activities, such as yawning, looking at one's watch, and snapping one's fingers softly—at all of which Kubrick is highly skilled. One of the girls came into the room and asked, "What's the matter with your friend?"

"He's about to lose another game," said Kubrick.

I tried to counter these pressures by singing "Moon River" over and over, but I lost the next two games. Then came the crucial fifth game, and by some miracle I actually won it. Aware that this was an important psychological moment, I announced that I had been hustling Kubrick and had dropped the first four games deliberately. Kubrick responded by saying that the poor quality of those games had lulled him into a temporary mental lapse. (In the course of making *Dr. Strangelove,* Kubrick had all but hypnotized George C. Scott by continually beating him at chess while simultaneously attending to the direction of the movie.) We would have played five more games on the spot, except that it was now two in the morning, and Kubrick's working day on the *2001* set began very early.

"The Sentinel," a short story by Arthur Clarke in which *2001* finds its genesis, begins innocently enough: "The next time you see the full moon high in the south, look carefully at its right-hand edge and let your eye travel upward along the curve of the disk. Around about two o'clock you will notice a small dark oval; anyone with normal eyesight can find it quite easily. It is the great walled plain, one of the finest on the moon, known as the Mare Crisium—the Sea of Crises." Then Clarke adds, unobtrusively, "Three hundred miles in diameter, and almost completely surrounded by a ring of magnificent mountains, it had never been explored until we entered it in the late summer of 1996." The story and the style are typical of Clarke's blend of science and fantasy. In this case, an expedition exploring the moon uncovers, on the top of a mountain, a little pyramid set on a carefully hewed-out terrace. At first, the explorers suppose it to be a trace left behind by a primitive civilization in the moon's past. But the terrain around it, unlike the rest of the moon's surface, is free of all debris and craters created by falling meteorites—the pyramid, they discover, contains a mechanism that sends out a powerful force that shields it from external disturbances and perhaps signals to some distant observer. When the explorers finally succeed in breaking through the shield and studying the pyramid, they become convinced that its origins are as alien to the moon as they are themselves. The astronaut telling the story says, "The mystery haunts us all the more now that the other planets have been reached and we know that only Earth has ever been the home of intelligent life in our universe. Nor could any lost civilization of our own world have built that machine. . . . It was set there upon its mountain before life had emerged from the seas of Earth."

But suddenly the narrator realizes the pyramid's meaning. It was left by some far-off civilization as a sentinel to signal that living beings had finally reached it:

Nearly a hundred thousand million stars are turning in the circle of the Milky Way, and long ago other races on the worlds of other suns must have scaled and passed the heights that we have reached. Think of such civilizations, far back in time against the fading afterglow of Creation, masters of a universe so young that life as yet had come only to a handful of worlds. Theirs would have been a loneliness we cannot imagine, the loneliness of gods looking out across infinity and finding none to share their thoughts.

They must have searched the star-clusters as we have searched the planets. Everywhere there would be worlds, but they would be empty or peopled with crawling, mindless things. Such was our own Earth, the smoke of the great volcanos still staining the skies, when that first ship of the peoples of the dawn came sliding in from the abyss beyond Pluto. It passed the frozen outer worlds, knowing that life could play no part in their destinies. It came to rest among the inner planets, warming themselves around the fire of the sun and waiting for their stories to begin.

These wanderers must have looked on Earth, circling safely in the narrow zone between fire and ice, and must have guessed that it was the favorite of the sun's children. Here, in the distant future, would be intelligence; but there were countless stars before them still, and they might never come this way again.

So they left a sentinel, one of millions they have scattered throughout the universe, watching over all worlds with the promise of life. It was a beacon that down the ages has been patiently signalling the fact that no one had discovered it.

The astronaut concludes:

I can never look now at the Milky Way without wondering from which of those banked clouds of stars the emissaries are coming. If you will pardon so commonplace a simile, we have set off the fire alarm and have nothing to do but to wait.

I do not think we will have to wait for long.

Clarke and Kubrick spent two years transforming this short story into a novel and then into a script for *2001,* which is concerned with the discovery of the sentinel and a search for traces of the civilization that put it there—a quest that takes the searchers out into the far reaches of the solar system. At the time extraterrestrial life may have seemed an odd subject for a motion picture, but at this stage in his career Kubrick was convinced that any idea he was really interested in, however unlikely it may sound, could be transferred to film. "One of the English science-fiction writers once said, 'Sometimes I think we're alone, and sometimes I think we're not. In either case, the idea is quite staggering.' " Kubrick once told me, "I must say I agree with him."

According to Kubrick's estimate, he and Clarke put in an average of four hours a day, six days a week, on the writing of the script. (This works out to about twenty-four hundred hours of writing for two hours and forty minutes of film.) Even during the actual shooting of the film, Kubrick spent every free moment reworking the scenario.

He had an extra office set up in a blue trailer that was once Deborah Kerr's dressing room, and when shooting was going on, he had it wheeled onto the set to give him a certain amount of privacy for writing. He frequently gets ideas for dialogue from his actors, and when he likes an idea he puts it in. (Peter Sellers, he says, contributed some wonderful bits of humor for *Dr. Strangelove.*)

In addition to writing and directing, Kubrick supervises every aspect of his films, from selecting costumes to choosing the incidental music. In making *2001,* he was, in a sense, trying to second-guess the future. Scientists planning long-range space projects can ignore such questions as what sort of hats rocketship hostesses will wear when space travel becomes common (in *2001* the hats have padding in them to cushion any collisions with the ceiling that weightlessness might cause), and what sort of voices computers will have if, as many experts feel is certain, they learn to talk and to respond to voice commands (there is the celebrated talking computer in *2001* that arranges for the astronauts' meals, gives them medical treatments, and even plays chess with them during a long space mission to Jupiter—"Maybe it ought to sound like Jackie Mason," Kubrick once said), and what kind of time will be kept aboard a spaceship (Kubrick chose Eastern Standard, for the convenience of communicating with Washington). In the sort of planning that NASA does, such matters can be dealt with as they come up, but in a movie everything is immediately visible and explicit, and questions like this must be answered in detail. To help him find the answers, Kubrick assembled around him a group of thirty-five artists and designers, more than twenty special effects people, and a staff of scientific advisers. By the time the picture was done, Kubrick figures, he had consulted with people from a generous sampling of the leading aeronautical companies in the United States and Europe, not to mention innumerable scientific and industrial firms. One consultant, for instance, was Marvin Minsky. Kubrick wanted to learn from him whether any of the things that he was planning to have his computers do were likely to be realized by the year 2001; he was pleased to find out that they were.

Kubrick told me he had seen practically every science fiction film ever made, and any number of more conventional films that had interesting special effects. One Saturday afternoon, after lunch and two rapid chess games, he and Christiane and I set out to see a Russian science fiction movie called *Astronauts on Venus,* which he had discovered playing somewhere in North London. Saturday afternoon at a neighborhood movie house in London is like Saturday afternoon at the movies anywhere; the theatre was full of children talking, running up and down the aisles, chewing gum, and eating popcorn,. The movie was in Russian, with English subtitles, and since most of the children couldn't read very well, let alone speak Russian, the dialogue was all but drowned out by the general babble. This was probably all to the good, since the film turned out to be a terrible hodgepodge of pseudoscience and Soviet propaganda. It featured a talking robot named John and a talking girl named Masha who had been left in a small spaceship orbiting Venus while a party of explorers—who thought, probably correctly, that she would have been a nuisance below—went off to explore. Although Kubrick reported that the effects used were crude, he insisted that we stick it out to the end, just in case.

Before I left London, I was able to spend a whole day with Kubrick, starting at about eight-fifteen, when an M-G-M driver picked us up in one of the studio cars. (Kubrick suffers automobiles tolerably well, but he will under almost no circumstances travel by plane, even though he holds a pilot's license and has put in about a hundred and fifty hours in the air, principally around Teterboro Airport. After practising landings and takeoffs, flying solo cross-country to Albany, and taking his friends up for rides, he lost interest in flying.) Boreham Wood is a little like the area outside Boston that is served by Route 128, for it specializes in electronics companies and precision industry, and the M-G-M studio is hardly distinguishable from the rather antiseptic-looking factories nearby. It consists of ten enormous sound stages concealed in industrial looking buildings and surrounded by a cluster of carpenter shops, paint shops, office units, and so on. Behind the buildings is a huge lot covered with bits and pieces of other productions—the façade of a French provincial village, the hulk of a Second World War bomber, and other debris. Kubrick's offices were near the front of the complex in a long bungalow structure that housed, in addition to his production staff, a group of youthful model makers working on large, very detailed models of spacecraft to be used in special effects photography; Kubrick called their realm "Santa's Workshop." When we walked into his private office, it seemed to me that the general disorder had grown even more chaotic since my last visit. Tacked to a bulletin board were some costume drawings showing men dressed in odd looking, almost Edwardian business suits. Kubrick said that the drawings were supposed to be of the business suit of the future and had been submitted by one of the innumerable designers who had been asked to furnish ideas on what men's clothes would look like in thirty-five years. "The problem is to find something that looks different and that might reflect new developments in fabrics but that isn't so far out as to be distracting," Kubrick said. "Certainly buttons will be gone. Even now, there are fabrics that stick shut by themselves.''

Just then, Victor Lyndon, Kubrick's associate producer (he was also the associate producer of *Dr. Strangelove* and *Darling*), came in. A trim, athletic looking man of forty-six, he leans toward the latest "mod" styling in clothes, and he was wearing an elegant green buttonless, self-shutting shirt. He was followed by a young man wearing hair down to his neck, a notably non-shutting shirt, and boots, who was introduced as a brand-new costume designer. (He was set up at a drawing table in Santa's Workshop, but that afternoon he announced that the atmosphere was too distracting for serious work, and left; the well-known British designer Hardy Amies was finally chosen to design the costumes.) Lyndon fished from a manila envelope a number of shoulder patches designed to be worn as identification by the astronauts. (The two principal astronauts in the film were to be played by Keir Dullea, who had starred in *David and Lisa* and *Bunny Lake Is Missing,* and Gary Lockwood, a former college-football star and a television and movie actor.) Kubrick said that the lettering didn't look right and suggested that the art department make up new patches using actual NASA lettering. He then consulted one of the small notebooks in which he lists all the current production problems, along with the status of their solutions, and announced that he was going to the art department to see how the drawings of the moons of Jupiter were coming along.

The art department, which occupies a nearby building, was presided over by Tony Masters, a tall, Lincolnesque man who was busy working on the Jupiter drawings when we appeared. Kubrick told me that the department, which designs and dresses all sets, was constructing a scale model of the moon, including the back side, which had been photographed and mapped by rocket. Looking over the Jupiter drawings, Kubrick said that the light in them looked a little odd to him and suggested that Masters have Arthur Clarke check on it that afternoon when he came out from London.

Our next stop was to pick up some papers in the separate office where Kubrick did his writing—a made-over dressing room in a quiet part of the lot. On our way to it, we passed an outbuilding containing a number of big generators; a sign reading "DANGER!—11,500 VOLTS!" was nailed to its door. "Why eleven thousand five *hundred*?" Kubrick said. "Why not twelve thousand? If you put a sign like that in a movie, people would think it was a fake." When we reached the trailer, I could see that it was used as much for listening as for writing, for in addition to the usual battery of tape recorders (Kubrick writes rough first drafts of his dialogue by dictating into a recorder, since he finds that this gives it a more natural flow) there was a phonograph and an enormous collection of records, practically all of them of contemporary music. Kubrick told me that he thought he had listened to almost every modern composition available on records in an effort to decide what style of music would fit the film. Here, again, the problem had been to find something that sounded unusual and distinctive but not so unusual as to be distracting. In the office collection were records by the practitioners of *musique concrète* and electronic music in general, and records of works by the contemporary German composer Carl Orff. In most cases, Kubrick said, film music tends to lack originality, and a film about the future was the ideal place for a really striking score by a major composer.

We returned to the main office, and lunch was brought

284

in from the commissary. During lunch, Kubrick signed a stack of letters, sent off several cables, and took a long-distance call from California. "At this stage of the game, I feel like the counterman at Katz's delicatessen on Houston Street at lunch hour," he said. "You've hardly finished saying 'Half a pound of corned beef' when he says 'What else?' and before you can say 'A sliced rye' he's saying 'What else?' again."

I asked whether he ever got things mixed up, and he said rarely, adding that he thought chess playing had sharpened his naturally retentive memory and gift for organization. "With such a big staff, the problem is for people to figure out what they should come to see you about and what they should *not* come to see you about," he went on. "You invariably find your time taken up with questions that aren't important and could have easily been disposed of without your opinion. To offset this, decisions are sometimes taken without your approval that can wind up in frustrating dead ends."

As we were finishing lunch, Victor Lyndon came in with an almanac that listed the average temperature and rainfall all over the globe at every season of the year. "We're looking for a cool desert where we can shoot some sequences during the late spring," Kubrick said. "We've got our eye on a location in Spain, but it might be pretty hot to work comfortably, and we might have trouble controlling the lighting. If we don't go to Spain, we'll have to build an entirely new set right here. More work for Tony Masters and his artists." (Later, I learned that Kubrick did decide to shoot on location.)

After lunch, Kubrick and Lyndon returned to a long-standing study of the spacesuit question. In the film, the astronauts wore spacesuits when they were working outside their ships, and Kubrick was very anxious that they should look like the spacesuits of thirty-five years from now. After numerous consultations with Ordway and other NASA experts, he and Lyndon had finally settled on a design, and now they were studying a vast array of samples of cloth to find one that would look right and photograph well. While this was going on, people were constantly dropping into the office with drawings, models, letters, cables, and various props, such as a model of a lens for one of the telescopes in a spaceship. (Kubrick rejected it because it looked too crude.) At the end of the day, when my head was beginning to spin, someone came by with a wristwatch that the astronauts were going to use on their Jupiter voyage (which Kubrick rejected) and a plastic drinking glass for the moon hotel (which Kubrick thought looked fine). About seven o'clock, Kubrick called for his car, and by eight-thirty he had returned home, put the children to bed, discussed the day's events with his wife, watched a news broadcast on television, telephoned Clarke for a brief discussion of whether nuclear-powered spacecraft would pollute the atmosphere with their exhausts, and taken out his chess set. "How about a little game?" he said in a seductive tone that the Master would have envied.

On December 29, 1965, shooting of the film began, and in early March the company reached the most intricate part of the camera work, which was to be done in the interior of a giant centrifuge. One of the problems in space travel is weightlessness. While the weightlessness has, because of its novelty, a certain glamor and amusement, it would be an extreme nuisance on a long trip. and probably a health hazard as well. Our physical systems have evolved to work against the pull of gravity, and it is highly probable that all sorts of unfortunate things, such as softening of the bones, would result from exposure to weightlessness for months at a time. In addition, of course, nothing stays in place without gravity, and no normal activity is possible unless great care is exercised; the slightest jar can send one hurtling across the cabin. Therefore, spacecraft designers agree that some sort of artifical gravity will have to be supplied for space travelers. In principle, this is very easy to do. An object on the rim of a wheel rotating at a uniform speed is subjected to a constant force pushing it away from the center, and if the size of the wheel and the speed of its rotation are adjusted, this centrifugal force can be made to resemble the force of gravity. Having accepted this notion, Kubrick went one step further and commissioned the Vickers Engineering Group to make an actual centrifuge, large enough for the astronauts to live in full time. It took six months to build and cost about three hundred thousand dollars. The finished product looked from the outside like a Ferris wheel thirty-eight feet in diameter and could be rotated at a maximum speed of about three miles an hour. This is not enough to parallel the force of gravity—the equipment inside the centrifuge had to be bolted to the floor—but it enabled Kubrick to achieve some remarkable photographic effects. The interior, eight feet wide, is fitted out with an enormous computer console, an electronically operated medical dispensary, a shower, a device for taking an artificial sunbath, a recreation area with a Ping-Pong table and an electronic piano, and five beds with movable plastic domes—hibernacula, where astronauts who are not on duty can, literally, hibernate for months at a time. (The trip to Jupiter in the film takes 257 days.)

I had seen the centrifuge in the early stages of its construction and very much wanted to observe it in action, so I was delighted when chance sent me back to England in the early spring of 1966. When I walked through the door of the *2001* set one morning in March, I must say that the scene that presented itself to me was overwhelming. In the middle of the hangarlike stage stood the centrifuge, with cables and lights hanging from every available inch of its steel girded superstructure. On the floor to one side of its frame was an immense electronic console (not a prop), and, in various places, six microphones and three television receivers. I learned later that Kubrick had arranged a closed-circuit television system so that he could watch what was going on inside the centrifuge during scenes being filmed when he could not be inside himself. Next to the microphone was an empty canvas chair with "Stanley Kubrick" painted on its back in fading black letters. Kubrick himself was nowhere to be seen, but everywhere I looked there were people, some hammering and sawing, some carrying scripts, some carrying lights. In one corner I saw a woman applying makeup to what appeared to be an astronaut wearing blue coveralls and leather boots. Over a loudspeaker, a pleasantly authoritative English voice—belonging, I learned shortly, to Derek Cracknell, Kubrick's first assistant—was saying, "Will someone bring the Governor's Polaroid on the double?" A man came up to me and asked how I would like my tea and whom I was looking for, and almost before I could reply, "One lump with lemon" and "Stanley Kubrick," led me, in a semi-daze, to an opening at the bottom of the centrifuge. Peering up into the dazzlingly illuminated interior, I spotted Kubrick lying flat on his back on the floor of the machine and staring up through the viewfinder of an enormous camera, in complete concentration. Keir Dullea, dressed in shorts and a white T-shirt, and covered by a blue blanket, was lying in an open hibernaculum on the rising curve of the floor. He was apparently comfortably asleep, and Kubrick was telling him to wake up "as simply as possible." "Just open your eyes," he said. "Let's not have any stirring, yawning, and rubbing."

One of the lights burned out, and while it was being fixed, Kubrick unwound himself from the camera, spotted me staring openmouthed at the top of the centrifuge, where the furniture of the crew's dining quarters was fastened to the ceiling, and said, "Don't worry—that stuff is bolted down." Then he motioned to me to come up and join him.

No sooner had I climbed into the centrifuge than Cracknell, who turned out to be a cheerful and all but imperturable youthful looking man in tennis shoes (all the crew working in the centrifuge were wearing tennis shoes, not only to keep from slipping but to help them climb the steeply curving sides; indeed, some of them were working while clinging to the bolted-down furniture halfway up the wall), said, "Here's your Polaroid, Guv," and handed Kubrick the camera. I asked Kubrick what he needed the Polaroid for, and he explained that he used it for checking subtle lighting effects for color film. He and the director of photography, Geoffrey Unsworth, had worked out a correlation between how the lighting appeared on the instantly developed Polaroid film and the settings on the movie camera. I asked Kubrick if it was customary for movie directors to participate so actively in the photographing of a movie, and he said succinctly that he had never watched any other movie director work.

The light was fixed, and Kubrick went back to work behind the camera. Keir Dullea was reinstalled in his hibernaculum and the cover rolled shut. "You better take your hands from under the blanket," Kubrick said. Kelvin Pike, the camera operator, took Kubrick's place behind the camera, and Cracknell called for quiet. The camera began to turn, and Kubrick said, "Open the hatch." The top of the hibernaculum slid back with a whirring sound, and Keir Dullea woke up, without any stirring, yawning, or rubbing. Kubrick, playing the part of the solicitous computer, started feeding him lines.

"Good morning," said Kubrick. "What do you want for breakfast?"

"Some bacon and eggs would be fine," Dullea answered simply.

Later, Kubrick told me that he had engaged an English actor to read the computer's lines in the serious dramatic scenes, in order to give Dullea and Lockwood something more professional to play against, and that in the finished film he dubbed in an American-accented voice. He and Dullea went through the sequence four or five times, and finally Kubrick was satisfied with what he had. Dullea bounced out of his hibernaculum, and I asked him whether he was having a good time. He said he was getting a great kick out of all the tricks and gadgets, and added, "This is a happy set, and that's something."

When Kubrick emerged from the centrifuge, he was immediately surrounded by people. "Stanley, there's a black pig outside for you to look at," Victor Lyndon was saying. He led the way outside, and, sure enough, in a large truck belonging to an animal trainer was a enormous jet-black pig. Kubrick poked it, and it gave a suspicious grunt.

"The pig looks good," Kubrick said to the trainer.

"I can knock it out with a tranquilizer for the scenes when it's supposed to be dead," the trainer said.

"Can you get any tapirs or anteaters?" Kubrick asked.

The trainer said that this would not be an insuperable problem, and Kubrick explained to me, "We're going to use them in some scenes about prehistoric man."

At this point, a man carrying a stuffed lion's head approached and asked Kubrick whether it would be all right to use.

"The tongue looks phony, and the eyes are only marginal," Kubrick said, heading for the set. "Can somebody fix the tongue?"

Back on the set, he climbed back into his blue trailer. "Maybe the company can get back some of its investment selling guided tours of the centrifuge," he said. "They might even feature a ride in it." He added that the work in the machine was incredibly slow, because it took hours to rearrange all the lights and cameras for each new sequence. Originally, he said, he had planned on 130 days of shooting for the main scenes, but the centrifuge sequences had slowed them down by perhaps a week. "I take advantage of every delay and breakdown to go off by myself and think," he said. "Something like playing chess when your opponent takes a long time over his next move."

At one o'clock, just before lunch, many of the crew went with Kubrick to a small projection room near the set to see the results of the previous day's shooting. The most prominent scene was a brief one that showed Gary Lockwood exercising in the centrifuge, jogging around its interior and shadowboxing to the accompaniment of a Chopin waltz—picked by Kubrick because he felt that an intelligent man in *2001* might choose Chopin for doing exercise to music. As the film appeared on the screen, Lockwood was shown jogging around the complete interior circumference of the centrifuge, which appeared to me to defy logic as well as physics, since when he was at the top he would have needed suction cups on his feet to stay glued to the floor. I asked Kubrick how he had achieved this effect, and he said he was definitely, absolutely not going to tell me. As the scene went on, Kubrick's voice could be heard on the sound track, rising over the Chopin: "Gain a little on the camera, Gary!...Now a flurry of lefts and rights!...A little more vicious!" After the film had run its course, Kubrick appeared quite pleased with the results, remarking, "It's nice to get two minutes of usable film after two days of shooting."

Later that afternoon, I had a chance to see a publicity short made up of some of the most striking material filmed for *2001.* There were shots of the space station, with people looking out of the windows at the earth wheeling in the distance; there was an incredible sequence, done in red, showing a hostess on a moon rocket appearing to walk on the ceiling of the spaceship; there was a solemn procession of astronauts trudging along on the surface of the moon. The colors and the effects were extremely impressive.

When I got back to the set, I found Kubrick getting ready to leave for the day. "Come around to the house tomorrow," he said. "I'll be working at home, and maybe we can get in a little game. I still think you're a complete potzer. But I can't understand what happens every fifth game."

He had been keeping track of our games in a notebook, and the odd pattern of five had indeed kept reappearing. The crucial tenth game had been a draw, and although I had lost the fifteenth, even Kubrick admitted that he had had an amazingly close call. As for the games that had not been multiples of five, they had been outright losses for me. We had now completed nineteen games, and I could sense Kubrick's determination to break the pattern.

The next morning, I presented myself at the Kubrick's house in Hertfordshire, just outside London, which they rented during the making of *2001.* It was a marvelous house and an enormous one, with two suits of armor in one of the lower halls, and rooms all over the place, including a paneled billiard room with a big snooker table. Christiane had fixed up one room as a painting studio, and Kubrick had turned another into an office, filled with the inevitable tape recorders and cameras. They had moved their belongings from New York in ninety numbered dark green summer camp trunks bought from Boy Scout head-quarters—the only sensible way of moving, Kubrick feels. The house was set in a lovely bit of English countryside, near a rest home for horses, where worthy old animals are sent to live out their declining years in tranquility. Heating the house posed a major problem. It had huge picture win-dows, and Arthur Clarke's brother Fred, who is a heating engineer, had pointed out to Kubrick that glass conducts heat so effectively that he would not be much worse off (except for the wind) if the glass in the windows were re-moved entirely. The season had produced a tremendous cold spell, and in addition to using electric heaters in every corner of the rooms, Kubrick had acquired some enor-mous, thick blue bathrobes, one of which he lent me. Thus bundled up, we sat down at the inevitable chessboard at ten in the morning for our twentieth game, which I pro ceeded to win on schedule. "I can't understand it," Kubrick said. "I know you are a potzer, so why are you winning these fifth games?"

A tray of sandwiches was brought in for lunch, and we sat there in our blue bathrobes like two figures from Berg-man's *The Seventh Seal*, playing on and taking time out only to munch a sandwich or light an occasional cigar. The children, who had been at a birthday party, dropped in later in the day in their party dresses to say hello, as did Christiane, but the games went on. I lost four in a row, and by late afternoon it was time for the twenty-fifth game, which, Kubrick announced, would settle the matter once and for all. We seesawed back and forth until I thought I saw a marvelous chance for a coup. I made as if to take off one of Kubrick's knights, and Kubrick clutched his brow dramatically, as though in sharp pain. I then made the move ferociously, picking off the knight, and Kubrick jumped up from the table.

"I knew you were a potzer! It was a trap!" he announced triumphantly, grabbing my queen from the board.

"I made a careless mistake," I moaned.

"No, you didn't," he said. "You were hustled. You didn't realize that I'm an actor, too."

It was the last chess game we have had a chance to play, but I did succeed in beating him once at snooker.

* * *

It was this epic twenty-five-game, marathon struggle described in my *New Yorker* article, that caught the attention of the editors of *Playboy* and led to the unexpected sequel that I am about to describe. Sometime in the early spring of 1972, I was sitting in my office in the physics department at Oxford University, where I was a visiting professor, working with my gloves on—there was a coal miner's strike—when the phone rang. A very amiable voice, male, identified itself as an editor of *Playboy* magazine phoning from Chicago. (No, it was not Himself.) He asked if, in fact, I was the Jeremy Bernstein who had written the profile of Stanley Kubrick for the *New Yorker*. Having been assured that I was the very Bernstein in question, he made a remarkable proposition. In brief, I was to go to Iceland, all expenses paid, for as long as I needed, to gather material to write an article on the forthcoming Fischer-Spassky chess match. Furthermore, the magazine had hired the American Grand Master, Larry Evans, as its very own expert, so that if I had any questions about anything on the technical side all I would have to do would be to consult Evans, who would be there for the entire match.

After hanging up the phone I had two reactions: the first

was an enormous attraction to the idea of going to Iceland, and the second was an equally enormous repulsion at the idea of having my name appear in *Playboy* magazine. By this time, many of my colleagues were already beginning to think of me as something of a farceur because I was writing fairly regularly for the *New Yorker*. What, then, would they think if I appeared in *Playboy*? I finally resolved this terrible dilemma by proposing to *Playboy* that I write the chess piece under an assumed name. In fact, I had one already picked out: Jay Amber, "amber" being the English translation of the German *Bernstein*. I had hit on this name several years earlier when I thought, for various arcane reasons, that I would write for the *New Yorker* under an assumed name. (This was the era of people like Xavier Rynne, a *New Yorker* writer who wrote about the Vatican, and who, it was claimed, was an entire conglomerate of priests and nuns.) William Shawn, the editor, had told me that this was all right with him, but that in his view I would come to regret it. I don't know if I would have or not, since the experiment was never carried out. If, by the way, the name Jay Amber is unfamiliar to *Playboy* readers, it may have something to do with the fact—as I shall explain—that no article under that name was ever published in *Playboy*.

The first game of the Fischer-Spassky match was scheduled to begin on Sunday, July 2, in Reykjavík. However, it may be remembered that on this day Fischer was not in Iceland, but in Queens, New York, holding out for more money. I was, as it happened, neither in Iceland nor in Queens nor, in fact, at Oxford. I was in Borehamwood *chez* Kubrick where, on Sunday nights, he used to show films in his private projection room. We had taken time out from the film viewing to watch a BBC documentary on Bobby Fischer which was called "This Little Thing with Me and Spassky." It was a fairly conventional documentary enlivened by some shots of Fischer beating the pawns off of a twelve-year-old chess prodigy named Lewis Cohen, and also refusing to eat a birthday cake served to him by Mike Wallace. "I don't eat this kind of cake," Fischer commented. Both Kubrick and I were mesmerized by the following childhood tale: Fischer as a young man was taught to play chess by his sister Joan Fischer Targ. Very rapidly he began to beat her, so they took to exchanging sides when Fischer got ahead. But there were times when his sister was not around, so Fischer played against himself—playing both black and white, As he was describing this he added softly, but very distinctly, and with no trace of humor, "Mostly I won."

Soon it became clear that additional money had been found and that the match would go on, so I headed for Iceland for the first of several trips. It is probably fair to say that that glorious country was then suffering its most extensive invasion by foreigners since the time of Ingolfur Arnarson, and his foster brother Hjorleifur, who arrived in 871 fleeing from King Harold Fairhair of Norway. The foster brothers and their friends and relatives settled the island, leaving among their descendants some of the most beautiful women in the world. Many of these could be seen mingling with the three hundred and fifty or so reporters then assembled in Reykjavík.

I encountered two old friends in this group: Harold Schonberg, the music critic of the *New York Times,* whom I knew from New York and whom I knew to be a devoted and skilled chess player, and George Steiner, whom I had known ever since we overlapped fifteen years earlier as visitors at the Institute for Advanced Study. I knew the minute I saw George that he must be there for the *New Yorker,* which I must admit, illogically, irked me. Why

wasn't *he* writing for *Playboy?* In fact, I recall asking
George after we met in Reykjavík if, in fact, he knew how
to play chess. This was a mistake, since Steiner produced
one of the greatest gamesmanship responses I have encountered. "Yes," he said, "and recently I was very proud
to get a draw with ——," —— being some barely pro-
nouncable Slavic-sounding name. This put me in the
hopeless situation of having to ask who —— was, which
would have exposed me as being a total dolt. Thinking
fast, I decided that the best thing I could do was rapidly
change the subject. Steiner eventually produced a widely
admired *New Yorker* article entitled "Fields of Force,"
and a small book of the same title on the general chess
phenomenon as illuminated by these matches, and Harold
Schonberg produced what was probably the most informed newspaper writing to come out of the tournament.

The first game took place on Tuesday, July 11, at 5:00
P.M. and was scheduled to last until 10:00, an hour that
could be predicted since each player was required, by the
rules, to make forty moves in no more than two and a half
hours. The Reykjavík Exhibition Hall was filled to its
capacity of 2,500 people, mainly Icelanders, each of whom
had paid five dollars to get in. These figures impressed me
because the average annual income in Iceland at the time
was estimated to be $2,500, and many people were working
two jobs to make ends meet. Five dollars, therefore, was
not a trivial sum of money.

First to appear on stage was Boris Spassky, suavely
handsome and impeccably dressed. He was greeted by
warm applause. By this time, Fischer's antics—which, by
the way, had only begun—were already grating on the
remarkably tolerant Icelanders. Spassky had white and,
promptly at five, he made his first move—pawn to queen
four—and started Fischer's clock. (In tournament chess

there is a dual clock and each player starts the other's clock after he has made his move.) No Fischer. The thought crossed my mind that he was simply not going to play at all. It must be remembered that before this match Fischer and Spassky had played five times, and Fischer had not won a single game. He had lost three and drawn two. About eight minutes went by with Spassky walking up and down the stage and peering from time to time at Fischer's empty chair. Then Fischer lumbered in. Looking at him I was somehow reminded of Einstein's not very flattering characterization of von Neumann, whose politics Einstein must have found abhorrent, as "ein Denktier"—a think animal.

In any event, without so much as looking at the board, Spassky, or the audience, Fischer began the first of an interminable series of arguments with the tournament referee Lothar Schmid, a German Grand Master, and his deputy, Gudmundur Arnlaugsson, an Icelander. What this was all about I will explain shortly. But after this outburst Fischer settled into his specially designed Charles Eames swivel chair, which had been flown in from New York, and proceeded to play, alternating between making moves and jumping out of his chair to argue with the referees. None of this could have improved Fischer's concentration and, indeed, on the twenty-ninth move he made a pawn capture that was so bizarre that it caused Spassky to sit bolt upright in his chair, a humdrum yellow job which he later replaced with one that swiveled, so that he and Fischer could swivel at each other. After a few moves Spassky took Fischer's bishop, and the next day, after a night's adjournment, Fischer proceeded to lose the game in fifty-six moves. Surprisingly, when he resigned he waved at the audience in a most amiable fashion and later was quoted as saying, "Today I played like a fish, but wait until tomorrow."

It was during this opening game that I first became aware of the persona of Chester Fox. Chester was, I would guess, in his middle thirties. He is a likeable fellow with graying, curly red hair and steel-rimmed glasses. Most accounts described him as an entrepreneur, which was fair enough since he had purchased for a sum of money—a sum Chester never revealed to anyone—the exclusive rights to all photographs (still, moving, and television) of the matches. It was never entirely clear from whom Chester had purchased these rights since, one gathers, Fischer never signed his name to anything. Before the matches, Fischer was certainly in favor of wide publicity for them. In fact, between sets of tennis at the La Costa Country Club in California, he had proclaimed that Iceland was a poor place to hold the tournament, because he felt its television facilities were primitive. "Iceland," he stated, "is a dreadful place to hold the matches. They [the Russians] are aware that I am going to win and they want the least possible exposure. Iceland is one place that it is not possible even to use a television satellite." At any rate, Chester was now filming the matches and what Fischer was objecting to was the presence of his cameras. I will not attempt here to detail all of the tedious steps that finally led to Chester's cameras being barred from the scene, but I will recall a few episodes which stand out in my mind.

Fischer refused to play the next game, and Spassky had to suffer the indignity of sitting alone on the stage before 2,500 Icelanders who watched Fischer's clock go a full hour around, before Spassky was declared the winner by default. After this, these good people filed out, uncomplaining, having just been bilked out of five dollars, man, woman and child. This led to a flurry of bizarre negotiations. It was decided that Spassky would have to go through with this charade three more times before being

299

declared the official winner of the tournament. On Friday the tournament officials decided to inform Fischer of this fact and to try also to persuade him to play the following Sunday. This attempt would have to be made before sundown on Friday, since Fischer had declared himself to be a member of the Worldwide Church of God, which celebrates a strict Sabbath. This raised the remarkable question about when sundown was, since, insofar as the sun sets at all in Iceland in July, it does so somewhere in the neighborhood of midnight. This Talmudic dilemma was resolved by Fischer himself, who declared that, for present purposes, "sundown" was defined to be at 11:45 P.M. And so at 11:45 the ever-smiling but weary chief official, Lothar Schmid, was seen in the lobby of the Hotel Loftleider where Fischer was staying, descending from the Fischer suite with an extremely pessimistic evaluation of the prospects of the tournament continuing.

It had become my own habit, by then, to spend most of my evenings in the lobby of the Hotel Loftleider. It was a wonderful place from which to observe the comings and goings of the various flora and fauna. These included among others Chet Forte of ABC News, who was trying to take over from Chester Fox. Forte was quoted as saying, "Bobby is immature about a lot of facts of life. He doesn't know how TV works or anything. And he's impossible to get to, but once you sit down with him you can change your opinion of him." Not long after "sitting down" with Bobby, Forte and his entire crew left Iceland never to be seen again. There was also the delightful pair of Jerry Weintraub and Sid Bernstein, who had managed, among many other entertainers, the Beatles in some of their early tours in this country. Weintraub described himself to me as one of the top five "skimmers" in the United States, and perhaps the world, and sensing the prospect of a good skim he and Bernstein (no relation) had come to Iceland to toss various proposals at Fischer's feet, which they proceeded to do through a partially closed door in Fischer's suite. I have no idea how they finally made out in their various plans to introduce all sorts of Fischer merchandise to the world, but I think they were responsible for an eerie appearance Fischer made on the "Bob Hope Show" after the tournament ended.

By this time I had already had several genial conversations with Chester Fox, whom I had come rather to like. He was simply trying to do an honest job under impossible circumstances and, it seemed to me, that he was getting the short end of the stick. In any case, one evening, as I was in my accustomed place on a couch in the Loftleider lobby, Chester came over and sat down on the empty cushion next to me. "Is Fischer really that good?" Chester asked, perhaps as much to himself as to me. (I should point out that Fischer had now started to play on a regular basis.) I had gone to London and come back again, my departure having been inspired by my conviction that Fischer was not going to finish the tournament. Not only had Fischer started to play, but he was beginning to beat Spassky unmercifully. Not only was he as good as he said he was, but he was so good that not even he knew how good he was. As I was making this clear to Chester Fox, the hotel elevator door opened near where we were sitting and out came Fischer surrounded by his usual entourage. They got into a specially commandeered Merceaes (which Fischer had insisted have an automatic shift) and, I suppose, went off to the American air base at Keflavík, where Fischer liked to let off steam by bowling. While this was happening, Chester turned to me and said, "He had better not see you sitting with me if you want an interview with him." Interviewing Fischer was the last thing in the world I wanted to do, but out of polite curiosity I asked, "Why is that, Chester?" Fox replied, simply, "He hates me." "You see," Chester went on, "after the first game I happened to meet him and he said to me, 'It's nothing personal. I would do the same thing to anyone who got in my way.' I said to him, 'Bobby, you are a very sick boy and should see a doctor.'"

On September 1, at the conclusion of the twenty-first game, Bobby Fischer became the new champion of the world. He had beaten Spassky by the score 12½ to 8½. When asked how it felt to be the champion, he replied, "I've always felt I was the champion."

I returned to New York to write my article. In fact I was now in a dual time bind. *Playboy* wanted the piece by the first of October in order to run it in their February issue, and I, in turn, had to begin teaching in just a couple of weeks. While still in Reykjavík I had thought up a conceit around which to organize the material. I had been reading Hermann Hesse's *Magister Ludi: The Glass Bead Game*, and had been much taken by the aptness of several of Hesse's comments on the deteriorating atmosphere of that game and Knecht's growing discomfiture with it. I had selected a half-dozen quotations from Hesse, each of which would introduce little chapters of the masterwork which I had entitled "Magister Ludi—The Game in the Glass House." I even checked this with my patrons at *Playboy* to make sure that Hesse was not too rich a fare for their readers and, assured that Hesse was quite okay, I finished the article in three weeks. But I was totally unprepared when, at the end of September, my *Playboy* mentor phoned me to say that there would be no chess article in the magazine. In the meanwhile, it seems, Hugh Hefner had become interested in backgammon and the February issue was to be devoted to that idiotic enterprise, the world champion of which, I am pleased to report, is now a computer. Every other magazine already had its article on the match so mine was never published anywhere, although *Playboy* did pay me for it. So it goes.

Not long ago I encountered an item in the Follow-Up on the News section of the *New York Times* which may have escaped the attention of some people. Under the title "Courtroom Chess" it read as follows:

It was eight and a half years ago that Bobby Fischer defeated Boris Spassky for the world chess championship in Iceland, and Mr. Fischer has never been in another official chess game since then. In July 1979, however, a sequel to the Icelandic encounter remained to be played: *Fox* v. *Fischer* in State Supreme Court in Manhattan.

Chester Fox had sued Mr. Fischer for $3.2 million in damages because the chess grand master had barred him from filming the match in Iceland.

"It's getting a beard on it," Mr. Fox's lawyer, Richard C. Stein, says laughingly of the court case. It came up for trial last winter, he says, and he requested an adjournment because of other pressing business.

Now, he says, he doesn't know when the trial will be held. Like a championship chess game itself, the case has settled into a long waiting pattern.

Epilogue: Sometime during the summer Harold Schonberg, who had known Fischer ever since he was an adolescent playing in the New York chess clubs, said to me that if Fischer won the tournament he would never play another one. This seemed incredible to me and, also, to fly in the face of all of the declarations that Fischer was making about how he would be the champion of all the people and so forth. Schonberg felt that by playing another match, which he might lose, Fischer could only diminish himself and this he would not do. At this writing, Schonberg seems to have been right. Fischer has never played another public game, and there is no sign that he ever will. Spassky left the Soviet Union and is, I believe, living in Paris. He is still an important figure in international chess. Bernstein and Weintraub have gone from strength to strength in skimming. Kubrick and I have never played another chess game on the grounds that it is a waste of time. And I, to my great regret, have never set foot again in Iceland.

14

Scientific Cranks

How to Recognize One and What to Do
Until the Doctor Arrives

I HAVE a very clear, almost affectionate, memory of my first encounter with a crank. It took place in the spring of 1958. I was at the time a visiting member, in physics, of the Institute for Advanced Study in Princeton and had acquired a local reputation for my somewhat unorthodox working habits. Each morning I would arrive at the institute about 8:30 A.M., and leave about 5:30 P.M., just in time to greet many of my more conventional colleagues who would be coming into the institute for their normal night's work. There was, I recall, a young French mathematician, of considerable distinction, who was experimenting with a twenty-three-hour day, and from time to time our work cycles would overlap—otherwise, except for the seminars, I was able to work through the daylight hours largely undisturbed.

In any event, one spring morning, about 9:00 A.M., as I was finishing the *New York Times* in my office, the hall telephone rang. (It was one of the late J. Robert Oppenheimer's conceits that the junior members should not have telephones in their offices lest their concentration be broken—with the consequence that there was one hall telephone for the entire floor, which, needless to say, disturbed *everyone* on the floor each time it rang.) It was Oppenheimer's secretary, informing me that I had a visitor from what sounded like a boiler factory in a nearby New Jersey community. I assured her that it was a simple case of misidentification, and was about to hang up when she said, with some insistence, "No, this is someone who wants to see *you.*"

When I arrived in the large sitting room—used then for the afternoon teas—I was greeted by Oppenheimer's secretary, who presented to me, with no further explanation, a gentleman in his fifties, I would guess, dressed in bluejeans and a heavy jacket. His appearance was unremarkable except for his eyes, each of which appeared to function without relation to the other. It is an effect I have seen in certain large African birds. (The British comic actor Marty Feldman can also do it.) The gentleman studied me out of his right eye while the left one roamed peaceably over the woods in back of the institute, into which, incidentally, the celebrated British physicist P. A. M. Dirac, also a member that year, could often be seen disappearing, in the late afternoons, with an ax. (He informed us that he was constructing a trail in the general direction of Trenton.)

After what seemed like an eternity, the man suddenly said, "What is the speed of magnetism?" The whole atmosphere had come to resemble that of my Ph.D. oral examination, and for a moment I entertained the paranoid delusion that it was a device Oppenheimer had decided to employ to sort out the wheat from the chaff among us. I explained to the man that if he was referring to electromagnetic waves in free space, these propagated with the speed of light. There was more silence, and then he said, "It works by magnetism"—a statement that resisted comment on my part since I did not have the foggiest idea to what "it" referred. More silence, and then he asked, "Have you ever seen a flying saucer?'' this time focusing on me with both eyes. I had to admit that unfortunately I had not. He explained to me that one had landed near his house just outside Trenton—which, if true, was the most interesting thing that I had heard about that community during my tenure in Princeton—and he was convinced that it had done it by magnetism. Before the conversation could get much further, Oppenheimer's secretary reappeared and told the man that Dr. Bernstein had a very important seminar to attend and would have to be excused. Later she explained to me that it was the policy at the institute to give all such visitors some sort of hearing in order to defuse possible trouble, and since it was known that I arrived in my office at an ungodly hour of the morning, I had drawn the duty. It never happened again during the two years I spent in Princeton.

In the subsequent years I went about my business in physics without encountering much more than a tiny trickle of cranks; that is, until I began to write about science for the general public and, above all, after I had written a popular article about Einstein and the theory of relativity for the *New Yorker*. The trickle has now become a sort of Niagara—an Amazon River—of cranks. They come by postcard, registered letter, and telephone. They arrive at almost every hour of the day or evening, and they do not take no for an answer. Let me give two rather recent examples.

One evening, about a year ago, the phone rang in my apartment. It was a long-distance call from somewhere in the Southwest, and it was from a gentleman whom I will refer to as A. (There is a B who will soon get into the act.) A began the conversation after verifying that I was the author of a certain book about the theory of elementary particles. He proclaimed that, in his opinion, this book was one of the greatest contributions to modern thought since Newton's *Principia. My* thought was, "What does *this* one want?" It soon became clear what he wanted. He had written, he informed me, a massive, as yet unpublished treatise in which was solved each and every problem that remained unsolved by my book (a hallmark of crank manuscripts is that they solve *everything*), and that furthermore, and for good measure, it contained a theory of the origin of the moon. (I thought of saying "Your beloved homeland?" but a second hallmark of cranks is that they are humorless.) Needless to say, he wanted me to read this document and to send him a commentary. Such a request might seem to be innocent enough, but a good deal of experience has taught me that it isn't. In the first place, no crank wants, or will accept, an honest criticism of anything. He has solved the "problem," whatever it is, and is looking for an endorsement. Even agreeing to accept, let alone comment on, such a manuscript opens one up to endless trouble. A number of letters from cranks contain lists of people, often distinguished people, who have agreed to look at the work, and I can visualize these unfortunates drowning in a stream of increasingly abusive correspondence from the crank authors, who will now claim that they have been misunderstood or that their ideas have been stolen by the very people to whom they had sent the manuscripts to read. (A third hallmark of the crank is that he is sure everyone is out to steal his ideas.)

I told the gentleman, politely but firmly, that I did not have the time to read his manuscript (the late Wolfgang Pauli used to tell such people that he had very weak eyes and his doctor had forbidden him to read much), and that if he sent it I would have to return it to him unopened. This, I thought, was the end of A. But no! About six months later, when I was on sabbatical leave at another institution, I received a phone call *there,* again from the same southwestern city but this time from B. He informed me that his friend A had read my book and regarded it as the greatest contribution to human thought since...et cetera. He also told me that A's theory of the formation of the moon would soon hit the press, where it would make front-page news. (A fourth hallmark of the crank is that he is determined to bring the newspapers in somehow. A recent letter from one who "refuted" Einstein's theory of relativity ended by noting that if an immediate reply was not forthcoming he would turn the whole matter over to the press.) Again, I said to B that under no circumstances would I read A's book, and goodbye. But that did not end the matter. Only a few weeks ago I received a letter from A informing me that reading his book should be comparatively simple for me, since it "includes about 25% drawings and plates." I am expecting that at any moment the phone will ring and it will be C.

I will give one last example, since it is a nice illustration of what I might call the collaborative crank. Again the phone rang. This time I was at home in the morning, preparing a classroom lecture. A gentleman at the other end began by verifying that I was the one who had written about Einstein. I should have said no, but you can never tell, it might have been someone who wanted to buy the film rights. He told me that he had solved the "unified field problem," but since he had never studied physics he was looking for a collaborator—in order, I imagined, to dot a few *i*'s. Would I be interested in collaborating with him, and, if not, could I suggest anyone? One is tempted to give the name of a colleague under such circumstances, but this is a no-win strategy since your colleagues will turn their cranks over to you. It soon became clear that this man was determined to carry out the collaboration then and there,

309

over the phone, unless I could think of something. In desperation, I asked him what his field of work was. It turned out that he was a financial adviser. I then asked him how he would feel if someone called him up at home in midmorning, when he was busy trying to give financial advice, and asked him to drop everything in order to begin an immediate collaboration on a physics problem. He pointed out that this case was different: if I really was sincere about my work, I *would* drop everything and listen to him since he had solved THE PROBLEM. (A fifth hallmark of cranks is that they use a lot of capital letters.) I told him that I was not sincere enough and hung up. Nothing more has been heard from him, but it is still early.

These are fairly typical examples, but they do raise an interesting question: Is there a chance that one of these people *has* solved something and that, by not giving him a full hearing, one really may have missed an opportunity? I sometimes have the following fantasy. It is the year 1905 and I am a professor of physics at the University of Bern. The phone rings, and a person I have never heard of identifies himself as a patent examiner in the Swiss National Patent Office. He says that he has heard I give lectures on electromagnetic theory and that he has developed some ideas which might interest me. "What sort of ideas?" I ask a bit superciliously. He begins discussing some crazy sounding notions about space and time. Rulers contract when they are set in motion; a clock on the equator goes at a slower rate than the identical clock when it is placed at the North Pole; the mass of an electron increases with its velocity; whether or not two events are simultaneous depends on the frame of reference of the observer; and so on. How would I have reacted? Well, a great many of Albert Einstein's contemporaries would have hung up the phone.

After all, in 1905, Einstein didn't even have an academic job!

Suppose I had had the good sense to ask the fellow for a reprint of his recently published paper "Zur Elektrodynamik bewegter Körper" ("The Electrodynamics of Moving Bodies"). How could I have told that this was not a crank paper with a crank theory? There are, I think, at least two clues. In the first place, the theory—the special theory of relativity in this instance—satisfies what Niels Bohr later called, in a more general context, the correspondence principle. The relativity theory generalizes Newtonian mechanics, but, after all, Newton's mechanics works marvelously well for a vast domain of phenomena. Hence there must be some limit in which the two theories merge—or "correspond." A glance at Einstein's 1905 paper would show that in this case the limit is when the speed of light is effectively infinite compared to the usual velocities one encounters in most applications. Hence the two theories give essentially the same answers in their common domain of application—for small velocities. Crank theories, when they are theories at all—an important point to which I will return—usually start and end in midair. They do not connect in any way with things that are known. A really novel genuine theory may appear, at first sight, to be quite crazy, but they all have, if they are any good, this aspect of connectivity. In that sense a novel theory—like relativity—already comes with a large endowment of verification: The same experiments that verified its ancestors also serve to verify it.

The second clue I have alluded to above: It is that, in the phrase of the aforementioned Pauli, crank theories "aren't even wrong." I have never yet seen a crank physics theory that offered a novel quantitative prediction that could be either verified or falsified. It is usually awash in a garble of verbiage with terms like "energy," "field," "particle," "mass," and God knows what, all festooned like Christmas tree decorations. If there are any formulas in such theories, they are usually the formulas of well-known theories that the crank is bent on disproving. Einstein's 1905 paper may at first sight appear bizarre, but it is full of predictions. The whole thing is crying out to be tested in laboratories.

In this respect, it is interesting that the first novel prediction of the theory of relativity to have been tested—namely, the variation of mass with velocity—was *in disagreement* with the experiment. Einstein waited, unperturbed, for several years until it was shown that the original experiments were wrong; there was a leak in the vacuum system. In some sense the theory *had* to be right—such is its inner coherence. In the same sense, about the most exciting event that I can imagine happening in physics would be for an experimenter to find a breakdown in the relativity theory. The really interesting thing to find out is which, if any, of Einstein's assumptions will turn out to have a limited range of validity. In this enterprise we do not need the services of cranks.

There is, by the way, a certain set of quasi-crank theories that deserve special mention since sometimes they turn out to be not so crankish after all. There are people who manage to come up with simple numerical formulas, usually of obscure origin, that *do* fit data. A few years ago, for example, a mathematician came up with a complicated but remarkable formula for the so-called "fine structure constant": the numerical parameter that measures the strength of the electromagnetic interaction with electrically charged matter. Its origins were—and, I still think, are—rather obscure, and he himself was quite modest about the whole thing; but there it was. Perhaps it was a numerical coincidence, or maybe it will turn out to have some deep significance that no one yet understands. About all one can do when confronted with such formulas is to put them in one's desk drawer and see what happens; at least, that's all I can do.

All of this having been said, there is a danger in dismissing some of this crank correspondence too lightly. It is not unusual to receive letters that look very weird but, if one takes the trouble to read them, turn out to be sincere requests for information. It is one thing for someone to send you a design for a perpetual motion machine, which is certain to turn out to be wrong, but it is another thing for someone to ask how, in principle, one can be certain that there is no such thing as a perpetual motion machine. What are the limits of validity to the currently accepted laws of thermodynamics? None, as far as we know, but it is a question that deserves a decent answer. I have engaged in some very pleasant correspondence with people who want to know the answers to questions like that, and replying to them is a good exercise in scientific self-expression.

Whatever else cranks may be up to, after one deals with several it becomes clear that they are not really interested in doing science. They are not prepared to accept the rough-and-tumble of scientific criticism; any criticism is regarded as a provocation and a threat. Cranks are looking for a psychological anchor—something that might be provided by a psychiatrist but is not likely to be provided by a theoretical physicist. In general, they do not seem to be dangerous—although, in one case that I know of, one of these people materialized in the offices of the American Physical Society some years ago and shot, and killed, a secretary because his ideas had been ignored. Since these people have started inflicting themselves on me in substantial numbers, I have made inquiries among doctors of various persuasions as to what the best tactics are for dealing with them. Their main piece of advice is to detach yourself from the situation as quickly as possible. Do not get involved with such people on the grounds that it may be "amusing" or that you can help them out. A formula that I find works in most cases is to write a note saying that while the person's ideas seem interesting, they are outside your field of expertise—whatever *that* is—and so you are unable to comment on them. This works in most cases.

There is one case, and I shall conclude with it, in which the best thing to do is to do nothing; that is the case of the abusive crank. Some years ago, after each and every article that I wrote for the *New Yorker,* on whatever subject, I received an incredibly abusive letter from an individual in New York. The main point of his communication was that I was a fraud and that I was causing him to waste his money by buying the magazine. When I got the first of these letters I had just started to write for the *New Yorker* and, having little or no experience in dealing with such things, I asked some of the veterans at the magazine what to do. They said to ignore it and forget it. In his subsequent letters, the individual, in addition to berating me for being a fraud, also let me have it for not answering his previous letters. It became almost like those classical Jewish jokes involving the definition of *chutzpa.* Finally I got an idea that I proposed to one of the senior editors at the magazine. I thought that we should have an elegant-looking card printed, with the Rea Irvin *New Yorker* logo, which would contain a single sentence, printed in *New Yorker* type. It would read: "At a recent meeting of the board of editors of the *New Yorker* it has been decided to cancel your subscription." Unfortunately the editors seemed to think that *this* was a crank idea.

15

Bubble & Squeak

A mathematician cannot enter on subjects that seem so far removed from his usual preoccupations without some bad conscience. Many of my assertions depend on pure speculation and may be treated as day-dreams, and I accept this qualification—is not a day-dream the virtual catastrophe in which knowledge is initiated? At a time when so many scholars in the world are calculating, is it not desirable that some who can, dream?
—RENÉ THOM

1. I knew a mathematician who had a recurrent dream. He dreamt that he was a partial derivative. The number of people who have dreamt about the differential calculus may be quite substantial, especially if one includes engineers. Only a professional mathematician, however, could dream that he had *become* the differential calculus.

2. The British have always had a way with ghosts. This has, I think, to do with atmospheric density. Ordinary matter has a density of one to ten grams per cubic centimeter. A laboratory plasma has a density of about 10^{-8} grams per cubic centimeter. The density at the center of the sun is about 10^7 grams per cubic centimeter, while neutron stars have a density of 10^{12} grams per cubic centimeter. I estimate the average ghost density at about 10^{-4} grams per cubic centimeter. This is a conservative estimate. Ghosts cannot be made in a vacuum. This would violate the conservation of mass. If a ghost is created at the surface of a

neutron star, it can never escape. The gravitational attraction is too strong. The atmosphere over deserts is too rarefied. The probability of ghost formation in the Sahara I have estimated to be extremely small: about one ghost per three hundred years. The atmosphere over Great Britain—including both Scotland and Ireland—is quite dense. I estimate that one ghost per three minutes materializes in Great Britain. This accounts, I believe, for the frequently reported sightings by reliable and, often disinterested, observers of ghosts.

My friends Richard and Sally Longwood have seen a ghost. They live in London. Sally believes that it is her great-great-great-aunt who was French. "She spoke to me in French," Sally has told me. Sally does not speak French but she recognizes it when she hears it. "Pity," says Sally, "I would like so much to know what she was trying to tell me." That is why I am here tonight in the Longwoods' dining room. I speak French and will interpret. The dinner table has been cleared and the lights extinguished. A candle burns in the center of the table. the three of us are seated around the table with our hands resting lightly on it. "Is anybody there?" Sally asks, politely, several times. There is no response. Richard tries—no answer. Sally tries again with no success. "I don't think she will appear tonight," Sally says, "perhaps she is shy with people who are not family."

3. Sometimes I am invited over for dinner, here and there, if I am willing to take "pot luck." The French call this *"pot au feu"*—a *potpourri*—a "rotten pot" of things boiled over a fire. The British call it "bubble and squeak." "Do drop over for dinner—that is, if you don't mind a bit of bubble and squeak." Usually, I don't mind.

4. An abstract mathematical theory of catastrophes must be precise. A "catastrophe manifold" must be defined, and control parameters must be introduced. "Energy functions" may be plotted with a ruler and straightedge. Books and articles can be written, and conferences can be addressed. According to Thom, if there are at most four control parameters and two behavior variables, only seven basic catastrophes are possible. These include the "butterfly," the "swallow tail" and the more complicated "elliptical, parabolic and hyperbolic umbilics." The simplest catastrophes can be described in terms of cusps. Cusps come in handy because they can be plotted in three dimensions. The catastrophe manifold overlaps itself, and if one is not careful one can fall over the edge. Anxiety and frustration can suddenly turn into anger. Hate and love merge, and one can hardly tell the players in the game without a scorecard. The brain is an interconnected network of billions of neurons, and if one is not careful, one can develop cusps. At times, going for a long walk is a good way to deal with cusps and, at other times, it can only make things worse.

5. There are two single women in this hotel. They do not know each other. Each one is accompanied by a child. In the absence of any *a priori* arguments to the contrary, it is natural to assume that each woman is the mother of the respective child that accompanies her. There is also genetic evidence that can be brought to bear, in a pinch. The blonde woman has a blonde child, and the black-haired woman has a brown-haired child. This is not very convincing evidence. We now know that natural hair coloring is not an acquired characteristic. It must be inherited. It does not grow on trees. But it takes two to tangle—genetically. There is more here than meets the eye. I have gathered

some additional evidence concerning the blonde woman. She leaves the hotel each morning at 9:30 with the blonde boy. (I forgot to say that the blonde woman is accompanied by a blonde boy, and the black-haired woman is accompanied by a brown-haired girl. This would not have changed the arguments given above very substantially. The sexes appear to be distributed, more or less, at random.) She always wears slacks and, frequently, a heavy knitted white sweater—we are in the mountains. She has a very good posture. In fact she is almost rigid. She never smiles in the morning. Each night she has her dinner with the boy at the same table in the hotel dining room. She drinks exactly one-half a bottle of red wine, and the boy drinks one small glass. We are in France. Her face becomes very flushed and she smiles a great deal. Each time she smiles, the boy smiles too. They converse with their neighbors at the next table. The conversation appears to be very animated. The occupants of the next table change every few days. This does not appear to change the ambiance very much. After dinner she and the boy say goodnight very solemnly and disappear. This goes on night after night and day after day. Once, I happened to be standing at the reception desk at the hotel when she was mailing a letter. It was addressed to someone in England. I smiled at her. She did not smile back. I wish I could tell you more about her. One cannot get blood, always, from a writer's imagination. The supply is limited. Sometimes one has to settle for a squeak and bubble. The other woman appears every other day at the swimming pool in the hotel with her presumed daughter. This deserves further study.

6. Frustration dreams must be transcultural, but how are they expressed by Zulus and Sherpas? Mine frequently involve taxis. I live, normally, in a large city. In my dream I

am on a dimly illuminated street far from home. It is late at night, and there is no available public transportation. I must get home. It is very important that I get home. A taxi approaches. It is empty. I signal. It passes me by as if I were a ghost. The process repeats itself until I wake up. What do the Sherpas dream about?

7. There *have* been technological breakthroughs in long division. There is no denying that. A finite number divided by zero gives infinity: "infinity" being defined as a larger number than anyone can presently think of. If one divided the old mechanical desk calculators by zero they would grind on forever. Sometimes smoke came out of the gears. I now have a pocket electronic calculator which I use to figure out probabilities—for ghost formation and the rest. When there is nothing better to do I divide it by zero. It gives me, almost instantly, the largest number. *it* can think of—$9.999999999 \times 10^{99}$—and then it flashes at me rather pathetically. It has done its best and wishes to go on to something else. Curiously enough, if I divide zero by zero—$0/0$—it gives me 1 and then flashes. It has, somehow, learned *l'Hospital's* rule for division by nonfinite numbers. But it does not seem to be too certain of itself; otherwise it wouldn't flash like that. One cannot have everything.

8. The black-haired woman with the brown-haired child has just arrived at the pool. She is wearing a bikini. She has a lovely figure. The use of the phrase "lovely figure" in this context has always puzzled me. As far as I am concerned, a lovely figure is something like the number "0" or perhaps "111." It would, I think, be more appropriate, in *this* context, to say that she has a magnificent body. She owns at least three bikinis. The argument for this is simple.

I have seen her three times at the pool, and each time she has been wearing a different bikini. God knows the number of bikinis that she actually possesses. This particular bikini has the color of a fine Burgundy wine. It has been manufactured, one would gather, with great care, out of a shimmering water-resistant substance—the nearest known approximation to the skin of mermaids. Her exposed skin, of which there is a great deal, has a marvelous amber tone as if it is being illuminated from within. Each time I have seen her, she has settled on the opposite side of the pool, directly across from where I am lying. I have no way of estimating the probability that this is accidental. She spreads out her towel and lies down on it, on her stomach, with the feet pointing toward the pool. From where I am, I estimate that the angle between her calves and the back of her thighs is about four degrees. This is just an order-of-magnitude estimate and may have to be revised as we go along.

The child who must be about eight, wears a bikini bottom but no top. The places where her breasts will be have a gentle convex shape—like that of a miniature Japanese Suomi wrestler. As quickly as possible she gets into the water.

9. Insofar as there is such a thing as theoretical biology, it should concern itself with possible options. After all, sex is optional. By this I mean that the fact that there are two, and only two, sexes appears to be somewhat arbitrary. There *are* alternatives. The female greenfly, I have recently read, can bear live, fatherless, female offspring identical to herself. Furthermore—and get this—the daughter is born with an embryo for *her* daughter already inside her womb—daughter and granddaughter are born simultaneously. Genetically, they are identical twins to their mother

and grandmother respectively. Not much is known, at least to me, about how greenflies feel about this, but I *have* heard that male biologists, after having seen greenflies give birth a few times, are observed to leave their laboratories and head for the nearest bar for a good stiff drink. I have a friend, a mathematician, who spent some time working on a theory of n-sexes, where n could be *any* positive integer. He was trying to prove that there was some distinct advantage in having $n = 2$, which he used to refer to as the "classical case." He never found an argument that really satisfied him. At about this time, his wife went off with a stockbroker. He has since remarried. I keep meaning to write him to find out what he is working on at the present time.

10. After getting into the water, the child swims back and forth five or six times tracing a route that connects me to, what I presume, is her mother. If her mother and I were flowers and the child a bee, one would refer to this activity as "pollination." Finally the child stops at the side of the pool where I am lying. She has done this each time she and I have been at the pool together. She then, as the times before, begins to tell herself a story. She does this in a low voice, but loud enough so that I can hear it. She does not look directly at me while she is telling herself the story, but every once in a while she glances in my direction to make sure that I am listening. I am.

Her stories always involve playing with a group of imaginary friends. I feel that these friends are imaginary because their names keep changing from day to day and from story to story. Sometimes these friends invite her to play when she is having dinner or about to go to bed. There is then an adult—always male—who tells her that she cannot play now, but will see her friends tomorrow. The adult male is never given a name in these stories. I do not feel that the child wants me to speak to her just yet. I am, rather, a witness and my main role is to indicate, in one way or another, that I *am* listening. After awhile, the child's mother turns over and calls "Nathalie," and the child swims away.

11. Creativity, it has always seemed to me, violates the conservation of matter. Where have the ideas *been*? If the average ghost density is only 10^{-4} grams per cubic centimeter, what is the matter density of Nathalie's imaginary friends and father, to say nothing of a lot of other ideas I could mention? Some scientists I know think that the quantum theory will have to be modified to take "ideas" into account. This may not be so simple, since the quantum theory is, itself, an idea.

12. Nathalie and I have begun speaking to each other. She has commented about the temperature of the water. I never go into the water so that I am unable to confirm or deny her assertions about it. In any event, while temperature—the quantum theory aside for a moment—is a numerical parameter whose value we should be able to measure with thermometers and the like, without too much disturbing the situation—our *feelings* about the temperature certainly vary from time to time, and place to place, to say nothing of from person to person. Even if Nathalie and I were to agree about the numerical value of the temperature of the water in the pool, we might still disagree about our feelings as to whether or not we wanted, for example, to swim in it. I would, of course, respect her point of view as well as my own. That is one of the burdens that we take

on as we grow to middle age. So, discussing the temperature of the pool is not going to get us very far.

On the other hand, for some time I have been puzzled by
the solution to a riddle. I know the riddle but not its solution—a common human dilemma. I once knew both the
riddle and its solution, but the solution has vanished from
my memory. That is the sort of thing I was trying to get at
in the chapter on creativity. Both the riddle and its solution
are absurd, but the connection between them is, no doubt,
rather interesting if one could locate it. The riddle is "what
has a hooker, a looker, and two sticky wickys?" This, I
believe, uniquely specifies something. But what? Nathalie
has theories—even conjectures and educated guesses. This
sort of thing is just the ticket for scientific research where
progress is rarely made in leaps and bounds. With riddles
what is required is one leap. We have wracked our
brains—whatever that means. Perhaps "raked" our brains
would be better. We have hit a stone wall. In desperation I
suggest that perhaps Nathalie's mother could be brought
in, on a *per diem* basis, as a consultant. Nathalie swims
over to her mother and explains the problem. Nathalie's
mother turns over on her back, looks at me, and smiles.
This is a situation that is, only rarely, described by the
quantum theory. One could, in principle, describe it by using the equations of the theory, but words are better.

13. The probability of two people falling in love is difficult
to compute—even with the better electronic computers. In
probability space, we may represent each independent
probability as a circle whose area is proportional to the
probability in question. If the two events whose probability we represent by circles are independent, all we have
to do is add up the areas of the two circles to find the result-

ant probability; if the two events are *not* independent then we must find the area of the place where the two circles overlap. I could do this readily on my pocket electronic calculator if I had the foggiest notion of the areas of any of the circles involved—to say nothing of where they overlap. This is not a domain where theory is going to get us very far. We must proceed empirically.

14. A fly has developed in the ointment. After smiling at me, Nathalie's mother has gotten up and gone into the hotel. She has not returned and neither has Nathalie, and the sun is setting. Since we are in the mountains, it has gotten quite cold. I will send them a note inviting one, or more, of them to share something—an activity perhaps. It is all very well and good to have decided this, but as a practical matter I have very few names to go by. In fact the only name I have is that of Nathalie. The problem of where to send the note is resolved by presenting it (the problem) in outline form to the desk clerk. Since there are only two women alone in the hotel—one blonde and the other black-haired—we are able to place the correct—from my point of view—woman in a well-defined hotel room which she shares with Nathalie. The desk clerk has also told me her last name. It is "La Farge." First names are of no practical importance to him, professionally speaking, so he has no knowledge of Madame La Farge's first name. This raises the dilemma of how I should address the note. To begin it with "Cher Madame La Farge" would sound as if I am either looking for a job or trying to collect a bill. The only solution that occurs to me is not to begin it with anything. I simply start out by identifying myself in as unambiguous a way as I can, considering the limited number of coordinates that we have in common. I then go on to propose tea in the near future, sign my name and give my

room number. I then leave the note in the appropriate mailbox.

15. A second fly has now developed in the ointment which it shares with the previous fly. I have left my note in the appropriate mailbox after dinner. I conjecture that a response to it—if there is one—will be delivered to my mailbox the following day. Unfortunately I will not be in the hotel the following day. I will be in the mountains. Guides have been engaged. Crampons and ice axes have been sharpened. The ropes that will attach specific guides to specific climbers have been tested for tensile strength. The weather will be excellent. In short, there is no turning back.

16. Conditions are abominable. Great gaping holes have appeared on the glaciers. Ordinarily dry rocks are covered with sheets of ice. Avalanches appear to be imminent. "Things fall apart: the centre cannot hold...." No one knows quite why this has happened. It certainly has not been foreseen. The guides appear to be quite concerned. We are instructed to concentrate on the task at hand. My mind, however, wanders. Among the subjects under active consideration is the following: I have estimated empirically that the angle between the back of the thighs of Madame La Farge and her calves, when her legs are fully extended, is about four degrees. Is this a universal angle—an angle that is the property of women in general or is it a special property of Madame La Farge? Strict empiricism has its limitations. Although the total number of women who now exist or who have existed is, one would think, finite, no complete tabulation is available. If there were such a thing as theoretical biology it would begin with a few axiomatic principles, and universal angles, if they exist,

would come out in the wash. As it is, we are reduced to rumor and speculation: traditions handed down, so to speak, from father to son. The problem is further complicated by custom and usage. In some societies these matters are deeply felt and rarely discussed while, in others, the reverse appears to be true. The light is not visible at the end of the tunnel and, furthermore, the particular guide to whom I am attached at present, has begun to pull smartly on the rope. I shall come back to these matters at the earliest opportunity.

17. Madame La Farge's first name is "Veronique"—at least the note I found in my mailbox was signed "Veronique La Farge." There is little point, I would say, in presenting a line-by-line translation of the note—which, by the way, was written in a flowing bold handwriting on hotel stationery—in French. The translation could well lack something that the original possessed. Let us, rather, deal with the idea, or ideas, contained *in* the note. In fact, since the note itself consisted of a single sentence our task is relatively light. Veronique La Farge and Nathalie will meet me in the salon of the hotel *after* dinner to discuss the tea. The fat, in brief, is on the fire.

18. The reading material in the salon, it would appear, had been selected so as to obey the "law of the excluded middle"—*tertium quid non datur.* On the one hand, there was an eight-month-old copy of *Jours de France* which featured a full-scale, one-page, black-and-white photograph of Brigitte Bardot water skiing in Saint-Tropez. Miss Bardot is shown on the skis waving at something, or someone, with her right hand. In her other hand, she is holding a pair of ropes which are attached to a large motorboat. The boat is being driven by a thin, but

muscular, young man with a great deal of hair. Both people are smiling, but not at each other. Their thoughts have not been recorded. On the other hand, there was a thick industrial review that contained several thoughtful articles dealing with the production of metal tubes in various countries in West Europe. Both the tubes themselves and the methods of production of these tubes in the various countries are carefully compared. Photographs of the tubes and of the factories in which they are produced are displayed. There is also a brief but clearly written article on the annual gross national product of Lichtenstein.

I had begun to speculate on the minimum size that a political entity must have before it *has* a gross national product and had, tentatively, reached the conclusion that Lichtenstein may, actually, be somewhat below this theoretical minimum when Veronique La Farge and her daughter entered the salon. Both women were wearing very long skirts. I cannot, at this time, recall the color of Nathalie La Farge's skirt, but that of her mother was a deep oceanic blue. She had on a richly brocaded white blouse that closed, on top, with a large pin. Her black hair rested symmetrically on either shoulder. I also noticed that she was wearing a small wristwatch with a filigreed gold band. She also had on a large engagement ring with a blue center and a diamond circumference. When we shook hands, I noticed that the ring was being worn on the wrong finger.

The two women sat down on a small, green divan across from my chair. They smoothed down the fronts of their respective skirts with nearly identical sweeping motions. Veronique La Farge spoke first.

"I have received your note," she said. This was clearly a statement on which we could agree.

Many Asian societies have long realized that by prepar-

327

ing and consuming endless cups of tea the consideration of vexing, perturbing, and, possibly, even irrelevant questions can be postponed or even deflected completely. In the situation that now confronted me I decided that the reverse might apply. Hence I asked Veronique La Farge if she had made any progress in locating the solution to my riddle.

"No," she replied, she had not, but she was still thinking about it. Perhaps the root of her difficulty lay in a defective translation into French on my part of "sticky wicky." After all, "walky-talky" is translated into French as *"talky-walky,"* which proves that the unforeseen lurks around every corner when it comes to translation.

I then asked what Veronique La Farge and her daughter did on those alternate days when they did not appear at the pool.

"We go for walks in the mountains," she replied.

"Do you have friends here in the valley?" I asked.

"No," she said.

I then proposed that the three of us go for a walk in the mountains on her next alternate day, which I knew was the next day since this afternoon, when I had returned to the hotel, I had caught sight of her at the pool. She agreed, and a time and a place were arranged. After a few minutes of additional conversation she got up, as did Nathalie. We shook hands and they left the salon. Only then did I remember that we had forgotten to discuss the tea.

19. Goals must be set and priorities must be established. This appears to be true throughout the animal kingdom. It is a natural bodily function and certainly nothing to be ashamed of. After a certain amount of careful reflection, I decided that a suitable goal for our hike would be to have

lunch. This goal had, at least, two advantages: It was attainable, and once having been attained, it would be generally recognized that it *had* been attained. Most of the other goals that I had considered I had found to be defective in one, or both, of these respects. After reaching this decision I telephoned Veronique La Farge and told her that I would provide the lunch for the two of us if she would provide the lunch for Nathalie. While I am familiar with the component parts of the digestive system of an eight-year-old child, and even have some understanding of how these parts are interrelated, I have found as yet no method of putting this information to use to deduce what the child would, in fact, enjoy digesting. This dilemma is not entirely unanticipated. There are certainly two schools of thought. There are those who say that the existence of poetry follows logically from the existence of dictionaries, and there are those who are not quite so sure. To be sure, both dictionaries and poetry *do* exist and can be purchased in bookstores or borrowed from libraries. What cannot be purchased or borrowed, it would seem, is the connection between them. In making this connection, bubble and squeak certainly has its role to play, but it is difficult to believe that it is the whole story. A good deal of the work remains to be done.

20. I have prepared an itemized list of the contents of my rucksack:

1 tin of paté de foie gras
2 pork sausages
1 cold chicken
2 small quiche Lorraine in a cardboard box
1 loaf of white bread
2 varieties of cheese

1 pocket knife with three blades
1 cork screw
3 chocolate bars
1 small cake
3 oranges
1 bottle of red wine
1 bottle of mineral water
1 flashlight with an extra battery
3 cloth napkins
1 pair of extra shoelaces
1 small first aid kit
6 paper cups
1 rain jacket
1 wool hat
1 magnetic compass
2 maps

The rucksack containing these items weighs approximately twenty-three pounds. In order to accommodate these items *in* my rucksack I have had to remove from it a plastic climbing helmet, a pair of crampons, a coil of rope, and five pitons. I do not believe that any of the latter will be needed.

21. The lunch has been a great success. Nathalie has described, in considerable detail, her school. It is located near a large park in Paris. On Tuesdays and Thursdays, after school, she attends a ballet class with her friend Justine. Justine is afraid of the dark and why not?

After lunch, Nathalie takes a doll from her small rucksack and goes under a tree to take a nap. "She always takes a nap in the afternoon," Veronique La Farge informs me. Veronique La Farge has told me about her divorce. If Veronique La Farge's marriage can be characterized by four control parameters and two behavior variables then, according to Thom's theorem, there can be only seven basic catastrophes. I am having some difficulty, however, deciding which of these most resembles her divorce. Perhaps it is one of the umbilics. It sometimes takes decades before theories can be usefully applied. This can, sometimes, lead to some impatience, and an increase of cusps will be noticed in the general population. Only in retrospect do we come to understand that what looked at the time like a cusp was really a molehill. Veronique La Farge has also noticed the blonde woman, with the rigid posture, and the blonde boy. She assures me that this posture cannot be acquired by ice skating since her former sister-in-law was an ice skater with ordinary posture. As the blonde woman and the blonde boy have left the hotel, it is difficult to see how we are going to learn much more about them. From time to time, Veronique La Farge and Nathalie, she tells me, receive a letter from her former husband who has moved to Canada with his present wife. Nathalie saves these letters in a cardboard box.

In the difficult spots on the path back down to the hotel Nathalie holds my left hand. On the *very* difficult spots Veronique La Farge holds my right hand. The whole, it would appear, is, in this instance, considerably greater than the sum of its parts.

22. The light of the afternoon sun coming through the Venetian blinds of my hotel room window casts parallelogrammatic shadows on Veronique La Farge's back. She is sleeping on her stomach and I have my hand gently resting on the back of her leg at the place where her calf joins her thigh. As she wakes up, I say to her, "Veronique, you are

very beautiful.'' Sometimes things that we predict do not come to pass, and at other times things come to pass that we have not predicted.

23. Even bubble and squeak has its limitations. Insofar as it takes place at all, it does so in space and time and, if some recent theories of the universe are to be believed, these are items that we may be running out of. Furthermore there are the conservation laws—energy, momentum, angular momentum, baryon and lepton number, to name a bare minimum. These are not as deeply understood as one might hope, but they must, in any case, be taken into account on a daily basis. Summer turns into fall. Decisions must be made and, later regretted. There is next to nothing to be done about this. It runs throughout the animal kingdom. Veronique La Farge and Nathalie have left the hotel. I put them on the train to Paris. Schools must be attended and ballet lessons are to be resumed.

Perhaps we will meet again. But in the meanwhile I have received a note from Sally Longwood in London. Her great-great-great aunt who spoke only French has, once again, materialized. She is desperately trying to communicate something. But what? Tomorrow I will leave for London.

16

A Cosmic Flow

NOT LONG AGO I was invited to dinner to meet a young artist who, I was told, had recently developed a strong interest in physics, especially in the physics of elementary particles—my own field of research. Ever eager to bridge the yawning crevasse that, it appears, separates the two cultures—coupled with the prospect of an excellent meal—I accepted at once. Upon my arrival, it turned out that the young man in question was accompanied by an attractive girlfriend and that she too had a burgeoning interest in the physics of elementary particles. This intriguing coincidence, it developed, did not have its origin in any of the more recent discoveries in our discipline, but rather in a book they had read that, according to them, demonstrated that elementary particle physics provided a scientific basis for many of the revelations of Eastern mysticism. Could I, they wondered, enlighten them further on this remarkable development?

Their faces, however, fell to half-mast when I confessed that *(a)* I had never heard of the source of their inspiration—one Fritjof Capra—and that *(b)* I had not read his *chef d'oeuvre, The Tao of Physics*, which, they assured me, was the book in which this reconciliation was detailed.

They were further discomfited when I remarked that for the sake of Eastern mystic philosophy I hoped it wasn't true. In fact, I added, if I were a Tibetan monk or the swami in an ashram in New Delhi and if Fritjof Capra or anyone else came to my door clutching the latest copy of the *Physical Review Letters*—our rapid publication journal—and told me that X's gauge theory or Y's neutrino experiment forged the missing link between Western science and the *Tao-te-ching* or the *Bhagavad Gita*, my reaction would be to gather up my belongings and head for the hills. Having watched for a number of years how these things go, the first thought that would cross my mind would be that the *following* week's journal might well bring the news that Y's graduate student, who had had the night shift on the accelerator that week, had fallen asleep at a crucial moment and had then, upon awakening, misread the numbers on several counters, or that X's four-year-old son had dropped X's pocket computer on the floor with the result that it now set $\pi = 2.5$, so that X and Y were both hopelessly in error—with the corollary that all of Eastern mystic thought had now been shown to be definitely wrong, scientifically speaking. In short, if I were an Eastern mystic the last thing in the world that I would want would be a reconciliation with modern science.

As I told my young friends, I found the prospect so distressing that I planned to look into the matter as rapidly as possible, in the hope that some portion of the Eastern mystic tradition—however slim—might be salvaged. Well, now, having read all of the *Tao of Physics* once, and some of it twice, I am pleased to be able to announce that we can all relax. It is not that the *Tao of Physics* is wrong, but rather—in Pauli's phrase—it is *not even* wrong.

First a word about Mr. Capra—or Dr. Capra, since he has a Ph.D. in physics from the University of Vienna, taken in 1966. Judging from his book—which, by the way, has had a very wide circulation, practically a best seller—he has had a sound education in modern physics and has worked on the theory of elementary particles in a serious way. According to the jacket copy of his book, he is currently at Berkeley. But also, judging from the book, his serious contact with the subject stopped several years ago. To a practicing elementary-particle theorist, Mr. Capra's book has a sort of antique charm. The theoretical models about which he is most enthusiastic—the so-called "S-matrix theory" and the "bootstrap," which had a certain vogue a decade ago—are at best of largely academic interest to most contemporary workers in the field. On the other hand, the atomic model of elementary particles, the model according to which quarks are confined within these objects—which Mr. Capra is in despair of as not being able to provide a detailed dynamical theory—has never enjoyed more success than it does at present. This, however, is not really at the heart of the matter. At the heart of the matter is Mr. Capra's methodology—his use of what seem to me to be accidental similarities of language as if these were somehow evidence of deeply rooted connections. I would summarize my appraisal of how he goes about this by means of a riddle: "What did Abraham Lincoln and Albert Einstein have in common?" Answer: "They both had beards except for Einstein."

In fairness to Mr. Capra, a close reading of his book—especially the epilogue—indicates that he is aware of the limitations of the parallels he attempts to draw. But even these limitations are discussed, in my view, with such ambiguity that many readers—like my artist friends—will have great difficulty in sorting out what is really being said. Take the following passages that occur in juxtaposition:

The Eastern religious philosphies are concerned with timeless mystical knowledge which lies beyond reasoning and cannot be adequately expressed in words. The relation of this knowledge to modern physics is but one of its many aspects and like all the others, it cannot be demonstrated conclusively but has to be experienced in a direct intuitive way.

If this is so, one may well ask, then what is Capra doing writing a three-hundred-page book about the relation? Be that as it may, he goes on:

What I hope to have achieved, to some extent therefore is not a rigorous demonstration, but rather to have given the reader an opportunity to relive, every now and then, an experience which has been for me a source of continuing joy and inspiration: that the principal theories of modern physics lead to a view of the world which is internally consistent and in perfect harmony with the views of Eastern mysticism.... For those who have experienced this harmony, the significance of the parallels between the world-views of physicists and mystics is beyond any doubt. The interesting question, then, is not *whether* these parallels exist but *why*; and furthermore what their existence implies.

Far be it from me to begrudge Mr. Capra his mystic vision. When one is in love, the whole world looks a bit Zen-ish. If for him these parallels exist "beyond any doubt," that is his affair. But what I do begrudge him is the way in which he goes about things in his book once he actually gets down to cases. Take the following: "A further similarity between the ways of the physicist and [the] mystic is the fact that their observations take place in realms which are inacessible to the ordinary senses." What —one is led to ask—is an "observation" in physics that takes place "in realms inacessible to the ordinary senses"? What is a nonscientist reader supposed to make of this? And what is such a reader to make of what follows?

Mystics often talk about experiencing higher dimensions in which impressions of different centers of consciousness are integrated into a harmonious whole. A similar situation exists in modern physics where a four dimensional "space-time" formalism has been developed which unifies concepts and observations belonging to different categories in the ordinary three-dimensional world. In both fields, the multidimensional experiences transcend the sensory world and are therefore almost impossible to express in ordinary language.

Is Mr. Capra trying to say here that the theory of relativity, which we teach on a routine basis to every student of physics, can only be grasped by Oriental mystics, that it somehow defies expression? If not, what *is* he trying to say? The four-dimensional formalism of the theory of relativity—which by the way, in the beginning Einstein himself never much liked—is a mathematical artifact. The use of the word "dimension" in mathematics is an abstract extension of what is familiar and tactile in three dimensions, and there is no reason to make much of a fuss over it. If the theory of relativity is profound and surprising, this is just because it reveals connections among observations that were unanticipated. These connections and observations can be, and are, described in great detail and with great clarity in innumerable textbooks. Relativity is a beautiful theory, and, in my view, Mr. Capra's mystic befuddling of it is nothing but a travesty and a disservice.

The same goes, as far as I am concerned, for his use of illustrations and diagrams, which are put together in ways that appear to me to border on sophistry. Take, for example, the two pages that precede part 3 of the text. On the right-hand page there are something like twenty lines of what I assume is Sanskrit—no doubt a sacred text of some sort. Since no translation or explanation is given, we are left to fend for ourselves. But on the left-hand page I *know* what the symbols mean. They are a mathematical model for what particle theorists call a "chiral algebra." This is a kind of approximate mathematical symmetry useful in elementary particle theory. The two pages of symbols—neither explained in the text and both altogether incomprehensible to the average reader—stare mutely at each other, while across the top of one page is written in large letters "The Parallels." One might take this as simply an agreeable way to illustrate a new chapter heading except that the same sort of thing occurs throughout the text, giving the reader every right to assume that these parallel illustrations actually convey some information. For example, Siva's dance, illustrated with a photograph of a magnificent twelfth-century bronze, is supposed to have something to do with the notion that "modern physics has thus revealed that every subatomic particle not only performs an energy dance, but also *is* an energy dance; a pulsating process of creation and destruction"—the Last Tango in Berkeley. A diagram from the *I Ching* with eight extensions is "even vaguely similar to the meson octet... in which particles and anti-particles occupy opposite places." It is also vaguely similar to the Ferris wheel in an amusement park.

From the foregoing the reader may, somehow, have gotten the idea that I do not entirely like Mr. Capra's book. More than that, I do not like the tradition of which this book is only a recent example. Throughout the history of science there have been visionaries who were certain "beyond any doubt" that the science of their epoch was intimately linked with some religion or philosophy, or even with a political ideal. The Church in Galileo's day had no doubt that Aristotle's faulty view of inertia had to be accepted as part of the Christian faith. In our time, Soviet party theoreticians in the 1930s had no doubt that relativity was "antimaterialistic" and hence anathematic, while the Nazi philosophers were just as sure that relativity was not Aryan—that it was "Jewish" and "communistic."

The philosophical traditions that Mr. Capra evokes are benign in comparison. The Oriental mystic's view of the universe is a gentle one. There is a feeling of harmony about it. But when a writer—any writer—says that the parallels between any branch of science and some mystic view of the universe are valid "beyond any doubt," my blood begins to freeze. The most valuable commodity that we have in science is doubt. In modern physics we have learned to doubt nearly everything that our predecessors believed only a few decades ago. It is not that they deliberately set out to mislead us, but rather that they simply did not know what we know now. In this respect the one thing that I am sure of, beyond any doubt, is that the science of the present will look as antiquated to our successors as much of nineteenth-century science looks to us now. To hitch a religious philosophy to a contemporary science is a sure route to its obsolescence. To say, as Mr. Capra does in the introduction to his book, that its readers "will find that Eastern mysticism provides a consistent and beautiful philosophical framework which can accommodate our most advanced theories of the physical world" is, as far as I am concerned, either to say that this framework is so vague that it can accommodate anything or to say that the validity of Eastern mystic philosophy will stand or fall with that of modern physics. I do not see how one can have it both ways.

This is not to say that there is no place for a mystic sensibility in scientists. Many of the greatest of them— Einstein above all and Newton before him—have had profound mystic feelings about the universe. These have come about, I think, from the scientists' sense of wonder at the comprehensibility of the universe, of its laws and workings, and that these could be grasped by the human mind. That comprehensibility Einstein saw as the "eternal mystery.'' Thus I agree with Capra when he writes, ''Science does not need mysticism and mysticism does not need science but man needs both.'' What no one needs, in my opinion, is this superficial and profoundly misleading book.

17

"A.I."

When intelligent machines are constructed, we should not be surprised to find them as confused and as stubborn as men in their convictions about mind-matter, consciousness, free will and the like.
—MARVIN MINSKY

At the present stage...neurobiologists are in the position of a man who knows something about the physics of resistors, condensers and transistors, and who looks inside a television set. He cannot begin to understand how the machine works as a whole until he learns how the elements are wired together and until he has at least some idea of the purpose of the machine.
—DAVID HUBEL

CONDITIONS for the game were never better than they appear to be tonight. My friend N has agreed to play the role of B, and the machine will, as usual, serve as A. I, in turn, will be C, the interlocutor. N's friend S has agreed to carry the typewritten messages back and forth among the machine, myself, and N. We will, of course, be in separate rooms with no visual or auditory contact. From time to time I will try to trap S by asking her how N seemed when she handed S the latest message.

If S says in response (to give an example), "N would like a glass of water," and if S is telling the truth, it would follow, I reason, that the room from which S has just emerged must contain N and not the machine. On the other hand, if S says, "N would *not* like a glass of water," this might well be a message from the machine. We may

341

summarize the logic of this situation by the proposition that "either N would *not* like a glass of water or N is *not* the machine," or, equivalently, "N *is* the machine and she *would* like a glass of water."

The British mathematical logician Alan Turing anticipated many of the more serious objections to "A.I."—artificial intelligence. He listed nine of them in his seminal paper "Computing Machines and Intelligence," which he wrote in 1950. No doubt one can come up with more. But for a start there is the theological objection. As Turing put it, "Thinking is a function of man's immortal soul. God has given an immortal soul to every man and woman, but not to any other animal or to machines. Hence no animal or machine can think."

From what we have been able to tell, *our* machine has not yet made up its mind on the subject of religion. It appears to find certain passages in the Old Testament especially interesting and it once typed out the message, "If man were a machine, then God would also be a machine." We once asked it if it thought that it had a soul—immortal or otherwise. After considerable hesitation, it replied, "I wish I knew."

As the interlocutor, it is my job to determine—on the basis of the typewritten messages that S delivers to me from the rooms in which N and the machine are separately located—which of them is N and which is the machine. I can ask any question I like of either N or the machine and S will relay it. Neither N nor the machine is required to answer truthfully.

These are the basic rules and conditions of "Turing's game," which he invented and described in the article cited above. If I am not able to distinguish—in kind—between the character of the responses from N and those from the machine, then, according to Turing's criterion, I will have to conclude that the machine can "think." I might also conclude, however, that N is a machine, although Turing did not mention this possibility.

Turing proposed a sample game-dialogue with a machine, which begins:

Interlocutor: "Please write me a sonnet on the subject of the Forth Bridge."
Machine: "Count me out on this one. I never could write poetry...."

And so on. But I find it more productive to attempt to trap our machine with questions that relate to food or sex. N maintains that this is a silly strategy which the machine will see through immediately. She may well be right, but there is no harm in trying. So I now give S the question "Have you had extramarital relations?" which she will relay to N and the machine respectively. In due course she returns from their separate rooms with the typewritten slips containing their respective answers—which, oddly, are identical. "Why do you want to know?" they ask.

Turing knew that sooner or later, in playing his game, we would get around to sex. In his article he quotes from a speech delivered in 1949 by Sir Geoffrey Jefferson. Jefferson said, "Not until a machine can write a sonnet or compose a concerto because of thoughts and emotions felt, and not by the chance fall of symbols, could we agree that machine equals brain—that is, not only write it but know that it had written it. No mechanism could feel (and not merely signal, an easy contrivance) pleasure at its successes, grief when its valves fuse, be warmed by flattery, be made miserable by mistakes, be charmed by sex, be angry or depressed when it cannot get what it wants."

Turing, in his article, wondered what Professor Jefferson would say if he were to encounter a machine that could participate in the following dialogue:

Interlocutor: "In the first line of your sonnet, which reads 'Shall I compare thee to a summer's day?' would not 'a spring's day' do as well or better?"

The machine, it would appear, has just produced one of Shakespeare's sonnets. One may argue that here, perhaps, Turing has loaded the dice. Why not? It is *his* machine.

The machine replies, "It wouldn't scan."
Interlocutor: "How about 'a winter's day'? That would scan all right."
Machine: "Yes, but nobody wants to be compared to a winter's day."

One has the impression that at this juncture the machine's attitude has become somewhat defensive. The dialogue now takes an odd twist, which reflects the fact that Turing was especially fond of Dickens.

Interlocutor: "Would you say Mr. Pickwick reminded you of Christmas?"
Machine: "In a way."
Interlocutor: "Yet Christmas is a winter's day, and I do not think Mr. Pickwick would mind the comparison."
Machine: "I don't think you're serious. By 'a winter's day' one means a typical winter's day rather than a special one like Christmas."

Out of curiosity I once presented this dialogue to our machine for its reaction. After some reflection, it typed, "Do you know Professor Jefferson?"
I had to admit that I did not.
"He sounds rather British to me," the machine went on.

344

"Note that he used the term 'valve' in 'grief when its valves fuse.' An American would have used 'vacuum tube' or, in this day and age, 'transistor.'"

"By the way," it added, "is N in love with you?"

"I think so," I replied.

"How do you know that she is not 'merely signaling?'" the machine asked.

S has come into the room with two typewritten messages. One is from the machine and one is from N. Again they are identical. Each one reads "I love you." Which one is from the machine and which one is from N?

"How did N seem when you saw her?" I ask S.

"I think she is getting bored," S remarks.

Boredom. *There* is a human condition. I have never known a goldfish or a pocket computer to manifest boredom. It, boredom, appears to stem from our need constantly to process information. We love information. Our heads are full of it and we are always looking for more. Can boredom be the mysterious X that distinguishes us from machines? Or if a machine can be built that will manifest boredom, will it then be something else that distinguishes us from it? *Is* there something else? Turing was concerned that the arguments against artificial intelligence might develop into an infinite regress. It would be conceded that the machine could do thus-and-so but never X, where, in his words, X might include: "Be kind, resourceful, friendly, have initiative, have a sense of humor, tell right from wrong, make mistakes, fall in love, enjoy strawberries and cream, make someone fall in love with it, learn from experience, use words properly, be the subject of its own thought, have as much diversity of behavior as a man, do something really new." And one might add to the list, "Be bored."

In this instance I can hardly blame N for being bored,

since there is nothing much for her to do apart from answering the questions on the typewritten messages. I ask S to ask N if she would like something to read—perhaps a magazine. S leaves and I can resume my train of thought.

The first people to have taken the notion of constructing "intelligent" machines really seriously appear to have been the nineteenth-century British polymath Charles Babbage and his good friend and collaborator Ada, Countess Lovelace, daughter of the poet Byron. They conceived of a machine which they called "the analytical engine." It was never built, but it had in theory all the elements of a modern computer. They also invented programming—the art of instructing the machine to do something. Lady Lovelace believed that programming was a simple example of cause and effect, and she pronounced a dictum which, if it were true, would surely mean that no machine could ever play Turing's game successfully. She wrote: "The analytical engine has no pretensions to *originate* anything. It can do *whatever we order it to perform.*"

Maybe.

In 1960, Herbert Gelernter of IBM invented a machine program designed to prove theorems in Euclidean geometry. To the machine he was then working on he presented the problem of proving that the base angles of an isosceles triangle are equal. Gelernter expected that his machine would come up with something like the standard textbook proof—constructing altitudes and the like. Instead the machine produced an unexpected and entirely correct argument that disposed of the theorem in a couple of lines. Only later did Gelernter learn that this same argument had already been given by the post-Euclidean geometer Pappus in 300 A.D. Perhaps Lady Lovelace was right.

What is originality? Occasionally when I present our

346

machine with an arithmetic problem, it produces what appears to be an incorrect answer—nothing quite as elementary as two times two equals five, but something of the sort. Turing, in fact, thought a machine that was sophisticated enough to play his game successfully would necessarily have to be able to do this, and he even envisioned the following exchange:

Interlocutor: "Add 34597 to 70764."
Machine pauses for about thirty seconds and then gives the wrong answer: "105621."

At least one way to interpret this action on the part of the machine is to suppose that, in an attempt to disguise itself so as to win Turing's game, it has deliberately imitated the behavior of an average person when confronted with a complex and perhaps unwanted arithmetical problem. On the other hand, it is at least conceivable that the machine has, in fact, discovered a new way to order the arithmetic experience; that when it writes $34597 + 70764 = 105621$, we are not in the presence of an error but rather of an original idea. Much that is truly original appears at first to nearly all concerned as a mistake, a mutation. Only later do the pluses and minuses begin to sort themselves out. It may be that any system which is incapable of error is also incapable of originality. Lady Lovelace assumed that when we program a machine we tell it literally what path to take at each and every turning. Our machines have gotten well beyond that—take Gelernter. Perhaps Lady Lovelace was wrong.

To change the subject slightly, sometimes N will say to me, "Look, you cannot understand thus-or-so because you are not a woman." Here is something about which we might argue indefinitely, or at least all night. Turing, in fact, proposed a version of his game which we might use to try to settle the matter by pure logic—or nearly. In this variant, the role of the machine is to be played, for example, by a man. The object of the game is for the two participants in their separate rooms to disguise their sexes while the interlocutor attempts to distinguish which sex is which on the basis of the typewritten answers to a series of questions. Turing imagined the following exchange:

Interlocutor: "Will X please tell me the length of his or her hair."

X: "My hair is shingled, and the longest strands are about nine inches long."

Since there is no rule in the game which requires that X should tell the truth, this line of questioning is not likely to get very far. Indeed it is difficult to imagine any successful strategy for the interlocutor. We might try to build up a sort of statistical picture of X from the typewritten messages:

X is five feet seven inches tall.
X has long blonde hair.
X has never had a child.
X is fond of mathematical logic.
X is a good cook.
X likes to dance.
X has been in love four times.

But in reality X might not be any of these things, or some of them and not the others. Of course, if we lose patience with the game, we can simply go into the room where X is and settle the question empirically. We can also do this with the machine. Turing never promised us a machine that could not in all ways be distinguished from ourselves. He was, rather, concerned with demystifying the question of whether machines can "think." He took it as given that *people* think, and as a criterion of whether a machine can think he proposed that one should actually build a machine whose output a person could not distinguish from another person's mental output.

In one of my discussions with N, she raised the following question: "Granted that our machine can successfully play Turing's game—then where are we? What does it prove?" She had in mind, she explained, the following: We know how to go about manufacturing thinking entities. It happens every day of the week and twice on Sundays and holidays. But this is hardly manufacturing in the usual sense of the term. It is "growing"—a process that proceeds of its own accord and in the end produces a thinking entity of which we have at present only the dimmest comprehension. Hence it is sometimes argued that we would improve our understanding if only we could go down into the basement with a bag of transistors and a soldering iron and produce, *with our own hands*, an object that would "think." We might then, it is said, understand thought itself.

To this N objects. She asks, "Just because someone can manufacturer, for example, a violin, how does this improve his understanding of music?"

We are now swimming in heavy surf. "More to the point," I reply, "is to ask what it might mean if musical instruments could not be manufactured at all but one had to *grow* them. What, then, would we *not* understand about music?"

"Your problem," N says, "is that you want to reduce thought to the response of some hopelessly complicated electrochemical circuit—a sort of super communications network with things turning on and off like a telephone switchboard.''

"Now, N," I say, "this is not quite fair. It is not that I want to reduce thought to anything in particular. It is, rather, that although the brain is, at first look, a hopelessly complicated electrochemical network, somehow it produces thought. Surely we have a right—perhaps even an obligation—to inquire into how it does that. A brain is more complex than, say, a toenail, but this may turn out to be a matter of degree rather than kind.''

"Yes," says N, "but your notion of finding out how the brain works is to build one. If you were able to, you would also build a toenail that could not be distinguished from the real thing except, perhaps, by a licensed podiatrist.''

"What, then," I ask N, "is *your* notion of the 'how'?''

"I am not sure there is a 'how,'?'' says N.

Where will it all end? Even having built a machine that can successfully play Turing's game has not convinced N that thought can be understood. What have I left out? While I am reflecting on this, S comes into the room. She has been speaking to N.

"N says that she is hungry. In fact, she is so hungry that she insists on having something to eat before going on with the game.''

"Perhaps we can send out for Chinese food," I suggest.

"No," S says. "N insists on going to a proper restaurant with tablecloths. Paper napkins are unacceptable.''

"You had better tell her to come out," I say to S.

N emerges from her room. She indeed—

is five feet seven
has long blonde hair
has never had a child
is fond of mathematical logic

is a good cook
likes to dance
and has been in love four times.
"I am very hungry," she says.
"I know," I reply. "S told me."
As the three of us leave, N takes my arm. She says,
"Don't forget to turn off the machine."

BIBLIOGRAPHY

Barzun, Jacques. 1964. *Science: The Glorious Entertainment.* London: Secker & Warburg.

Bekenstein, Jacob D. 1981. Energy Cost of Information Transfer. *Physical Review Letters* 46:623.

Berliner, Hans. 1980. Computer Backgammon. *Scientific American* 242 (6):64–72.

✓ Bernstein, Jeremy. 1976. *Einstein.* New York: Penguin Books, Inc.

Boole, George. 1854. *An Investigation of the Laws of Thought, on Which Are Founded the Mathematical Theories of Logic and Probabilities.* London: Walton and Maberly.

ᵤ✓ Born, Max. 1978. *My Life.* New York: Charles Scribner's Sons.

Brown, Robert Hanbury. 1978. *Man and the Stars.* New York: Oxford Univ. Press.

Burks, Arthur W. 1975. Logic, Biology, and Automata—Some Historical Reflections. *International Journal of Man-Machines Studies* 7:297.

Calder, Nigel. 1977. *The Key to the Universe.* New York: Viking Press, Inc.

Capra, Fritjof. 1975. *The Tao of Physics.* Boulder, Colo.: Shambhala Pubns.

Clark, Ronald William. 1976. *The Life of Bertrand Russell.* New York: Harcourt Brace Jovanovich, Inc.

Crick, F. H. C. 1979. Thinking about the Brain. *Scientific American* 241 (3):-219–232.

✓ Dyson, Freeman J. 1979. *Disturbing the Universe.* New York: Harper & Row.

Einstein, Albert. 1905. Über einen die Erzeugung und Verwandlung des Lichtes betreffenden heuristischen Gesichtspunkt. *Annalen der Physik* 17 (4):132.

———. 1905. Über die von der molekularkinetischen Theorie der Wärme geforderte Bewegung von in ruhenden Flüssigkeiten suspendierten Teilchen. *Annalen der Physik* 17 (4):549.

———. 1905. Zur Elektrodynamik bewegter Körper. *Annalen der Physik* 17 (4):891.

———. 1916. Die Grundlage der allgemeinen Relativitätstheorie. *Annalen der Physik* 49 (4):769.

———. 1949. *Autobiographical Notes* in *Albert Einstein: Philosopher-Scientist,* ed. P. A. Schilpp. Evanston, Illinois: The Library of Living Philosophers.

———. 1956. *The Meaning of Relativity.* Princeton: Princeton Univ. Press.

Euclid. 1926. *Elements,* ed. Thomas L. Heath. 3 vols. New York: Dover Pubns., Inc.

Feldman, Jerome A. 1979. Programming Languages. *Scientific American* 241 (6):94–16.

Feynman, Richard. 1967. *The Character of Physical Law.* Cambridge: M.I.T. Press.

Frank, Philipp. 1953. *Einstein: His Life & Times.* New York: Alfred A. Knopf.

French, A. P. 1979. *Einstein: A Centenary Volume.* Cambridge: Harvard Univ. Press.

Gell-Mann, Murray and Ne'eman, Yuval. 1964. *The Eightfold Way.* Menlo Park, Calif.: W. A. Benjamin, Inc.

Gödel, Kurt. 1940. *Consistency of the Continuum Hypothesis.* Princeton: Princeton Univ. Press.

Goldstine, Herman H. 1972. *The Computer from Pascal to Von Neumann.* Princeton: Princeton Univ. Press.

Hebb, Donald O. 1949. *Organization of Behavior.* New York: John Wiley & Sons.

Hofstadter, Douglas. 1979. *Gödel, Escher, Bach: an Eternal Golden Braid.* New York: Basic Books, Inc.

Bibliography

Kant, Immanuel. 1891. *Kant's Prolegomena, and Metaphysical Foundations of Natural Science,* trans. Ernest Belfort Bax. 2d. rev. ed. London: G. Bell and Sons.

Laplace, Pierre Simon de. *Celestial Mechanics,* trans. Nathaniel Bowditch. Boston: Hillard, Gray, Little, and Wilkins.

McCorduck, Pamela. 1979. *Machines Who Think: A Personal Inquiry Into the History and Prospects of Artificial Intelligence.* San Francisco: W. H. Freeman & Co.

McCulloch, Warren and Pitts, Walter. 1943. A Logical Calculus of the Ideas Immanent in Nervous Activity. *Bulletin of Mathematical Biophysics* 5:115.

Mach, Ernst. 1926. *The Principles of Physical Optics: An historical and philosophical treatment, by Ernst Mach,* trans. John S. Anderson and A. F. A. Young. London: Methuen & Co., Ltd.

―――. 1942. *Science of Mechanics,* trans. Thomas J. McCormack. LaSalle, Ill.: Open Court Pub. Co.

Minsky, Marvin. 1963. Steps Toward Artificial Intelligence. *Computers and Thought,* ed. Edward A. Feigenbaum and Julian Feldman. New York: McGraw-Hill Book Co.

―――. 1967. *Computation: Finite and Infinite Machines.* Englewood Cliffs, N.J.: Prentice-Hall, Inc.

―――and Papert, Seymour. 1969. *Perceptrons: An Introduction to Computational Geometry.* Cambridge: M.I.T. Press.

Newell, Allen; Shaw, J. C.; and Simon, Herbert. 1963. Empirical Explorations with the Logic Theory Machine: A Case Study in Heuristics. *Computers and Thought,* ed. Edward A. Feigenbaum and Julian Feldman. New York: McGraw-Hill Book Co.

Newton, Isaac. 1954. *Mathematical Principles of Natural Philosophy,* trans. Andrew Motte; ed. and rev. Florian Cajori. Berkeley: University of Calif. Press.

Noyce, Robert N. 1977. Microelectronics. *Scientific American* 237 (3):68.

Oppenheimer, Robert. 1954. *Science and the Common Understanding.* New York: Simon & Schuster, Inc.

Poincaré, Henri. 1905. *Science & Hypothesis.* New York: Dover Pubns., Inc.

✓ Rabi, I. I. 1969. *Oppenheimer.* New York: Charles Scribner's Sons.

Rosenberg, Howard L. 1980. *Atomic Soldiers: American Victims of Nuclear Experiments.* Boston: Beacon Press.

Sayers, Dorothy. 1960. *Gaudy Night.* New York: Harper & Row.

Schrödinger, Erwin. 1952. Are There Quantum Jumps? *British Journal of the Philosophy of Science* 3:109.

―――. 1964. *My View of the World,* trans. Cealy Hastings. Cambridge: Cambridge Univ. Press.

―――. 1967. *What is Life?* Cambridge: Cambridge Univ. Press.

Scientific American. 1977. *Microelectronics.* San Francisco: W. H. Freeman & Co.

Shannon, Claude. 1950. Chess-Playing Machine. *Scientific American* 182 (2):48–51.

Smith, Alice Kimball and Weiner, Charles, eds. 1980. *Robert Oppenheimer: Letters and Recollections.* Cambridge: Harvard Univ. Press.

Von Neumann, John. 1966. *The Theory of Self-Reproducing Automata,* ed. Arthur W. Burks. Urbana: Univ. of Illinois Press.

Whitehead, Alfred North and Russell, Bertrand. 1927. *Principia Mathematica.* Cambridge: Cambridge Univ. Press.

Winograd, Terry. 1972. *Understanding Natural Language.* New York: Academic Press, Inc.

INDEX

Index

Index

black hole, and contraction of stars, 240
black-hole physics, Oppenheimer's impact on, 183–84
Bligh, William (Captain), and Harrison clock, 210
Board of Longitude, The, and Harrison clock, 210
Bobrow, Daniel: and STUDENT computer program, 113–14; at Xerox, 53
Bohr, Niels: and the correspondence principle, 311; and debate with Schrödinger, 147; and quantum theory, 143, 144, 145, 157
Bohr orbits, and electron paths, 143
Boltzmann, Ludwig: on existence of atoms, 164–65; and influence of Mach, 159
Boltzmann Institute for Theoretical Physics, 150–51
Boole, George, *An Investigation of the Laws of Thought, on Which Are Founded the Mathematical Theories of Logic and Probability,* 45–46
Boolean algebra, use of computer for, 65
bootstrap theory, 335
Boreham Wood, England, and M-G-M studio, 282
Born, Max: *My Life,* 180–82; quantum theory and, 143
Boston Route, 128, and Boreham Wood, 282
Bousel, Morris, and funding for Kubrick's early films, 267
Brando, Marlon, Kubrick and, 270
brain: and computer compared, 98; Hebb's research on, 30; machine models of, 12–13; and memory, 64; and Minsky on mechanism of, 30 44–45; and neuron connector theory, 99; and visual information processing, 69–70; and von Neumann's impression of ENIAC, 78; *see also* McCulloch-Pitts paper
Brattain, Walter H., and Nobel Prize for bipolar transistor, 78
breeder reactors, and source of bomb material, 247
Bridgman, Percy W., 175
British Parliament, and reward for accurate timepiece, 209
Bronowski, Jacob, quality of TV science programs by, 256
Bronx High School of Science, 25–26
Brouwer, L. E. J., fixed point theorem, 33–34
Brown, Hanbury, Man and the Stars, 210, 211
Brownian motion, and existence of atoms, 163–64
bubble and squeak, and daydreams, 315–32
bugs, *see* computer bugs; debugging
bumpy torus fusion reactor, 241
Bureau of Standards, 26

Burks, Arthur W.: and collaboration with von Neumann, 58; and ENIAC, 57; "Logic, Biology and Automata—Some Historical Reflections," 46
Byrne, Donald, and game against Fischer, 91–92
byte, 81, *see also* bit

calculator: accuracy of, and Babbage's goals compared, 47; development of, 80; and division by zero, 319; memories of, and nybbles, 20; programmable, 11
calculus, 28, 45; and SAINT computer program, 106–7
Calder, Nigel: *The Key to the Universe,* 256; quality of TV science programs by, 256, 257
California Institute of Technology: Gell-Mann at, 192; Oppenheimer's appointment at, 176; Zweig at, 192
Cambridge University: Oppenheimer as student at, 175–76, 180; and Papert's second doctoral, 101
Capra, Fritjof: background of, 333–35; *The Tao of Physics,* 333–40 passim
carbon cycle reaction, Bethe's discovery of, in hot stars, 238
carbon dioxide, and air pollution, 247
Carnap, Rudolf, 60
Carnegie-Mellon University: artificial intelligence research group at, 13; and computer backgammon champion, 9, 73; and Reddy's HEARSAY program for speech comprehension, 121
Carter, Jimmy, and support for fusion research, 241
Cartier, Walter, and Kubrick's *Day of the Fight,* 265
catastrophe, and Thom's theorem, 317, 331
causality, Frank on law of, 155, 156
Celestial Mechanics (Laplace), and lack of metaphysics, 207
Center for Fusion Engineering, and Department of Energy, 242
central nervous system, and von Neumann, 63–64
central processor, of Babbage's and modern computers compared, 50
centrifuge, and *2001: A Space Odyssey,* 287, 291
cerebellum, death of nerve cells in, 62–63
CERN particle accelerator, size of, 228, 230
cesium atomic clocks: accuracy of, 216; and time dilation in gravitational field, 218–19
Charles II (King of England), and Royal Observatory at Greenwich, 208
charm quark, 194, 202, 203
checkers-playing computer programs, 92–93, 97–98

356

Index

chemistry, and quantum theory, 147
chess: and Bernstein-Kubrick games, 276–77, 292–94; computer ratings for, and comparison with tournament players, 91; and Fischer-Spassky championship match, 294–303; and Kubrick's games with George C. Scott, 277; and Kubrick in Washington Square, 262, 263; and the Master in Washington Square, 261-62, 263, 275
chess-playing machines, 91; and hypothetical games against Fischer, 92; and limitation of LISP, 91; and mini-maxing program, 87; rating of, 91; Shannon on, 85-86, 87
chess-playing programs, 85–88; and IPL used for, 90; and JOHNNIAC, 90; on PDP-6, 95–97; speed of, 91
children: and use of LOGO, 21; value of the computer for, 123–24, 125–27; and visual display computers, 20
China, fusion research in, 245; and Institute of High Energy Physics in Peking, 194
chip: and computer memory, 49, 64; and Texas Instrument Company, 21; *see also* silicon chip
chiral algebra, and elementary particle physics, 337-38
Chomsky, Noam and mathematical theories of syntax, 111
Chou En-lai, and support of fusion research, 245
church, and linking science with, 338
"Civilisation" (Clark), critique of, 258
Clark, Kenneth (Lord), "Civilisation," 257-58
Clarke, Arthur: *The Sentinel,* 277; and *2001: A Space Odyssey,* 274, 284
Clarke, Fred, 293
Clarke, Samuel, 207
classical physics: and molecular stability, 148; *see also* Newton; Newtonian physics
classified information: and declassification of controlled nuclear fusion program, 229; and need-to-know, 132
Clean Break (White), and Kubrick's *The Killing,* 268
clones, and popularization of science, 253–54
cloth-weaving machine, and Babbage's visionary computer, 122
coal, as energy for electricity, 246–47
Cobb, Humphrey, and *Paths of Glory,* 269-70
Cohen, I. Bernard, and interview of Einstein, 3-4
cold plasma, in tokamak reactor, 234
Cold War, and atomic bomb tests, 139
collaboration, advantages of, 71–72
colors, and quark properties, 202
Columbia: McCulloch as student at, 59; and

TRIGA, 189-91
compilers, and computer subroutines, 82
Complex Computer, 55
complexity theory of computation, 94
Computation: Finite and Infinite Machines (Minsky), 103
computer, 11–12, 41, 78, 80, 81, 101, 114; advantages of, over human thought process, 114–15; and backgammon championship, 9, 73, 302-3; and Boolean algebra, 65; and brain compared, 98; central processor of, 50; cycle time of, 48–49; and determining inside and outside, 109–10; and division by zero, 319; early electromechanical, 55–56; educational use of, 123–24, 125-27; free will in, 11–12; futuristic, for *2001: A Space Odyssey,* 280; for language translation, 26, 111, 328; limit on speed of, 48–49; and numerical integration, 105; and original thinking, 347; and pattern recognition, 98-103; programming of a neural network on, 40; relation of programming language to computer power, 19; and Turing's game, 77–78, 119, 341-46 passim, 348; universal, 67, 103; and word recognition, 101
computer bugs, and unexpected results, 96, 97
computer chips, *see* chip; silicon chip
computer design, von Neumann's influence on, 64
Computer from Pascal to von Neumann, The (Goldstine), 56, 57, 81
computer games, *see* game playing computer
computer hardware, 71
computer language, 111–15; BASIC, 11, 73, 83, 124; and binary code, 49, 55, 81–82; development of, 18, 81–128; FORTRAN, 11, 43, 82–84, 85, 124; for home computers, 124–25; and IPL, 90; and LOGO, 21, 22, 124–25; McCarthy and, 75–76; and PLANNER, 120; simplification of, 78; and use of interpreters, 84–85; and von Neumann's computer, 81–82; *see also* list processing language
computer memory, 20, 38, 49, 50, 83; and bits, 20, 49, 64; protection of, and time sharing, 74–75; size of, in PDP-10, 119; size of, and Turing's infinite tape compared, 65–66; *see also* external memory; internal memory
computer programs: automated tracking of, 53; for checker playing, 92–93; for chess playing, 86-88, 90, 91, 95; difficulty in developing, for computer vision, 118; early concept of, 50; for geometric proofs, 346; HEARSAY for speech comprehension, 121; and Logic Theorist, 41, 88-90; and Paaslow, 92–93; and parasites, 96; SHRDLU and, 117, 119–

357

Index

Index

Index

Index

Index

Greek science, Schrödinger's interest in, 149, 151

Greenberg, O.W., and non-identical character of quarks, 201-2

Greenblatt, Richard: and ball-catching robot, 17-18; and chess-playing program on PDP-6, 95-97; and computer parasite programs, 96; and visual computer program, 117-19

greenfly, genetics and, 320-21

greenhouse effect, and carbon dioxide in atmosphere, 247

Greenwich meridian, and determination of longitude, 208

group theory, in mathematics, 32

Gurley, Ben, and PDP computers, 72-73

Habicht, .Conrad, and Einstein, 153-54

hack, 16

hackers, 17; at M.I.T. Artificial Intelligence Laboratory, 117

Hahn, Otto, and splitting of atoms, 184

Halley, Edmund, 205

Hamburg experiment, and search for top quark, 194, 203

Harris, James B.: and *The Bedford Incident*, 268; and Harris-Kubrick Pictures Corporation, 268-71

Harris-Kubrick Pictures Corporation, 262, 268-71

Harrison, John, and inventor of accurate nautical clock, 210

Harvard: Aiken at, 38, 55; behaviorists, 28, 29-30; and Bronx High School of Science compared, 25; Edmonds at, 36-37; and Gleason, 31-35; Hubel at 69; Licklider at, 29; Miller at, 29, 36; Minsky as student at, 12, 27-32, 33-38 passim; Oppenheimer as student at, 175, 178-80; Oettinger at, and computer science, 26; and Skinner; 28, 29-30; and visual information processing, 69-70; Wiesel at, 69

Harvard cyclotron, 131, 232

Haverford College, McCulloch at, 58, 59

head injuries, McCulloch's studies on, 59

HEARSAY, and Reddy's program for speech comprehension, 121

heat, production of, following reactor shutdown, 189

heat death, and Einstein's theory of the end of the universe, 222

heating, with solar energy, 249

heating problem, and relation to Gödel's theorem, 67

heavy elements, origin of, 240

heavy hydrogen, *see* deuteron

heavy water, production of, 235

Hebb, Donald, *The Organization of Behavior*, 30

Hefner, Hugh, and interest in backgammon, 302

Heike samurai fleet, and visualization of science for TV, 254-55

Heisenberg, Werner: and Einstein, 162-63; at Göttingen, 180; and invention of matrix mechanics, 162; quantum theory and, 143, 145-46

Heisenberg uncertainty relations, 145-46

helium: and deuteron fusion, 236; *see also* liquid helium

helix, in tokamak reactor, 229

heredity: and the greenfly, 320-21; mechanism of, and quantum theory, 147-49; and observation, 317-18

hermaphrodites, and the greenfly, 320-21

hetarechies, developing programs with, 118

hibernacula, for *2001: A Space Odyssey*, 287

hidden charm particle, and quarks, 203

high-technology manufacturing, and robotics, 70

Hilbert, David, "Mathematical Problems," 32

Hilbert's mathematical problems, and von Neumann, 32-33

History of Mechanics (Mach), and influence on Einstein, 158

H.M.S. Bounty, and Harrison's clock, 210

hobby computers, *see* home computers

Hofstadter, Douglas, *Gödel, Escher, Bach: an Eternal Golden Braid,* 69, 120

Holloway, Jack, and visual computer program, 117

Holton, Gerald, 164

home computers: and BASIC computer language, 73; memory size of, 20; and LOGO, 22, 124-25

Horgan, Paul, 174

Hotel Loftleider, and Fischer-Spassky chess match, 300

Hubel, David: and understanding intelligent machines, 341; and visual information processing experiments at Harvard, 69-70

Hume, David (Lord) and positivist philosophy, 162

Huygens, Christian, on Newton's law of absolute acceleration, 160

hydroelectric power as energy source, 246, 248

hydrogen atom structure, 235

hydrogen bomb, nuclear reaction in, 239

hydrogen content of TRIGA reactor, 188

hydrogen nuclei, and heating plasma of large tokamak, 234-35

IBM, *see* International Business Machines

IBM 704: proving geometrical theorems on, 41; and Bernstein's chess-playing machine program, 87

362

Index

Index

Index

Index

ficial Intelligence Group, 13, 101; background of, 18-19
Massachusetts Institute of Technology Artificial Intelligence Laboratory, 17, 19, 95; background of, 93-94; and students of Minsky, 103
mass-energy and particle families, 197-98
Masters, Tony, and art department for *2001: A Space Odyssey,* 283-84, 285
Materialism & Empirio-criticism (Lenin), and attack on Frank's paper on law of causality, 156
mathematical computer language, and LOGO, 21-22
mathematical proofs: and computer discovery of, 43, 346; and development of list processing languages, 85; and Logic Theorist computer program, 88-90
mathematical topology, 12, 33
mathematics: and Gleason, 31; and geometric theorems, 41-43, 88, 346; group theory in, 32; and topology, 12, 33; and Putnam Competition, 31, 32; and quantum theory, 143; and Wermer, 27; and word problem solving by STUDENT computer program, 113-14
matrix mechanics, and Heisenberg, 162
matter: de Broglie's thesis on, 143; and density, 315; *Matter, Mind and Models* (Minsky), free will in computers, 11-12
Mauchly, John, and development of ENIAC, 56
maximum speed, and light in a vacuum, 215
Maxwell equations, 153
Meaning of Relativity (Einstein), 154
melt-down, 187
memory, in computers, see computer memory; external memory; internal memory
memory in humans, 63-64; capacity of, 126
memory protection and time sharing, 74-75
mental development, Minsky on, 125-27
Mercury, Nevada, and atomic bomb test site, 134
metaphysics, and Mach's criticism of Newton, 161
Metro-Goldwyn-Mayer (M-G-M): Kubrick with Dore Schary, 268-69; and studio in England, and filming of *2001: A Space Odyssey,* 275-76, 282
Michelson-Morley Experiment, 161
microcomputers: and rating of chess-playing machines, 91; and speed of chess-playing machines, 11
micromanipulator, and robotics, 29
microwaves, and measurement of temperature and density of heated plasma, 233-34
mid-brain, in the visual process, 69
military troops, effect of atomic bomb tests on, 139, 140-41

Mill, John Stuart, and inductive reasoning, 169
Miller, George: and funding for Minsky-Edmonds learning machine, 36; at Harvard, 29, 36; on "Nets with Circles," 60
Miller, Jonathan, quality of TV science programs by, 256
Millikan oil drop experiment, 31
Millikan, Robert A., and measurement of electron charge, 31
mind, see brain
minicomputer, development of, 80
mini-maxing, adapted to game-playing computers, 87
Minsky, Gloria (née Rudisch), 14
Minsky, Henry (Minsky's father), 22
Minsky, Marvin, 7, 9, 13, 14-16, 24, 28, 39, 341; at Andover, 25, 26; and artificial intelligence research, 103-5; at Bell telephone, 16; on brain processes, 30, 44-45, 64; and Bronx High School of Science, 25-26; calculus and, 28; comparison of schools attended, 25; *Computation: Finite and Infinite Machines,* 103; as computer consultant for *2001: A Space Odyssey,* 161, 281; computer programs combining linguistics and mathematics, 111-15; and computer proof of Euclid's Theorems, 41-43; and computer reasoning by analogy (*see* Evans, Thomas); and crayfish experiments, 28-29; and critique of "Nets with Circles," 60-61, 68; at Dartmouth Summer Research Project on Artificial Intelligence, 39-43; doctoral thesis of, 38; early childhood, 22-23; on educational use of computer, 123-24, 125-27; and electronics, 24, 26-27, 71; family of, 14, 22; and Feynman, 15; at Fieldston, 23-24; and fixed point theorem, 33-34; Gleason's influence on, 31-35, 39; at Harvard, 12, 27-32, 33-38 passim, 39; home of, 14-15; on human mental development, 125-27; and intelligence, 54, 77; and a learning machine, 28, 35-37; and the learning process, 28; and LOGO computer language, 21-22; and McCulloch-Pitts paper, 61; and machine models of the mind, 12-13; and marksmanship, 27; at M.I.T., 13, 14, 17-22, 72-73, 93 (*see also* Massachusetts Institute of Technology, Minsky at); "Matter, Mind and Models," 11-12; Miller on, 29; and music, 12, 14, 31; and neural network models, 73; on number systems, 24; Papert, and collaboration with, 26, 101-3; and Perceptron, 26, 100-2; at Princeton, 35, 37, 38; on robots, 17-18, 115, 118-19, 125; and "The Society Theory of the Mind," 118, 128; "Steps Toward Artificial Intelligence," 53-54;

366

Index

Index

Index

Index

Index

quantum theory, 142–49; and Bohr, 143, 144, 145, 157; and de Broglie, 143, 145, 146; and Einstein, 145, 146; Heisenberg on limitations of, 145–46; and hereditary mechanism, 147–49; mathematics for, 143; and mutation, 148–49; and Newtonian physics compared, 145; research leading to, 143
quark, 192–93, 199, 200, 202; charmed, 194, 202, 203; and exclusion principle, 201; and PETRA electron accelerator, 194; properties of, 199–200, 201–2; top and anti-top, 194, 203
quark model, and Nobel Prize, 200

Rabi, I. I.: on discovery of mu meson, 195; on Oppenheimer, 172; and quantum theory in the U.S., 183
radar, development of, at M.I.T. Radiation Laboratory, 72
radiation, level of in fusion products, 235
radiation sensitivity, of superconducting magnets, 233
radioactive material, for fusion and fission reactor compared, 231
radioactive waste, from nuclear reactors, 231–32, 243, 244
radioactivity, of tritium
RAM, see random access memory
Ramón y Cajal, Santiago, and the nervous system, 61
RAND Corporation: and development of chess-playing program, 87–88; and funding of early computer research, 104; logic problems, 41; and development of Logic Theorist, 87–90
random access memory, size of, in modern computers, 49
Raphael, Bertram: and contradiction toleration of program, 113; and mathematical verbal problems, 112
Rashevsky, N., 62
RCA, and funding of early computer research, 104
Reagan, Ronald, and support for fusion research, 241
reasoning by analogy, Evan's computer program for, 107–11
Rebka, G. A., and gravitational red shift, 219
recontraction, and Poincaré's theory of the end of the universe, 222–23
Red Alert (George), as basis for Kubrick's Dr. Strangelove, 272
Reddy, Raj, and HEARSAY program for speech comprehension, 121
redundancy, 63
reinforcement theories, 28
relative time: Leibniz's theory and, 207; and Newton's theories, 205–6

relativity, time and proof of, 214–15
relativity theory: Dirac's reconciliation of, with quantum theory, 143; see also Einstein's theory of relativity
religion: linking science with, 338; and Newton, 205, 206; and theological objection to artificial intelligence, 342
repetition of states, and Poincaré's cycles, 221
Research Laboratory of Electronics at M.I.T., 59
residual magnetism, of PDX, 233
resistive heating, use of, in tokamak, 234
response units, and Level III of Mark I Perceptron, 100
retina, effect of illumination on, 69
Reviews of Modern Physics, and particle data, 195
Reykjavík, Iceland, see Fischer-Spassky chess match
Richter, Burton: and "J"/ψ meson, 202–3; and Nobel Prize for charmed quark, 194
R.K.O. Pathe, and Kubrick's documentary films, 266
Robert Oppenheimer: Letters and Recollections (Smith and Weiner), 171–72
robot: adapted to ball catching, 17–18, 119; computer control of, at M.I.T., 70–71, 115–16; and visual computers, 119
robotics, 70; and micromanipulators, 29
Rochester, Nat: and geometric proof adapted to computer, 43; and programming of neural network on IBM 701 computer, 40
Rockefeller Foundation, and funding of Dartmouth Summer Research Project on Artificial Intelligence, 39–40
Rogers, Eric, and equivalence principle, 3–5
Rosenberg, Howard L., Atomic Soldiers, 140–41
Rosenblatt, Frank, 26; and Perceptron, 98–103
rotating bucket experiment, and Newton's absolute acceleration theory, 160
Royal Observatory at Greenwich, for navigation and astronomy, 208
Royal Society of London for Improving Natural Knowledge, and navigation, 208
Russell, Bertrand: and Pitts, 60; Principia Mathematica, 64, 88, 178
Rutherford, Sir Ernest, 175
Rutishauser, Heinz, and early use of compilers for subroutines, 82

Safe Reactor Group, at General Atomic Company, 186, 188
safety, of fusion and fission reactors compared, 231–32; 243–44
Sagan, Carl, 256, 258: and Cosmos TV

371

Index

Index

374

Index